EXCESS BAGGAGE

EXCESS BAGGAGE

One Family's

Around-the-World Search

for Balance

Tracey Carisch

SHE WRITES PRESS

Published: 2018
Printed in the United States of America
ISBN: 978-1-63152-411-0 paperback
978-1-63152-412-7 ebook

Library of Congress Control Number: 2018935585

For information, address:
She Writes Press
1563 Solano Ave #546
Berkeley, CA 94707

She Writes Press is a division of SparkPoint Studio, LLC.

Interior design by Tabitha Lahr

Dedicated to RJS and our Sad Country Fridays

If you're always trying to be normal,
you will never know how amazing you can be.
—Maya Angelou

CONTENTS

A NOTE FROM THE AUTHOR

Dear Reader,

This book is a true account of our family's travels through twenty-four countries over the course of eighteen months. I recreated events, locales, and conversations from my memories of them. In order to maintain their anonymity, in many instances I have changed the names of the individuals and organizations involved.

My husband, Brian Carisch, is a phenomenal amateur photographer. His photos from our adventure have been organized into a catalog which visually supports the storytelling in this memoir. To follow along with the imagery of our journey, please visit:

www.traceycarisch.com/photos

Finally, thank you for letting me share this adventure with you! As I've written this book and given speeches about the lessons our family learned on our journey, I've had the opportunity to connect with so many amazing people around the world. Please feel free to reach out on social media or through the web site to share your thoughts, feedback, and personal experiences. I'd love to hear from you.

Sincerely,
Tracey Carisch

PINOT NOIR AND PANIC ATTACKS

Inbox count: 596

Weekly errands: 23

Loads of laundry to fold: 4

Moments of joy and bliss: Data unavailable

Hands weren't typing. Eyes weren't scanning my inbox. Feet weren't stomping up the school's concrete steps in the mad dash to pick up my kids from the aftercare program. For the first time since waking up, my body was motionless. Totally and completely still.

Warm spring air floated over my arms and reached down into my chest, filling me up like a balloon and pulling a sigh from my lungs. I leaned my head back against the patio chair's fat cushion and gazed up into the clear evening sky, where wispy pink clouds streaked across the atmosphere and a few bright stars twinkled through the darkening shades of blue.

The waitress brought my glass of pinot noir and set it on the table in front of me, but I didn't reach for it. Instead, I closed my eyes and relished the moment. Sitting. Breathing. Doing absolutely nothing.

What a glorious thing this is, I thought. *I should do it more often.*

And then the silence was broken, replaced with greetings and air kisses as a parade of friends began to arrive.

"This place is adorable! How long has it been open?"

"Did you get your hair cut? It looks great!"

"Oooh . . . cute purse! Where'd you find it?"

It was exactly what I needed: an evening of zero obligations. No dirty dishes or homework drama or loads of laundry to fold. Just easy conversation with good friends who expected nothing of me, except to pass them the wine.

When the appetizers had been ordered and everyone had a glass in hand, one friend asked the group in her charming southern drawl, "So, ladies, what'd y'all do this week?"

And that's when it happened.

Evidently, a mind-altering revelation can surface anywhere. I wasn't having a near-death experience or praying at the feet of a spiritual guru. I suppose, given my love for wine, it shouldn't come as much of a surprise that my life-changing epiphany made its grand entrance in the middle of Chattanooga's new French wine bar. But there it came, in all its agonizing glory. My chest tightened as tiny beads of sweat erupted onto my forehead. A buzzing sound rushed through my ears, drowning out my friends' voices and making it sound as though they were talking into the over-sized wine glasses they held in their hands.

The only thing more surprising than the onset of these symptoms was the innocuous topic provoking them. *What did I do this week?* I honestly couldn't remember. It was all a blur of meetings, errands, car pools and house chores. In my attempt to answer a friend's simple question, a wave of disheartening clarity crashed in on me like a tsunami. *My life has become a repetitive, uninspiring to-do list.*

Get everyone to work and school on time.

Check.

Read and send emails at all hours of the day.

Check.

Sit in countless meetings.

Check.

Go to the grocery store, pick up dry cleaning, make dinner.

Check.

Check.

Check.

Was nothing in this entire week worth remembering? Am I just going through the motions to the point that I'm practically catatonic?!

The longer I sat there trying to think of something that could distinguish this week from the last, the harder my heart slammed against my rib cage. My lungs fiercely rejected the air I attempted to gulp down through shallow, shaky breaths, and my hands went completely numb. In one brief moment, I'd gone from laughing girls-night-out gal to petrified panic attack victim. Looking for an escape, I mumbled something about needing to pee and beelined for the bathroom.

After a few minutes alone in a small ladies' room adorned with faux finishes and Parisian posters, I could feel my heart returning to a normal rhythm. The numbness slowly faded from my fingers. Sucking in deep breaths, I gripped both sides of the sink and leaned in to study my reflection. A sheen of sweat had smeared my make-up into a bad case of raccoon eyes. The long blonde hair, blown into submission that morning with an expensive hair dryer, was now tangled and damp at the roots. A red wine stain ran down the front of my designer shirt, evidence of a frazzled flee from the overstuffed patio chair. Looking at that panicked face, I knew every inch of it. Every freckle and every little wrinkle, down to the tiny chicken pox scar on my jaw line. And yet, it felt like I was looking at a complete stranger.

"What in the hell is wrong with you?" I said out loud. Of course, it wasn't lost on me that I'd simply replaced a panic attack with the equally-worrying issue of talking to myself in a mirror.

I blotted at the wine stain with a damp paper towel, and then smoothed out my hair and makeup as best I could. Taking a deep, slow breath, I squared my shoulders and gave my reflection a cold, hard stare.

"Get back out there and just *be happy*," I said with conviction. Once again . . . talking to myself in the mirror. Not a good sign.

I returned to my friends, determined to sweep this crazy little episode under the rug. Taking their cues, I laughed, nodded and tried to look deeply interested in everything they said. I put on a show and acted like my normal self. It was a performance deserving of an Oscar, because the truth was, I would never be my normal self again. Something in me changed that night. It wasn't just a panic attack. It was a cataclysmic shift. An unexplainable, unalterable, uncontrollable upheaval in the way I looked at everything in my seemingly perfect life.

I got home that evening and stood in my kitchen contemplating another drink. When I opened a cabinet to grab a wineglass, I noticed the shelves of martini and margarita glasses we never used. Pulling open the next one, I saw the juicer I bought after watching a documentary on Netflix. Another cabinet held the new Tupperware I'd picked up at Target that week, not because I needed it, but because it looked so much cuter than the Tupperware I already owned. My heart began pounding again as I frantically yanked open doors and rummaged through drawers.

When's the last time I used this melon baller? Did I ever figure out how to work this julienne peeler? And why on earth do I own an egg slicer?

Within seconds, our kitchen looked like something out of a poltergeist film. Every single drawer and cabinet was wide open, and a terrified woman stood in the middle of it all. As I took deep breaths and tried to avoid a second panic attack, I suddenly remembered a story I'd recently heard. My Power Yoga instructor told it during the "quiet meditation" she did at the beginning of that Tuesday's class. I'd barely listened to it at the time, but now the symbolism in her little Zen tale seemed to perfectly describe my life.

A horse was galloping at great speed, and it appeared the rider was going somewhere very important. As the hooves thundered through a village, a young boy watched the man ride by and called out "Where are you going?" The man on the horse turned back to the boy and yelled, "I don't know! Ask the horse!"

SHORT ROAD TO MIDLIFE

College degrees: 3

Diaper changes: 9,225 (give or take)

Home square footage: 4,239

Vacation days: 14

I remember him standing in the doorway of our classroom. His blonde hair was damp, his tall frame sported swim trunks and a ratty T-shirt, and under one long, tan arm he held a massive black wakeboard. Seeing me in the back row, he threw a nod in my direction and strolled through the room to the empty seat on my left. After propping the wakeboard up on the wall behind us, he folded himself into one of the new ergonomic chairs installed during Indiana University's summer renovations.

"Hey. How was your summer?" he asked.

"Good. I interned with Arthur Andersen in the Chicago office."

"Cool." His hands drummed out a quick rhythm on the desk. "I waterskied."

"That sounds about right," I said with a grin.

"Can I borrow a pen?"

I pulled a cheap Bic from the front pocket of my backpack, assuming that was the last I'd ever see of it. "Tough day hitting the books, Carisch?"

He smiled and leaned back. "Come on, it's three in the afternoon and this is my first class of the day. How could I not do something fun before walking into this?" He stretched out his arms and gestured to the windowless room full of bored upperclassman. Then he winked and added, "You're lucky I even showed up."

"Oh, am I?" I handed him a sheet of paper before he could ask for one.

"All right people!" yelled a gruff, matronly woman as she strode through the door to the front of the classroom. "I'm Professor Taylor, and *this*," she punched the air with a piece of paper, "is the seating chart for Telecomm Tech 412. Write your name in the box where you're sitting and sit there for the rest of the term. This is how I take attendance, so don't even *think* about skipping my class."

As the room heaved a collective groan, he swung his chair around to face me. "Well, Trace," he said, his slate-grey eyes twinkling mischievously. "Looks like you're stuck with me."

And stuck with him I was. If anyone had told me on that first day of our senior year that Brian Carisch and I would fall madly in love, I probably would have laughed in their face. I was too rigid and scheduled to know how much I needed this wakeboard-toting frat boy in my life. He was the opposite of what I thought I wanted, but as our friendship grew into an unexpected romance, we found in each other the balance we both needed in our lives.

And, as they say, the rest is history.

"Do you have kids?" my colleague asked.

I choked on a sip of Diet Vanilla Cherry Coke and almost sprayed the reports stacked in front of me. "Um, no," I sputtered, responding as though his question was completely preposterous and outside the realm of all universal reason.

Seeing my dramatic reaction, he smirked and said, "You realize you're in Utah, right? Most women here have their first kid before they're twenty-one."

After graduating, Brian and I wound up in Salt Lake City with jobs in the booming technology market of the late '90s. Within just a couple years we had a mortgage and a marriage certificate. As typical twenty-something yuppies, we worked hard and played hard. By day, I built a formidable reputation at my consulting firm and got promoted into a management role. By night, I hosted Pampered Chef parties that turned into full-blown drunkfests. At one rowdy gathering I remember screaming onto my quiet street, "I can't fucking wait to use my new garlic press!" Needless to say, parenthood was not a topic of conversation for us at the time.

I shook my head at my colleague's question and went back to the stack of papers filled with system security settings. "My husband

and I aren't even going to think about having kids until we're at least thirty," I said.

"Yeah, well, don't wait too long," he replied. "All your eggs will dry up."

I looked up to give him a long, brooding stare. "Interesting information," I said. "Now let's talk about your testicles, shall we?"

Although rather irritating, this dose of office chauvinism got me thinking. Brian and I knew children would be in our future someday, so maybe we should consider putting our careers on hold and sowing our wild oats together before all my eggs "dried up." After a couple conversations over beers on our back porch, the two of us were pricing around-the-world plane tickets and reading travel books. We calculated the money we'd need for our grand journey, and then cut our spending dramatically. I clipped coupons. Brian dropped his season ski pass. We got rid of one of our cars and started taking the bus. After saving up for almost two years, we decided we'd pull the trigger on our dream trip as soon as I finished grad school. When I graduated from my MBA program at the University of Utah, we'd set off into the wild blue yonder.

One April weekend, as we crossed off the last weeks before our big adventure, Brian went camping with some friends while I stayed home with a paper for Financial Modeling. I'd planned to spend my Saturday hammering out pages of boring analysis on capital budgets, but as I started working, a random thought popped into my head.

Something really important was supposed to have happened by now.

Twenty minutes later, after some date calculations and a frantic trip to the pharmacy, I stood in my bathroom holding a pregnancy test gleaming a bright blue plus sign. I stared at the plastic stick in disbelief for a few minutes, letting the magnitude of it sink in.

Then, like any good Type A personality, I launched myself into a hysterical whirlpool of turbulent emotions. One minute I was in awe and near tears over the miracle growing inside me. Moments later, I'd melt into the fear Brian would be just as freaked out as I was, which then morphed into illogical rage, because *this is our child, Brian! Why are you so unhappy about having a baby with me, jerk!* I spent the entire day coming up with new and creative varieties of knocked-up turmoil, running the gambit from the rising costs of childcare in the metropolitan area to the fetal alcohol syndrome I'd probably caused with my most recent Pampered Chef party.

Yet, when I finally got to sleep that night, a calm and collected voice whispered through my dreams. *Chill out, girl. Everything's working out just as it should.* The next morning, I woke up believing that voice. This might not have been *my* plan, but somehow this unexpected twist in our story was part of a bigger plan. The nagging question was if Brian would see it the same way. How would he feel about scrapping our around-the-world adventure and being thrust into fatherhood?

The next day Brian returned from his camping trip, and seconds after he walked in the door, I dumped a bag of five positive pregnancy tests onto the coffee table. I watched his eyes widen in surprise.

Please don't be disappointed.

He looked up at me, brow furrowed. "Seriously?" he asked hesitantly.

Too anxious to speak, I just nodded.

Slowly, an enormous smile spread across his face, and the next thing I knew my feet were off the ground as he stood up and lifted me into a hug. "Holy shit, honey," he whispered in my ear. "We're having a fucking baby."

Relief and joy blasted through me as his arms squeezed me tighter and he planted a kiss on my lips. Despite all the emotional turmoil of the last two days, I knew one thing for certain. We were seriously going to have to do something about our potty-mouths before this kid arrived.

A few days before Christmas, we welcomed our little Emily. Even with the sore nipples, poopy diapers, and middle of the night screaming sessions (usually the baby, but sometimes me), motherhood brought a sense of balance to my life. I saw the world from a new perspective and found a more accepting outlook when it came to life's challenges. This tiny thing that couldn't talk or even control her appendages turned out to be an amazing therapist to a recovering perfectionist.

In fact, I loved motherhood so much I got a little baby crazy over the next few years. When Emily started walking and drinking out of a sippy cup, I started to feel the tug for baby number two. That fall, we made a cross-country move to Chattanooga, Tennessee, and while unpacking boxes, we learned another little Carisch would be arriving. Liv joined the family before Emily was out of diapers, bringing her white-blonde hair, big blue eyes, and quiet smile with her.

Of course, it wasn't long before Liv started trying to be like her big sister and saying things like "No, Mama. I do it me-self." The little maternal pull started up again, and along came Ali—curious, funny, creative Ali. The chaos of a busy family of five meant she learned to entertain herself a lot, which occasionally involved Sharpies and a wall or a box of tampons and the Christmas tree. Ali's ingenuity and our periodic parental neglect led to some memorable situations with the baby of the family.

So, it would be three little girls for us. Brian found himself seriously outnumbered, but I was impressed at how quickly he got comfortable in his new world of femininity. I'd be in the middle of changing a diaper when he'd look over my shoulder and yell, "Trace, you have to go front to back! You're getting poop in her cooch!"

A couple years into our parenting career, Brian and I were forced into a long-term, intimate relationship with stuffed animals. Emily developed a serious emotional attachment to a Winnie-the-Pooh bear I'd received as a baby gift. I hadn't realized how important a toy could be in a child's life, until the evening we accidentally left Pooh Bear at a restaurant. After witnessing the insane, hysterical, screaming drama that ensued in his brief absence, I quickly bought a second Pooh Bear as backup. Of course, Emily passionately rejected him, saying he looked "too new." Luckily, backup Pooh Bear still got to fulfill his cosmic toy purpose. One day, Liv pulled him out from the pile of stuffed animals, and soon he was her most treasured possession. Our third bear, Bobo, came on the scene about the time Ali was learning to walk. Imitating her big sisters, she picked out the toy in her room most resembling the Pooh Bears and started carting it around everywhere. Being slightly larger than the other two bears, we called him "Big Bear", which Ali's two-year-old tongue pronounced Bobo. (Unfortunately for Bobo, his name means "idiot" in Spanish.)

Those three bears rode in baby strollers, attended tea parties, and cuddled up in bed with their respective little girls each night. Missing a bear at bedtime equated to a Code Red security crisis, so they went on every vacation and every trip to visit the grandparents. We had three little girls and three little bears pretty much everywhere we went.

The bears grew tattered over the years as our family transitioned out of the baby equipment and into the big girl beds. The girls started day care, then elementary school. We signed them up for swimming clinics and soccer leagues, ballet classes and piano lessons. Life rolled along, the days and weeks blending together with the routines of family life.

In the midst of all this, my career took off. My rising expertise in the field of high-tech workforce development had me giving speeches at conferences and appearing on television to talk about things like "twenty-first century skills" and "project-based learning strategies." While I led meetings with corporate leaders and government officials, both my salary and my list of powerful contacts grew. In short, I was doing the thing we're supposed to do. Go to college, work hard, impress people, and keep getting promoted to the next rung up the ladder.

So then, what in the hell was my problem!? Panic attacks in wine bars? Really, Tracey?

In the weeks following that girls' night out, everything changed. While part of me had melted into a panic-stricken mess, the other part separated from the crazy lady and became the observer of my life.

Are you seriously doing this right now? Observer Tracey would ask as she watched the ridiculousness of a woman in a pencil skirt and heels hunching around the driveway with a bottle of Roundup. *Your top priority after bringing the kids home from school and spending a long day at work is to spray weeds?*

Observer Tracey pointed out how much time I spent whirling through the thoughts in my head and ignoring the world around me. As I slid into a parking spot ready to rush into the next store on my list of errands, she'd say, *You don't even remember driving here. You barely paid attention to the process of maneuvering a two-ton vehicle through rush hour traffic!*

She also took note of how much time I spent cleaning, organizing, and redecorating our house. Some backward part of my brain apparently held the belief that our busy life wouldn't seem so chaotic if I cleaned out a closet. Or put a new color scheme in the den. Or reorganized the laundry room so the detergent was tucked away in a cabinet instead of sitting on the washing machine. *Good grief, I can't believe you're making an issue out of laundry detergent*, Observer Tracey would say in that admonishing tone of hers. *And here's a news flash for you: No one cares about the positioning of your throw pillows either!*

This neat freak routine was all a lie, though. My talent for purging my way through a junk drawer until it was a shining example of Martha Stewart-inspired perfection was rivaled only by my equally-impressive aptitude for jamming every compartment in our house with random crap. The place might look good at first glance, but open a closet and there was a good chance something would fall out and crack you on the head. Our home became a metaphor for my life. Everything seemed perfect on the outside, but a bundle of chaotic confusion lurked in the hidden chambers of my mind, waiting for someone to open a door and let all the scary, sticky drama come spilling out.

I didn't talk to Brian about my panic attack or my conversations with Observer Tracey for fear he'd think I was headed for the psychiatric ward. But one night, my confused resentment came bubbling out. We were sipping beers on our porch and chatting about the things we needed to get done over the weekend, when my eyes landed on a flower bed.

I'd spent an entire Saturday afternoon in the blazing sun planting petunias, and for the next four months I'd have to deal with them. Weed them. Water them. Deadhead them. I hated yardwork, and yet, in an effort to impress the neighbors and random strangers, I'd created a horticulture hell for myself. Staring at those flowers erupted a seething anger in me, sending heat to my cheeks and a pounding tension across my forehead.

"Oh my god," I muttered through gritted teeth. "I hate those goddamn petunias."

Brian gave me a look of amused confusion. "What are you talking about? Are you okay?"

Then, without warning, a flood of unbridled fury came spilling out of me in a surge of flailing arms and wild eyes. "What in the hell are we doing!?" I yelled. "Why are we talking about going to Home Depot? Is that really how we want to spend our weekend? Seriously, Brian, is it?"

He opened his mouth to saying something, but I cut him off. "Do you know what I caught myself doing the other day," I said with disgust. "I was spraying weeds in a business suit! Yeah, that's right. I came home from work and I saw these stupid dandelions in the driveway and so I got out of the car, went straight for the weed killer, and spent fifteen minutes of my life walking around in high heels spraying weeds! WEEDS!" Feeling the start of another panic attack, I took a deep breath to calm myself down while Brian stared at me with a baffled look on his face. "Is this how we want to spend the next twenty years?" I asked. "Meetings and emails and Home Depot and weed killer and deadheading stupid flowers? Is this what we really want?"

We stared at each other for a long moment as the world moved around us. I heard kids laughing on our street. The neighbor's dog started barking. A car passed by. And we just sat there looking at one another. I watched his expression slowly change from confusion to contemplation, and then to certainty.

"No," he said firmly. "No, it's not what we want."

A sigh escaped from my chest. "Then what are we doing?"

Half an hour later, after I'd spewed about the meaning of life and house chores until I was blue in the face, I'd managed to pull Brian into my vortex of midlife depression.

"My god, you're right," he muttered, taking a long drink from his beer. "It's totally blurring by us."

"Yep."

"Maybe we need to think about career moves," he suggested. "You know, find jobs we're really passionate about. Follow our bliss . . . or whatever."

I smiled sadly and shook my head. "It's not our jobs, Brian. It's everything. I'm tired of the rat race we're in."

As he turned to look out over our yard, his eyes fell into pensive sadness. I felt a heavy cloud of tension envelop us as it suddenly dawned on me what he was experiencing—his spouse of thirteen years going on a rampage about how unhappy she is with the life they've built together. That couldn't feel good. A deep, aching regret pulled at my heart as I considered how much my honesty could be hurting him.

What am I doing? Am I wrecking everything we have?

Brian took a slow breath and turned to look at me with intense, determined eyes. He wrapped his strong hand around mine and held it tightly. "Trace, if we're tired of the rat race, then let's get the hell out of it."

CRAZY HAIRBRAINED IDEAS

Amazing, life-changing decisions: 1
Second thoughts: 437
Irrational projections of self-doubt: 1
Plane tickets: 5

I t's a weird feeling, this whole discontentment-in-the-midst-of-happiness thing. After all, Brian and I were living the American Dream, weren't we? We had successful careers, beautiful kids, and a lovely home with lots of lovely stuff in it. What more could we possibly ask for? And yet, life seemed to be rushing by in a flurry of to-do lists, carpools and home improvement projects.

We started calling it The Blur: a frightening phenomenon wreaking havoc on the human psyche by fast-forwarding the days and replacing fun activities with obligatory ones. It ate up our weekends with soccer games and errands, and then consumed the evenings with homework and laundry baskets. Routine and distraction seemed to feed the beast, so we tried to defeat The Blur by mixing things up a bit. We went on family hikes and camping trips. We checked out new events in town, and we threw more parties. During my weekly yoga class, I tried to intently focus on staying calm and centered, instead of turning it into a heart-pounding, fat-burning sweat session. But nothing seemed to work. As the weeks rolled into months, our confusion grew. And then one day . . . Brian and I began to shape a wild, outlandish idea.

What if we just walked away from it all and traveled the world for a while?

That's crazy.

No, we could never do that.

Could we?

The longer the idea lingered, the less crazy it seemed. In fact, with each demanding day, stepping away from our busy, modern-American life felt like finding sanity. Maybe letting go of all the material stuff we'd accumulated and the hectic schedule we'd created for ourselves would help us find the balance that seemed to be so lacking in our lives.

As we considered the logistics of taking our girls on a trip around the world, Brian and I arrived at a startling conclusion: we could actually do this. His job as an independent software developer could support us financially since he could work from anywhere. If we sold our house, cars, and almost everything we owned, we'd be free to travel for as long as we wanted without being tied to financial obligations back home.

Of course, we rationalized the whole thing by leaning hard into the cultural learning our daughters would experience. We wouldn't be doing this for *us*. No, no, no, we'd do it for our *children!* Think of the languages they'll learn and the exotic places they'll see! This has nothing to do with two middle-aged workaholics trying to claw their way out of the rat race. No, siree . . .

After weeks of talking each other into it, Brian and I finally convinced ourselves this was the right thing for our family. So, we set the plan in motion. We put our house on the market with the confidence that when it sold, everything else would fall into place. I'd leave my job, we'd sell most of what we owned and put the rest in storage so we could begin a new life together. *We could actually do this.* The day the for-sale sign went up in our yard, a buzz of excitement rushed through me every time I looked at it.

However, it wasn't long before the excitement wore off and the uncertainty set in. Many of our friends and family thought we'd lost our marbles, so we got to hear all their horror stories about a cousin or an aunt or a friend of a friend who'd gone through a catastrophic travel disaster.

"He contracted a rare tropical disease and went into liver failure!"

"Their tour guide stole their passports and all their money and left them stranded in the middle of nowhere!"

"She had to flee to the American embassy when a revolution broke out!"

On and on it went, and eventually it started to work. I obsessed over news stories about plane crashes and hostage situations, and I questioned if I'd ever be able to rebuild my career after walking away from it for a midlife-crisis-inspired jaunt around the planet. In the back of my mind I drew up a tally, with all the unknowns of this journey on one side and the good things we had in Chattanooga on the other.

Maybe this isn't the way to fix whatever it is I think is broken, I thought. *Maybe we're making a huge mistake.*

I was leaving a meeting one day when an acquaintance caught up with me in the parking lot.

"Tracey! Hold on a minute!" Susan waved at me and trotted across the pavement. "So . . . I heard a pretty wild rumor about you," she crooned, like a teenager with some juicy gossip. "Are you guys really leaving Chattanooga to travel the world?"

Oh, great. Here we go.

"Yes, that's the plan," I said matter-of-factly.

She gasped and put a dramatic hand on her chest. "You've got to be kidding me! That's crazy! You're just going to pull your kids out of school?"

"We'll be homeschooling them." *Careful, Susan. You're in dangerous territory.*

"But what about your work? You're just going to up and quit?"

"Eventually, yes, I'll be leaving. But our house hasn't sold yet, and that could take quite a while."

"Oh, it's such a shame, though. All the education and work-force programs you've helped put in place. What's going to happen to it all when you leave?"

"It will be fine, Susan. I'm starting to transition the work so things will go smoothly regardless of who's running the programs."

"Do you even know where you're going?" Her voice dripped with judgment.

Stay calm. Don't bite her head off. "Not yet," I said, feigning cheerfulness. "We're just going to wait and see how everything goes." I started rummaging through my purse for my keys, hoping she'd take the hint and we could be done with this conversation.

"My goodness, I can't believe it's true," she said, shaking her head in disbelief. "I mean, I heard that and I said to myself there's no way Tracey Carisch would do this. I just never could have imagined something like this out of you."

That's it, lady. "Well, we aren't exactly friends, Susan, so you don't know me very well. If you'll excuse me, I have to go." I turned on my heel and marched to my car.

Driving home, I regretted being so curt with her. It wasn't Susan's fault she'd caught me on a day when I felt more uncertain than excited about all this. After all, she was only giving voice to the questions in my own head. My fingers tightened around the steering wheel as I thought about leaving the career I'd worked so hard to build. *I still have some time with this decision,* I reassured myself. *Nothing is irreversible at this point.*

But that irreversible point of no return arrived the very next day when we got an offer on our house.

"What do you think?" Brian said, his eyes twinkling with excitement as he wrapped his arms around my waist. "This is it, Trace! The start of our amazing adventure!" Seeing the enthusiasm on his face put a knot in my stomach.

"Yeah, um . . . Let's talk about it after the girls are in bed." I slipped out of his embrace and walked into the kitchen to start dinner, where I mindlessly diced and sautéed my way through a fog of confusion.

After the girls were tucked in, I walked through our home surveying all the stuff we'd accumulated over the years. As my eyes roamed over the electronics, knickknacks, and mass-produced wall art, an overwhelming exhaustion slouched my shoulders. *Is this a good enough reason not to travel the world? Because I'm too lazy to pack?*

I knew I had two options: a) reject the offer and keep our lovely life just as it was, or b) throw off the bindings of my predictable existence and do something no one would have ever expected of me.

Hoping to avoid the decision a little longer, I stopped in front of our living room bookshelves and scanned the titles. How-tos on home organization, time management, parenting, and new age positive thinking stared back at me. For so many years, I'd been looking for someone else to tell me how to live my life.

My eyes paused on a book about efficient cleaning techniques, and without thinking, I pulled it off the shelf to thumb through its pages. One section talked about the merits of taking the time to clean the kitchen sink each night. The idea being postulated by the author was that I should scrub my sink to a spotless shine before I go to bed because I *deserve* the wonderful feeling it would give me in the morning when I feast my eyes on a sparkly, shiny faucet. I chuckled and shook my head as I remembered fervently agreeing with this idea when I first read it. *Yes! I totally deserve to clean my kitchen sink! Hallelujah, sister!* But after a panic attack and a few months listening to Observer Tracey, the thought that I "deserved" to clean my sink sounded utterly preposterous.

And at that moment, I knew the direction my life would take.

I went out to the garage and grabbed a cardboard box. When I walked back inside, I passed Brian in the kitchen.

"Hey," he said, watching my determined march with curiosity. "What are you doing? We kind of need to talk about this offer on the house, Trace."

"Uh-huh, just a sec," I mumbled, searching through a junk drawer. I grabbed a Sharpie and scrawled the word DONATE across the cardboard. Then I gently placed that book on efficient cleaning inside the box and gave Brian a big smile. "Let's sell this place and do something crazy."

Two days later our house was under contract, and the reality of our massive life change swept through like a hurricane. Boxes tumbled into every room. Closets vomited their contents into piles designated for donations, yard sale, or storage unit. Craigslist ads brought all manner of strangers into our home, scrounging the rubble for good deals on furniture and small appliances. Within just a few weeks, we'd wrapped up our American life and closed the door of our home for the last time.

Brian and I stood on our porch and watched the girls run down the street to say one last good-bye to their friends. As we leaned against the railing together, he grinned at me and shook his head.

"We're two professional, well-educated thirty-somethings," he said. "And we don't even own a couch."

I laughed and tucked my shoulder under his arm. "We've got each other, baby," I said, smiling up at him. "We don't need no stinkin' couch."

TOGETHERNESS

Sibling fights: Too many to count
Gorgeous fjords: 12
Dollars over budget: Data ignored
Pearl divers: 5

NORWAY

'd been watching the streets of New York City zip by when a piercing scream erupted from the back seat. Jerking around to the third row of our airport shuttle, I found Ali clutching her arm, face beet-red and mouth contorted into a high-frequency shriek only dogs could hear. Next to her, Emily stared out the window with a guilty look on her face.

"What happened?" I yelled. Unable to speak, Ali uncovered her arm to reveal a bloody mark and then pointed to the culprit on her right. "You *pinched* her?" I asked Emily in disbelief.

My gentle, kind-hearted child looked back at me with a willful yet confused look on her face, as though even she was shocked at what she'd done. I comforted Ali and gave Emily some of the standard disappointed, motherly comments. "What has gotten into you? We don't pinch!" Then I closed my eyes and let out a heavy sigh. This was not how I'd imagined the start of our life-changing world journey.

The girls had been so calm and agreeable, it honestly hadn't occurred to me this whole thing might be freaking them out. When Brian and I told them about our decision to travel, all three of them seemed to immediately trust us on it. There weren't any dramatic "You're ruining my life!" tantrums. No screaming fits or emotional meltdowns. On the surface, they seemed to have handled these changes easily, and since I desperately wanted that to be true, I'd chosen not to question it. *Oh, they're fine! I'm not a bad parent for ripping my children away from everything they've ever known and throwing them into a world of uncertainty . . . right?*

Emily let out a little sob, and I turned to see her wipe a tear from her cheek. She'd always been the typical, self-motivated firstborn child, spending most of her time trying to please everyone around her. This approval-seeking personality made Emily an extremely easy kid to raise during her decade of life, but caring so much about other people's opinions had its downside. Over the past year, she'd struggled through the classic mean girl dramas.

One girl in particular provoked the Mama Bear response in me. For purposes of anonymity (and also because it brings me a weird satisfaction) we'll call her Little Bitch. Without fail, this child generated tears in our household on a weekly basis. Sometimes she targeted Emily directly, while other days her vendetta against some other poor kid created the drama.

"I don't know what to do," Emily would mutter through confused tears. "She said she's mad at Sierra and if any of us talk to her then she'll be mad at us, too."

It took every ounce of willpower in my being not to handle the situation with brute force. When I'd catch a glimpse of Little Bitch at school, I'd feel the impulse to push her against a wall *Goodfellas*-style and tell her where she could stick her manipulative bullshit. However, I restrained myself, knowing that any intervention on my part would only make matters worse for Emily . . . and get me arrested.

Perhaps it was the relief of walking away from this emotional roller coaster that made Emily so enthusiastic about the new turn her life was taking. She talked about the countries she wanted to visit and the good things that would come out of this adventure. I'd convinced myself she was nothing but excited, and yet, here we were watching her flirt with a life of violence. Pinching her five-year-old sister to the point of drawing blood was so far out of character for Emily I knew it had to be a glimpse of the anxiety she was hiding beneath the surface.

Ali's crying subsided to sniffles and eventually disappeared. Within minutes, she was back to her happy self, showing her bear the pretty highway graffiti. "Bobo, look at those fancy rockets!" she exclaimed, pointing to a series of ornately-decorated cock and balls which had been spray-painted onto the wall of an underpass.

This was the classic 180-turnaround we'd come to know and love from our easy-going youngest child. The girl was a pure example of "living in the now." She didn't worry about the future or hold resentment over the past. One minute, she's screaming because her sister pinched her, and the next she's appreciating the phallic beauty in New York's concrete jungle. The only sign of psychological disturbance Ali exhibited in the weeks before our departure came in the form of her deep emotional attachment to all material objects. During the packing process, she turned into one of those people featured on the show *Hoarders.*

"Mama! You can't give away these pants! I *love* these pants!"

"Alison, those are size 3T. They don't fit you anymore."

"But Mama! I had so much *fun* in these pants. I can't just give them away!"

Broken toys, outgrown clothes, puzzles missing a third of their pieces . . . she wanted it all. Understanding this new hoarding tendency to be some sort of coping mechanism, I'd given Ali a lot of leeway. We had stuff in our storage unit that would go straight into the trash or donation box when we unpacked it. But sometimes as a parent you have to pick your battles. I didn't need to start one over a pair of 3T pants.

I turned to look at Liv sitting next to me on the second-row bench seat. The sun streamed through the window and reflected off her towhead like a halo. She was the big question mark for me. I could never tell what was going on in that little seven-year-old brain of hers. Even as a toddler, she'd held her cards close to her chest. She'd take little toys into the closets or under the beds so she could play hidden away by herself. At least twice a week I'd be frantically searching the house for her, convinced she'd wandered into the street and been immediately abducted.

Shortly after Liv turned four, I started noticing how her eyes scanned back and forth across the pages as she sat looking at picture books.

"Livvy, can you read those words?" I asked on several occasions.

"No," she'd said each time. "I'm just looking at the pictures, Mama."

Then, one day Emily was sounding out a word in her first-grade reading homework. "Fuh . . . an . . . fuh . . . an . . ."

As she slowly struggled through the first syllable, Liv looked up from her Legos and glanced at the page. Rolling her eyes in exasperation she said, "Fantastic. The word's fantastic, Emmy."

"Liv!" I exclaimed. "You *can* read."

She gave me a startled look, clearly surprised to see me in the room. "No, I can't," she insisted. "I just . . . guessed."

Liv liked to have her secrets, apparently. She was the one I'd been watching closely for signs of emotional distress in the days leading up to our trip. Her imaginative mind could conjure up scary scenarios eight ways to Sunday, so I worried she'd struggle the most with all the uncertainty of our new nomadic life.

When our shuttle pulled up to JFK International Airport, Brian turned around and looked back at me from the front passenger seat. "Alright, Trace," he said, putting his hand on my knee. "This crazy trip is really starting. You ready to do this?"

"I guess so." I watched the girls climb out to the walkway. "But I don't think our kids are."

He shrugged and said, "Well, they kind of have to be at this point." Then he pushed his door open and walked to the back of the van to help the driver with our bags.

Brian was right. No amount of worrying about the psychological state of my children would change the fact that we were now a homeless family of globetrotters.

"Let's play Spot the Rat!" Ali yelled to her sisters.

"Kiddo, we're not in New York anymore," Brian said. "That would be a really boring game here."

We stood in the immaculate station of the Flytoget Airport Express Train in Oslo, Norway. Not a piece of trash or speck of dirt spoiled the gleaming perfection of the sleek, modern terminal. We could have eaten off the floor.

The first stop of our international adventure was one of the most expensive countries on the planet because, ironically, the transatlantic flight into Oslo was rock bottom cheap. We could have immediately flown out to another European nation, but we figured we might as well see a little of this land, once home to our family's ancestors. After all, how expensive could Norway really be?

Um . . . eye-poppingly, mind-numbingly, thank-god-we're-only-here-for-ten-days expensive. We accidentally ordered a beer that cost $24. We filled our rental car with gas at a whopping $12 a gallon. When we stayed at a hotel with a free breakfast, we forced the girls to practically eat their weight in food and then stuff their pockets with muffins. That's how expensive Norway was.

Aside from the hit to our budget, the country proved to be an incredible start to our journey. Oslo's clean and tidy streets were lined with a harmonious mixture of contemporary and historic buildings. The city's parks and greenspaces invited us to sit on a bench and breathe in the crisp air, while the girls climbed on spotless playground equipment. And everyone in the country spoke English, so no language barrier!

We made our way across the southern coast, driving along gorgeous fjords lined with deep green forests and passing through a labyrinth of tunnels cut into the mountainous terrain. However, we were frequently reminded that even occupying the road was an expensive activity in Norway as the navigation system constantly reported automatic tolls being added our rental car bill.

"Prepare for toll ahead," the GPS lady's voice would say in her proper British accent.

Moments later, we'd hear the loud double beep indicating we'd just paid yet another Norwegian road tax. The sound might as well have been a *cha-ching!*

Our GPS lady had some other idiosyncrasies that kept driving a little interesting. Sometimes her staccato enunciation gave us directions almost impossible to understand. "In two point three key low meat us turn left and con tin you point four key low meat us." Other times, she'd say something completely vague like, "Stay on this road for a long time."

A highlight of our time in Norway was our trek up to Preikestolen, a flat, pillared cliff rising almost half a mile above the waters of the magnificent Lysefjord canyon. The three-hour hike up to the top was a testament to our girls' physical endurance as well as Brian's paternal motivational skills, which basically involved ignoring all the whining and walking thirty yards ahead of the rest of us. Despite the arduous morning required to reach it, our time on Preikestolen proved to be a breathtaking experience. Of course, for me, this was due to both the gorgeous view and the fact that air was forcefully ripped from my lungs each time one of the girls made what I considered to be a careless move that could result in her fall to a watery death. Such moves included: Running, hopping, walking, reaching for a sandwich, and turning one's head quickly.

Somewhere around my tenth dramatic gasp, it finally occurred to me that my children aren't lemmings and actually do possess a self-preservation instinct. I was able to put the 2000-foot sheer drop out of my mind (sort of) and enjoy the calm beauty of the experience. A warm breeze floated up the cliff's face as I stood looking out over the deep gorge cutting through to the ocean. The sky and the water mirrored the same shade of brilliant topaz blue, and between them ran the rich, warm marbled browns of the canyon walls. I tried to imagine what the land looked like millions of years ago, before a sheet of slow-moving ice irreversibly transformed the landscape, turning it from a gentle green slope into a majestic sculpture of stone and water. Slight changes, imperceptible from one day to the next, had accumulated over time to create something extraordinary.

I took a deep breath of fresh, clean air and felt a wish form inside me—the wish that this journey would be the colossal force changing our family forever. It had become very apparent we were in desperate need of some serious life changes.

My shocking discovery in the first weeks of this trip (besides the $17 chicken breast at a Norwegian grocery store) was the realization that our family didn't get along very well. At all. Our new mode of 24-7 togetherness revealed how little of it we'd had back home, where most of our waking hours had been spent separated from one another at work, school, or one of those many kid activities we rushed around to. For the first time, the girls weren't spending their days in their own classrooms, and Brian and I weren't heading off to our respective offices. There were no playdates or sports practices or parties with friends. It was just the five of us. Together. All. The. Time. As a result, we were getting precipitously close to strangling one another.

Our rental car seemed to be a catalyst for a lot of the drama. The girls' proximity and the sound of their fights bouncing off the walls of the vehicle were a constant recipe for tension.

"GIRLS!" Brian's voice boomed from the drivers' seat during a backseat altercation over a wadded-up piece of paper. "THAT'S ENOUGH! I'M SERIOUS!"

"She started it," Liv mumbled.

Brian flashed his angry eyes in the rearview mirror. "I will seriously pull this car over," he said in a tone giving me a flashback to my own childhood. I couldn't help but stifle a laugh.

"What's so funny?" he barked, jerking his head to glare at me.

"Whoa," I said defensively. "Don't get mad at *me*."

He stayed silent, but I could see his knuckles go white as he tightened his grip on the steering wheel.

"You know, your attitude isn't helping the situation," I said.

"And what *would* exactly? All they do is fight! It's driving me nuts!"

"Yeah, well, yelling at the top of your lungs over their fighting makes it worse."

"Oh, so *I'm* the problem? I shouldn't intervene when my kids act like this? I'm supposed to be like you and just pretend it's not happening?"

"What's that supposed to mean?"

"It means I always have to be the bad guy because you never do anything about it! Ignoring them isn't working, Tracey."

"Good grief." I crossed my arms and turned toward my window. "This conversation is ridiculous."

"You know what? You're right. This is ridiculous." The tires squealed as he hit the brakes and veered into a parking lot.

"What are you doing?"

"I'm going back to the hotel. I need to work." He wheeled the car around and turned back onto the road. "We're blowing through money like crazy in this country. I'd rather get some client hours in than deal with this kid drama. You can take them to the beach on your own."

We sat in silence on the drive back. When we pulled into the hotel parking lot, Brian got out and I walked around to the driver's seat without either of us exchanging a word. As he approached the hotel door, I couldn't help myself.

"Hey! While you're in there, clean up your side of the suitcase! It looks like a friggin' tornado went through it!"

I drove away from the hotel with a deep, simmering rage brewing in me. I tried to follow GPS lady's cryptic directions to the public beach, but kept missing turns. By the time another fight started up in the backseat, I was at my wit's end.

"Ali, get your head off me!" Emily yelled.

"I'm tired. I need a pillow," Ali whined.

"No, you don't, just sit up straight. Or lean on Liv!"

"She never lets me lean on her."

Scuffling, grunting, followed by Liv's entry into the drama. "Ali, get off!"

"Ow! See! I told you, Emily!"

"You don't have to be so mean, Liv!"

"Shut up, Emily! You don't want her on you either!"

"I! WANT! A! PILLOW!"

And . . . *snap.*

"BAAAAAH!" Foot hits the brake. Tires screech. Car fishtails into the road's gravel shoulder. Dramatic, wild-eyed woman jerks around to the shocked, open-mouthed faces of her offspring. "GOD DAMMIT! WHAT IS WRONG WITH YOU?! YOU KIDS ARE DRIVING ME APESHIT! I CAN'T TAKE IT ANYMORE! JUST SHUT UP! FOR ONE GODDAM MINUTE, SHUT THE FUCK UP! IF I HEAR ANOTHER WORD OUT OF ANY OF YOU, I SWEAR TO GOD I WILL LEAVE YOU ON THE SIDE OF THIS GODDAMN ROAD!"

Whoops.

I sat there twisted around to the back seat, panting like an animal, while the girls stared at me, afraid to move. It had finally happened. My inner demon exploded with the fury of a screaming banshee, and regret instantly consumed me. I'd gotten mad at the girls before, but it had *never* been anything like this. I started to stammer out an apology, but the voice of the GPS lady interrupted me.

"Stay on this road for a long time."

Lady, I'm not sure we can without killing each other.

A little while later, we finally found the beach, and I sat digging my toes into the cool, damp sand as a crisp breeze chilled my cheeks. The sun shone down, bouncing sparkles between the anchored boats bobbing on the waves. It would have been a very pleasant way to spend an afternoon, were it not for the girls' constant bickering over their sand castle project. Listening to them whisper insults at each other, I felt a tension grip my stomach.

Maybe this family isn't cut out for a nomadic life.

I sighed and scooped up handfuls of sand, letting the shiny grains slide through my fingers. And then, an old memory came . . .

A scene from my college days glided across my mind's eye. I'd been sitting in the bathroom of Kilroy's Pub, my brain swimming from one too many Bud Lights, when I noticed some unexpected words scrawled in thin black ink on the back of the stall door.

Pearls don't lay by the seashore, bitch.

I'd squinted and read it again, surprised to see an old proverb (minus the cursing) displayed next to derogatory comments about people and their private parts. If I'd come across that same phrase on a motivational poster, I probably wouldn't have given it a second thought. But being slightly drunk with my ass parked on a toilet seat, I sat there thinking about its meaning. Like a pearl sitting inside an oyster under meters of cold ocean water, the most beautiful things in life aren't found within easy reach. Worthwhile rewards require some effort . . . and a little discomfort.

Sitting on a quiet beach in Norway, I understood those words more than ever. Our family had taken a plunge into cold water, and now it was time to go diving for some pearls.

'Cause they don't lay by the seashore . . . bitch.

IDIOTS ABROAD

Incidences of moronic behavior: 52

Unneeded items in luggage: 28

Sexual propositions to strangers: 1

Visa violations: Almost 5

ANDORRA

My most embarrassing moment in life took place when I was brand new at the mother-of-two gig. Liv was barely a week old and Emily was two and a half when I decided I must venture to the grocery store with my two daughters. This was totally unnecessary, since Brian worked from home and friends had stocked us up with casseroles. Nevertheless, I was determined and could not be dissuaded. Taking the girls to the store felt like a rite of passage I needed to complete now that I was the mother of multiple children. Plus, I wasn't exactly thinking clearly since I was all jacked up on postpartum hormones.

I prepared for this intimidating task by changing Liv's diaper while Emily toddled around my bedroom grabbing everything in sight, so she could promptly dump it all onto the floor. It occurred to me she'd probably continue this annoying behavior when, for the first time in her life, she'd have the freedom to move of her own volition in a grocery store. Liv's infant seat would be in the shopping cart, so Emily would be running free.

Things were going surprisingly well as we started off in the produce section. I had to repeat my sing-songy, "Nooo," a few times, but overall Emily was behaving much better than I'd expected. I was feeling rather proud of my obedient child, and, of course, my stellar mothering skills that had yielded all of this wonderful obedience.

Yet, I kept noticing people were looking at us strangely. As I passed other customers, their heads turned and they gave me confused looks. While arranging items in my cart, I noticed out of the corner of my eye a man staring at us from the other end of the aisle. When I looked up at him, he quickly turned away. One little old woman shuffled passed me with an utterly horrified expression on her face. By the time we'd made our way to the dairy case, I felt like a total freak show. *Really people? Is it that off-putting to see a mother and her two children in a grocery store?* In my hormone-induced state, I felt a passionate anger toward these judgmental jerks who apparently hated children. And mothers. And grocery shopping! Just as we were approaching the checkout lane, Liv suddenly burst into her shrieking, newborn cry. Emily, seeing her chance, went straight for the candy display. Before I knew it, all maternal hell broke loose. I tried to comfort Liv while pulling candy bars out of Emily's hands, which led to the obnoxious, two-year-old whining we'd managed to avoid up to this point. And to top it off, my boobs started leaking! I cringed with embarrassment as two dark circles widened their way across my red maternity tank top.

After about sixty seconds of mayhem, I couldn't take it anymore. I might have been able to handle being a social outcast among the other customers, but dealing with a screaming newborn, a whiny toddler, and leaky tits all at the same time sent me over the edge. I hooked Liv's infant seat in the crook of my elbow, snatched up Emily's hand, and left my cart sitting in the checkout lane.

Once I'd gotten the girls buckled in, I threw myself into the driver's seat and melted into a blubbering mess, hands clutching the steering wheel as I hiccupped heaving sobs. After a few minutes, I pulled it together and managed to drive home without dissolving into a pile of tears. When we got into the house, I turned on an episode of *Dora the Explorer* for Emily and left Liv sleeping in her infant seat while I went to the bathroom to splash some water on my puffy, tear-stained face.

And that's when my most embarrassing moment happened. If you'd thought it was fleeing the grocery store and turning into a sobbing lunatic in the parking lot, you'd be wrong. So very, very wrong.

I was reaching for the hand towel when I caught a glimpse in the mirror of something white on the back of my red shirt. I slowly turned and discovered, with sickening horror, the enormous maxi pad stuck down the middle of my back.

Oh! My! God!

I'm not talking about a normal maxi pad, either. This was one of those foot-long, postpartum mega pads that could hold the contents of a small swimming pool. My brain flashed back to the moments before we left the house, when I'd been sitting on the floor changing Liv as Emily toddled around my room. I could distinctly remember her coming over and patting me on the back, which I'd thought was a cute gesture of affection. Nope. It was her sneaky little hand slapping the damn mega pad on me!

How had I not noticed this cotton monstrosity of humiliation!? Once again, I will blame postpartum hormones.

I tell you all of this because the mega pad incident was a turning point in my life. For one, I vowed to always tell someone when I see they have a maxi pad of any size stuck to their body. However, since no one in the history of mankind has ever dealt with this issue like I have, the more pertinent concept I took from the situation was my new definition of idiocy. Once you've walked around in public wearing a maxi pad on your back, you've pretty much set the gold standard for being an idiot. Every embarrassing situation after that kind of seems like small potatoes.

This turned out to be a very helpful attitude to acquire prior to our trip, because as the weeks progressed on our family's global adventure, we started each day knowing one thing for certain—no matter what we were doing or where we were doing it, at some point we were going to feel like morons. This is, evidently, the nature of international travel. You aren't going to know everything. Ever. You're going to muck it up. A lot. So just swallow your pride, take the lesson learned, and put it in your repertoire of Things I Figured Out the Hard Way.

One day, I panicked in a parking lot because I thought I'd locked the keys in our rental car. But a helpful Norwegian saved the day by simply pulling on the door handle and magically opening it. *Ta-da!*

Another time, I left Brian's cell phone on a rock while we were hiking, which required my poor husband to do the trek twice in one day and return to the spot where his phone was miraculously still sitting there untouched.

I left my wallet on a plane and let it fly off to another country, and then lucked out when an airline employee put it on the next flight back.

I bought hemorrhoid cream thinking it was toothpaste.

I could go on, but for my pride's sake I'll just stop there for now and call it good. Despite being embarrassed on a regular basis, very few of our travel blunders reached "mega pad on the back" proportions, so I found myself taking it all in stride pretty well. After our excruciatingly expensive days in Norway, we flew south to stay with relatives in Andorra, a tiny country tucked among the Pyrenees mountains between Spain and France. Brian's stepsister, Mari, her Spanish husband, Ori, and their four young children welcomed us into their home. Somehow, amazingly, all eleven of us lived in their four-bedroom apartment in harmony. Having their cousins around gave our girls a reprieve from the constant sibling togetherness. Brian worked out of Ori's office and established a regular schedule with his clients. Mari and I bonded over coffee or wine, depending on the time of day, and fell into an efficient routine of splitting the household duties.

"So, around the world, huh?" Mari said one afternoon as she swayed back and forth soothing her six-month-old while I tested my skills on her Nespresso machine. "What's on the docket for this trip, lady? You guys haven't given us any details."

I pushed a button to start a loud whirring sound, and after a few moments, the opaque liquid streamed into the cup. "Well, that's because we don't have any. We're here for a few weeks, and then after your place . . . we don't really know."

She raised her eyebrows. "No idea?"

"Nope."

"No plan whatsoever?"

"Huh-uh," I said with a laugh.

Mari smiled and shook her head. "Wow. You guys are really doing this thing. I mean, talk about going with the flow."

"I know. It's crazy, right?" A mixture of surprise and pride floated on my voice. "Sometimes I have to stop and wonder what happened to me. Who is this woman so comfortable with all this uncertainty?"

"It's definitely not the Tracey I've always known," she said with a grin.

"Me neither." I slid her cup across the table. "But I think I like this version of me better."

She smiled and took a sip. "Well, whoever she is, she makes a mean *cortado.*"

In exchange for my *cortado*-making skills, Mari and Ori made everything easy for us. Staying with them was like global travel with built-in tutors. They helped us navigate the new culture and take some important next steps in our travel plans, like getting our last round of vaccinations and finding a long-term rental car. In the evenings, Brian and I had the luxury of conversations with other grown-ups, and on the weekends our families took trips into the Spanish and French countryside together.

Despite all this assistance, the moments of idiocy were still frequent and plentiful. A few weeks into the trip, it became poignantly clear how asinine I'd been in the process of packing. Some of the items I'd elected to bring were utterly breathtaking in their stupidity. Take, for instance, my Babyliss Pro Ceramix Xtreme hair dryer. I'd thought I couldn't live without it, that having good hair days was somehow a critically essential element of this cultural experience. So I'd packed the damn thing, assuming it would work with the electrical outlet converters we'd brought with us. The first time I plugged it in, the lights dimmed and a rancid burning odor filled the room. I'd also foolishly brought an entire medicine cabinet of over-the-counter drugs. Pain relievers, cold medicine, motion sickness pills, antibacterial ointment. Even Band-Aids! Not only did we not need any of it, but if we did require some sort of health aid, it could all be easily purchased at one of the multitude of drugstores on the European continent, which, incidentally, sold the stuff for much cheaper than what I'd paid back in the US.

We had many other discoveries of our own absurdity. When we picked up our long-term rental car in France, it only took us an hour to get completely lost and almost run out of gas. One day, we dutifully presented our family's stack of passports to a very confused cashier at a toll booth. By far the best of my idiotic moments was when I tried to thank a man for holding a door open for me. I smiled at him and said, "*Yo soy muy amable.*" He gave me a strange look and walked off, which I thought was a bit rude until I realized I'd just said, "*I* am very nice" instead of "*You* are very nice." Apparently, mixing up "*Yo soy*" and "*Usted es*" quickly transforms a person from appreciative stranger to propositioning prostitute.

Yes, those humbling moments were always out there waiting for me, sitting along my life path making daisy chains until it was time to jump out, trip me up, and turn me into a fool. You'd think this travel learning curve would get exhausting after a while, but I was surprised to find it all strangely exhilarating. Every time we didn't know what we were doing, we eventually figured it out, and when we did, a little seed of pride blossomed in my chest. It was like being a little kid and mastering something for the first time. But instead of, "Look, I tied my shoes all by myself!" it became "Look, I said thank you to someone without suggesting I have sex for money!"

Brian and I were sitting in the living room with Mari and Ori one evening when we discovered one massive travel blunder that would change the course of our trip.

"Trace, did you know about this Schengen thing?" Brian asked, his brow wrinkled with concern. He sat next to me on the couch staring at his laptop.

"What Schengen thing?"

Ori looked up from the book he'd been reading. "The Schengen Agreement? Yes, it is why we do not have checkpoints at all the borders in Europe now. It is much better than before."

"Well, according to this, it's not better for us," Brian said, staring intently at his screen.

"Why would it be a problem?" Ori asked with a shrug.

I leaned over and began scanning the article Brian had pulled up. "Oh no," I groaned. "We're already locked in on our rental car, aren't we?"

"Yep."

"What's the matter?" Mari asked as she walked over to look at Brian's computer.

"Americans only have a ninety-day visa for the Schengen Zone," Brian said. "And it looks like most countries in Europe are part of it."

"So, you can only be in Europe for ninety days total?" Mari asked.

"No, no, no," Ori interjected as he got up to join the rest of us around Brian's computer. "You can go to a country not in the Zone and then come back and the ninety days start again, yes?"

"No, because look at this," Brian said, pointing to a line of text on the screen. "We can be here 90 days out of every 180 days. The visa doesn't start over if we leave the Zone and come back."

A simultaneous dawning of realization came to Mari and Ori's faces. "Well, that sucks," Mari said flatly.

"Yeah, especially since we just paid for five months on our rental car," I added.

We all sat there in silence for a few moments until Brian spoke up. "It'll be fine," he said confidently. "This just means we're going to spend a lot of time in the countries that *aren't* in the Schengen Zone." He squinted at the screen. "All three of them."

REMEMBERING AMONG THE RUINS

Urges to punch a human in the face: 12
Bored children: 3
Dead policemen: 1
Talking pigs: 1

FRANCE ◎ CROATIA

As one of the few countries not part of the Schengen Zone, Croatia became the next destination of our journey. We knew very little about it, other than the news reports we'd seen back in the '90s when the country went through a bloody civil war after the fall of communism. However, we'd heard it was now one of the most beautiful, peaceful, and inexpensive places in Europe, so we searched online and found a tiny apartment situated in the coastal town of Labin. A seven-day road trip would take us out of Andorra, across France, Italy, and Slovenia to our new temporary home on the Istrian peninsula. After hugs and goodbyes with our family, we set off in our little rental car, ready to meet the truly unknown—a country where we didn't speak the language and didn't know a soul.

We drove straight from Andorra to Nimes, France, and spent the afternoon walking among the town's eclectic mix of classic French and Roman architecture. Streets of white, limestone buildings led to a restored coliseum, a remnant of the region's era under ancient Roman rule. After wandering the city for a while, we stopped in a courtyard and found a café where we could order a few crepes. When in France, right?

"Do you people know what you want?"

The monotone French-accented English came from behind me, accompanied by a heavy sigh. I turned and saw our waiter looking down at me through a swath of scraggly, bleached-blond bangs. I could almost read his mind. *Stupeed Ah-meri-cahns.*

We brushed off his rudeness, ordered our crepes, and happily ate them in our quaint little courtyard. As the sun began to set, a shadow crept its way up the stone walls of the buildings, and the air turned cool. Brian paid the bill and we started the walk back to our hotel, but within seconds he stopped, his eyes wide and his hands frantically searching his pockets.

"Oh my god, Trace. Where's my wallet?" He went through those first bewildered moments of denial. "It has to be here somewhere. I *just* had it." He checked his pockets again, and I checked my purse. We returned to our table at the café and searched, but it was nowhere to be found. Soon we were resentfully making all the necessary calls to the credit card companies and figuring out how to get Brian's driver's license replaced.

After two hours of stolen wallet drama, I went out to get us a much-needed bottle of wine. As I walked by the ornate fountain in the central square, a gloomy sulk pulled my face into a scowl. It wasn't just the theft. It was the taunting statement this situation seemed to be making about our own naivety in this travel endeavor. It felt as though we'd already been defeated just barely out of the gate, like the universe was mocking us. *Oh, you think you can travel around the world, do you? Let's see how you handle a petty crime within the first twelve hours of your grand European road trip, suckers.*

As I wandered the streets in search of a wine shop, I passed by the café again and saw our waiter sitting at a table smoking a cigarette. He'd been poignantly absent from the scene when we'd come back to search for Brian's wallet. Later, as we retraced the events of the afternoon, we suspected him of stealing it. We had no proof, but something told me this guy was guilty, and I felt an undying need to call him out on it. A quiet fury festered in me as I watched him from across the courtyard, the cigarette dangling from his lips while he talked to the pretty waitress sitting across from him.

Suddenly, I found myself marching toward him, my sandals slapping against the cobblestones and sending an echoing racket off the buildings as an internal force propelled me forward with dogged purpose.

"Excuse me," I blurted out when I reached his table. "I think you picked up my husband's wallet."

The young man slowly pulled the cigarette from his mouth and glanced up at me from under half-open eyelids. *"No anglais,"* he muttered.

"But you were speaking English when we were here before?" I said, pretending to be confused. "You know, when my husband's wallet went missing?"

He shook his head and gave me a dismissive wave. "I do not understand you."

I repeated my words slowly and loudly as though speaking to an elderly person with hearing aids. "I think . . . you have . . . my husband's wallet. I. Want. It. Back."

He tossed a lock of greasy hair out of his droopy eyes and muttered something in French to his coworker. She laughed as he looked up at me and said, "Lady, I do not know what you speak of. Please leave me alone."

As he spoke, I noticed his teeth were a strange brown color, giving me a moment of motherly concern for his health. Then he took a long drag and stared at me with a smirk, letting the smoke float from the corner of his mouth up into my face. When I coughed and waved it away, he blew a snide laugh through his nostrils. It felt like a challenge. *You can't prove anything, you dumb Ah-meri-cahn.*

Unfair as it might be, I decided then and there he was undoubtedly a thief. He and his greasy hair and his half-open eyelids and his weird brown teeth were going to get away with stealing money and credit cards, as I was sure he'd done before and would do again. I wanted to punch him and scream in his face. I wanted to grab a fistful of that nasty hair and yell, "Listen, you pathetic little leech on French society! Keep the damn money to support the drug habit that's turning your teeth that lovely shade of baby diarrhea, but give me back the credit cards and driver's license so we don't have to go through the hassle of replacing things that are *totally worthless to you!*"

Suffice it to say, I didn't scream in his face. Instead, I stalked over to the manager and made a big show of ranting about our wallet situation. As he courteously checked to see if it had been turned in, the waiter's furtive glances at me from across the patio further solidified his guilt in my mind.

"I am so sorry, Madame, but no one found a wallet today," the manager said as he walked back to me. "Do you wish for me to call the local police officers so you can give a report?"

I wanted to win this wallet war in some way. Having a little

French squad car show up and scare the bejesus out of Brown Tooth Boy seemed like an effective option.

You do realize none of this is going to make you any happier, right? Observer Tracey popped the thought into my head. *You're choosing to make this harder than it needs to be.*

I took a deep breath and rolled my eyes at myself. The hot fury churning in my gut began to cool, and the tension melted from my shoulders. Like so many other times in life, this wasn't about what had happened, but rather how I would choose to react.

Why am I trying to create more drama? This isn't worth it.

I looked over at the kid I'd been demonizing moments before, and he seemed different somehow. Still greasy and aloof, but a little less villainous and a little more vulnerable. If he was going around stealing wallets from tourists, he was having a much harder time in life than I was. He stubbed out his cigarette and threw me a quick glance before walking into the café.

"Madame, shall I call the police to come?" the manager asked again.

Do you want to be right? Or do you want to be happy?

I turned and gave him a resigned smile. "No. No, I don't think that will be necessary."

Then I politely thanked him for his help, strode out of that courtyard, and let the whole thing go. Life is about choices, and that day I chose to be happy.

A few days later, I was driving our car along the winding roads and rolling hills of Croatia's Istrian peninsula, rarely passing another vehicle. A ceiling of low, grey clouds hovered over the small towns we passed, each with its own stone bell tower keeping watch over the region. We arrived in Labin shortly after sunset and found ourselves driving aimlessly around dark, unfamiliar streets. Our rental car's GPS system couldn't locate the address of our apartment, and in a classic idiotic move I hadn't bothered to get directions from the owner. We finally stopped at a restaurant to use the phone, and as luck would have it, the manager happened to be good friends with our landlord.

Within minutes, a red compact car pulled up with a smiling man behind the wheel. "*Dobrodošli*, my friends!" he called in heavily-accented English as he heaved his stocky frame from the vehicle. "I am so happy to see you! I am Cornelje! You stay in my family's property!" He grasped Brian's hand with both of his and shook it vigorously. "Welcome, welcome! We are so happy you come!" Cornelje took me by the shoulders to plant a kiss on each cheek, and then peered into the backseat of our car. "And here are your beautiful children! Wonderful!" Cornelje banged on the glass and waved enthusiastically. "MY MOTHER IS VERY—ah, what is word...*uzbuden*...ah yes—EXCITED! MY MOTHER IS VERY EXCITED TO MEET YOU! SHE GIVE YOU SWEETS! YOU LIKE SWEETS, YES?"

Emily, Liv, and Ali smiled nervously and exchanged looks as Cornelje clapped his hands together. "We shall go, yes? Let us go to the house! Come!"

Soon we were following our jovial friend's car down a long, dark driveway to a house we never would have found on our own. After helping with our luggage, Cornelje led us around the back of the large stucco home and up a few steps to our little two-bedroom apartment on the first floor. We stepped into the small but immaculately clean kitchen/dining room/living room. "My parents live in top of house," Cornelje explained as he pulled one of our bags into a tiny bedroom. "They come soon."

As if on cue, a tall woman with short, dark, wavy hair and a broad smile stepped through the doorway, followed by a gentleman who looked like an older, more serious version of Cornelje.

"This is my mother, Jele," Cornelje said. Jele smiled and laughed as she moved down the line of our family, giving quick kisses on each cheek. When she got to Ali, Jele pulled her into a big hug and began talking excitedly.

"My mother say she hope you help in garden and orchard," Cornelje said to Ali. "You can pick fruit and eat as much as you want." Ali smiled shyly and nodded.

"This is my father, Zdravko," Cornelje said. Hearing his name, Zdravko smiled and stepped forward, thrusting two bottles at Brian.

"Thank you," Brian said, taking a bottle in each hand and

turning them to read the labels. Zdravko nodded and said a few words to his son, gesturing at the bottles.

"My father want me to tell you the wine is from our family's grapes," Cornelje explained, pointing to one bottle. "And this one, it is a Croatian spirit. My father make it and it . . . how do you say? It will put hair on chest!" He let out a boisterous laugh and turned to walk out onto the patio. "Come! Let's get you drinking!"

After a glass of their family wine and a couple shots of Zdravko's whisky, my brain buzzed and my stomach burned. I leaned my head back on the patio chair and gazed up into the inky blackness of the moonless night sky, listening to the conversation around me. It had been a long day of driving, and my eyes began to droop as Brian told Cornelje and his parents our family's story. While Cornelje translated, Jele beamed and nodded, her hands clasped at her chest in rapt attention. When she began talking, her voice bubbled with enthusiasm and her arms gestured out to the land around the house, invisible to us in the darkness.

"My mother say this is a . . . how do you say . . . a *noble* adventure." Cornelje refilled wine glasses as he talked. "She want your time here to be special. For you to learn how we use our land. This will be good, yes?"

The next morning, we could see how every inch of the family's large lot had been put to use. A collection of trees dripping with heavy fruit occupied half the yard, and neat rows of vegetables lined the rest. A thriving grapevine had been carefully architected to form the roof over the carport and then edge its way along the perimeter of the property, creating a natural fence. The large house was subdivided into several apartments, each with its own balcony or patio looking out over the surrounding fields. Everything about our new home exuded a fierce independence, a survivability capable of feeding and sheltering an extended family through hard times.

This stoic personality could be felt among the citizens as well. Like our hosts, many locals maintained gardens, fruit trees, and grapevine carports, giving their homes both beauty and bounty. The people we encountered around Labin were guarded and efficient. No smiles from strangers or friendly greetings from store clerks, just serious faces focused on minding their own business.

Our first week there, I ran into Cornelje at an outdoor café. When I walked over to say hello, he looked up from his newspaper, gave me a quick nod, and then turned back to the words on the page. His brusque response left me a bit confused, because back at the house things were very different. When Cornelje stopped in to see his parents, he always came by our apartment to sit on the patio and share stories for a while. He introduced us to his wife and their two-year-old daughter, and he gave us advice on things we should see in his country. We fell into an easy friendship with his parents, too. Zdravko brought us bottles of wine, and Jele was always whipping up a baked treat for us. Each morning when Jele came into the garden, Ali tiptoed out in her nightgown and followed her around the yard. "Ah-leeeee!" Jele would sing out when she had a special job for her or a perfectly ripe piece of fruit to share. The two of them developed a wordless friendship spanning across the generations. Yet, one day when Ali and I saw Jele at the grocery store, she gave us the same curt nod I'd gotten from Cornelje at the café. Public and private personas seemed to be very different for the Croatians we knew.

On Cornelje's recommendations, we took day trips from Labin and toured around to the other coastal towns of the Istrian peninsula. A canyon road near our house curved down through hills of olive and cypress trees, delivering us to the seaside resort town of Rabac, where the Adriatic pushed its aquamarine waters onto a diverse array of beaches. Small, smooth stones blanketed large sections of the shore, while others bloomed gardens of white, weather-worn boulders. In some inlets, a barrier of dark jagged rocks jutted into the water, seeming to protect the land from the sea. A restored coliseum in the port city of Pula and the polished stone corridors winding through the town of Rovinj revealed remnants of the Roman Empire once occupying Croatia's coastline. This taste of the local history motivated us to take a road trip south for a few days and visit the country's oldest cities.

Our first stop was Split, a town transporting visitors back in time with its ancient ruins and narrow stone alleyways. As our family sat among the pillars of Diocletian's Palace and climbed the steps of the Saint Domnius bell tower, Brian and I were in constant awe of the antiquity surrounding us. The girls, on the other hand, didn't seem to share our enthusiasm. They walked along without complaint, but as the day wore on, their bored looks and slouching shoulders made it clear they weren't enthralled with the wonder of it all like we were.

The next day, we arrived in Dubrovnik where the courtyards and ancient gates left me feeling like I'd stepped back into the Middle Ages. We walked along the top of the massive stone wall surrounding the city, and I marveled as every turn in the walkway offered a different panorama. Gazing out to the islands off the coast, I tried to imagine medieval trading ships gliding into the port. When I looked below us into the city streets, I could almost hear the rattle of horse-drawn carts echoing off the stone walls. Brian and I were mesmerized by it all, and yet, once again, the girls seemed bored to tears.

"How much longer are we gonna be up here?" Liv asked.

Emily sat down on a stone bench built into the wall's walkway. "Yeah, we've been walking around this place all day."

"Can we get something to eat?" Ali added dramatically. "I'm *starving.*"

"Seriously, girls?" I said. "Look at where we are! Isn't it amazing to be standing up here seeing all this? Hundreds of years ago, people walked on these same stones and sat on that same bench you're sitting on. Isn't that kind of cool?"

In response, I got three blank looks and a monotone, "Uh-huh."

For a moment, I felt a visceral anger course through me. *What is wrong with these little brats? Don't they have any appreciation for this amazing piece of history they're getting to see?*

But in an instant, I remembered another period in history. It was 1986 and I was with my family in Washington, DC, following my parents from one historic landmark to the next. The Lincoln Memorial, the White House, the Washington Monument, the Vietnam Wall. Almost thirty years had passed, but the details of that family vacation still stuck out among my childhood memories. Staring up at those grand monuments, so rich with our nation's history, left a deep impression on me. Yet, looking back on it, I realized that in Washington I'd been doing exactly what my kids were doing in Dubrovnik. I wasn't oohing and aahing. I was uh-huhing.

That's when I had a big parenting epiphany: kids hate walking around and looking at stuff. They're not going to appreciate a 2000-year-old coliseum or a grapevine that's been growing a hundred times longer than they've been alive. I could remember a time when I was the one with the bored expression on my face, but I also knew that somewhere in the girls' young minds connections were being made, shaping their memories and perspectives without them even realizing it. Their Dubrovnik was my Washington, DC. So, I managed to let go of my desire to see them ooh and aah, and took comfort in the fact that someday they'd look back on all this and appreciate every minute of it.

"We're supposed to turn right at a dead policeman."

Brian shot me a confused look. "What in the hell does that mean?"

I stared at the directions I'd copied down from the email. "I have no idea."

Brian shook his head and steered the car onto the shoulder. "Let me see these directions." He took the paper from my hands and began reading out loud. "Turn right at the church tower. Go down the hill. Turn right after the dead policeman. Go up a hill and you will see our farm." He stopped and looked at me skeptically. "Are you sure you copied this down right?"

I rolled my eyes. "I don't think I would have accidentally written the words 'dead policeman' without realizing it. I emailed her yesterday to ask what it meant, but never got a response."

Brian shrugged. "Maybe it's a statue or something," he suggested. "Like a memorial." He pulled the car back onto the road and drove slowly down the hill as we looked for something that could be described as a dead policeman.

That morning, we'd left our apartment at dawn and driven two hours inland to the outskirts of Zagreb. I'd found a web site connecting travelers to volunteer work around the world, and it led us to a family needing some extra helping hands on their small, organic farm. The wife and I had gone back and forth over email several times to set up our day with them, but finding the property was clearly proving to be more difficult than I'd anticipated.

"Is that it?" Liv asked, leaning forward from the back seat and pointing to a white rectangular stone box in the middle of a small park.

"What is that?" Brian asked. "A tomb?"

"That has to be it," I said, looking at the paper. "The directions say to make a right turn after this dead policeman thing, and look. There's a road up ahead on the right."

We passed the monument, turned right, and drove up a hill. As the directions indicated, we quickly came to a farm. A large weather-worn house with a wide front porch sat close to the gravel road, tucked behind an overgrown hedgerow. Wooden outbuildings stood behind it with various pieces of farm equipment leaning against the walls. As our car's tires rolled to a stop on the shoulder, a small, smiling woman with long dark hair pulled back in a neat ponytail walked down from the front porch and waved at us.

"You found us!" she called out in perfect English, with just the slightest hint of an accent. "It can be hard to explain how to get here. I always worry people will get lost. I am Dunja Kovačić," she said. "It is nice to meet you in person, Tracey. And you must be Brian." She shielded her eyes from the sun as she looked up at him. "Wow. You are very tall," she added with a laugh.

As the girls introduced themselves, a little head peaked out from behind Dunja's leg. "This is Josipa. She is four years old," Dunja said, putting a hand on her daughter's head. "That little man hiding on our porch is her younger brother, Simun. And this," she said, placing a hand on her swollen belly, "this is a little someone we will meet in a few months."

"I didn't know you're expecting," I said. "Congratulations."

"Yes, it is why we need extra help. I am not able to do as much as usual."

"Well, that's why we came," Brian said, clapping his hands together. "Put us to work."

Soon we all had jobs to do. Ali and Josipa gathered eggs from the hen house. Brian and Dunja's husband, Renato, worked together on a section of fence near the barn. Emily and Liv cleaned out the horse stalls and spread fresh straw on the dirt floors, while I pulled weeds in the garden with Dunja. Within a couple hours, we'd fallen into an easy camaraderie with the Kovačić family. I heard Brian and

Renato laughing a lot over their construction work, and the children giggled as they ran around the property together.

After making my way down a row of Swiss chard, I stood up to stretch and look out over the landscape. The quiet fields surrounding the house sloped gently toward a dense forest, which spanned out over the undulating hills like a deep green carpet. An abundant tangle of pumpkin vines lined a fenced pasture, where several horses gathered around a metal trough. Chickens, ducks, and pigs roamed freely throughout the farm, while a small herd of goats stood staring at me from their pen. Following my gaze, Dunja answered my unspoken question.

"If we let the goats out, I have no garden," she said. "Those animals eat everything they see."

"Then they'll love these weeds." I gestured to the wheelbarrow overflowing with scraggly plants. My eyes scanned the land again, and I could make out another farm sitting off in the distance. "I had no idea what Croatia would look like before we came here. You live in a very beautiful place, Dunja."

"Yes, it is beautiful. Very peaceful. I don't think many Americans know what we have," she said thoughtfully as she lowered herself onto a stool. "They only seem to know of our civil war."

"Honestly, that's really all I knew about before we came here. I was in high school then, but I remember it got a lot of coverage on the American news networks. Was that a hard time for your family?"

"No. I was not here for most of my childhood." Dunja pushed a strand of hair from her eyes with the back of her hand. "My father worked overseas, so I attended the international schools where we lived. That's why I speak English so well. There were a lot of American students and everything was taught in English. I wasn't here at all during the war." She paused and looked off in the direction of Brian and Renato, her demeanor shifting to a serious tone. "Renato, though . . . His family struggled through it, and it's been hard on them ever since. His parents lost—" She stopped midsentence and took a deep breath, seeming to shake off a painful thought. "Well, they lost a lot of faith in this country. They complain they have the same jobs as before, but they make less money. There are still many who want the old government back."

Dunja paused and I wanted to ask her more, but she quickly smiled and slapped her hands onto her legs. "I think we will put some meat on the grill for lunch," she said. Standing up awkwardly from her stool, she walked out of the garden toward our husbands, who were chatting at the fence. Dunja called out to Renato in Croatian, and he immediately began laughing.

"That is what she said!" he called back, smiling and nodding at Brian.

Dunja turned to me with a confused look. "What did he say?" she asked.

I rolled my eyes and sighed. "Sorry. My husband's corrupting him with dumb American jokes."

She paused and tilted her head. "This is an American joke? To say to someone 'that is what she said'?"

"Umm . . . yeah, sort of. It's kind of hard to explain."

An hour later, we were all sitting around the family's large kitchen table in front of plates piled high with grilled vegetables and steak. As we ate our meal, a large sow came wandering in through the open back door. When Renato scolded her in Croatian, the pig turned to glare at him. He pointed to the door and spoke louder, but the pig didn't move, responding only with a long series of grunts. Renato tried again, but the pig stood her ground and blasted two loud snorts at him. Finally, he unloaded a diatribe on her, shouting angrily as his gestures punched the air with frustration. The pig gave him a long stare and finally blew out an impetuous sigh. Then she stalked to the door, muttering quiet grunts to herself.

Dunja smiled at me and said, "Renato told her if she does not leave the kitchen she will not get any scraps from our lunch." She shook her head and stabbed her fork into a piece of steak. "I swear, those two are always fighting."

After lunch, Brian and Renato finished up the fence, and I cleared the last weeds from the garden. When the afternoon sun began casting long shadows over the farm, Renato decided it was time for horseback rides. He slid a bridle and lead rope onto a handsome white horse and led each of the children around the pasture. I stood with my arms resting on the fence and watched the sun stream through a patch of clouds, each ray lighting up a little piece of land in the distance. It had been a memorable day with their family, and I was sad to see it end.

"Tracey, I am very thankful your family spends this day with us," Dunja said, walking toward me with Simun on her hip. Then she laughed and added, "And not just because that fence is finally fixed and the garden has no more weeds." She set Simun down, and we watched him climb through the fence to join the girls in the pasture. Then she leaned against the railing and looked at me with kind eyes. "It is good to have new people to visit with. You have a wonderful family."

"So do you." I smiled and glanced down at her belly. "Although, I hate that we won't get to meet the newest little member of it."

"Do not say that!" Dunja exclaimed, lightly slapping my arm. "Someday you will be back to meet her . . . or him."

It was almost dark by the time we ended our day with the Kovačić family. As we gave everyone hugs and said good-bye, Renato insisted on sending us back with some dates and plums from their trees. We were loading into the car when I remembered a question I'd been meaning to ask all day.

"Hey, what happened to the police officer?" I asked.

Dunja gave me a perplexed look. "What police officer?"

"That memorial we passed on the way here," Brian explained. "You know, before turning onto your road."

Renato shook his head and looked at Dunja. "A what? What is this word . . . memorial?"

Dunja attempted to explain it to him, speaking a few words in Croatian. She shrugged and said, "I do not know this memorial. We don't have anything—" Suddenly, she stopped and widened her eyes. "Oh! The dead policeman?"

"That stone tomb is for a policeman that died, right?" I asked.

Dunja began laughing. "No, no, no . . . a dead policeman is a . . . I do not know what you call it. It is a hump in the road. To slow down cars."

"A speed bump?" Brian asked.

"Yes! A speed bump!"

Brian and I smiled and shook our heads at our own ridiculousness in thinking someone would actually refer to a memorial as a dead policeman.

"So, what is that white stone tomb for?" I asked out of curiosity.

Dunja and Renato looked at each other and shrugged.

"This is very good question," Renato said. "We find out and we tell you next time you come."

PEACHES AND COCONUTS

Friendly strangers: 0
Medieval torture devices: Too many
Episodes of kid drama: Too many
New-old friends: 4

CZECH REPUBLIC

"Why does everyone look so mad?" Ali asked, warily eying the crowd swarming around us.

"Because we're the dumb tourists, sweetie," I said as I stared up at the signs over each staircase and attempted to get my bearings. Standing in the middle of Prague's Staroměstská metro station during rush hour was not making us any new friends among this mob of tired Czech commuters trying to get home.

After a month in warm, scenic Croatia, we had to leave Jele, Zdravko, and our little apartment with its yard of grapevines and fruit trees or else risk violating our thirty-day visa. So, we ventured back into the Schengen Zone, arriving in Prague on a rainy day. We drove along the Vltava river and then crossed over it to find our apartment in the Vinohrady area of the city. Utilitarian structures from the Soviet era had been squeezed in between classic art nouveau buildings, combining the bluntly stark with the lavishly ornate.

Urban life proved to be a big change from our days in rural Croatia. We left our car parked in a garage and navigated through the city by foot, bus, and train, finding historic areas to explore and parks where the girls could play. Outside the large windows of our second-floor apartment, the street woke up before dawn with the sounds of car horns and bus engines and heels clicking on the sidewalk. We managed to shift into urban mode quickly, and by the end of our first week in the city, I was the one rolling my eyes at the confused tourists standing in the middle of the metro stations.

A short walk to a green line metro train gave us easy access to the many historic sites around Prague. This eclectic city has withstood the test of time. At the start of World War II, it was one of few major metropolitan areas in Europe that hadn't been scarred by battle. Its gothic monuments and medieval castles remained preserved, while a modern city flourished around them.

One of the city's more recent additions was the Rudolfinum, a concert hall and art gallery constructed in the late 1800s and decorated with statues of the world's great musicians along its roofline. When the German army invaded in the spring of 1939, Hitler declared Prague the jewel of his growing empire, but he wasn't pleased to learn Rudolfinum's sculptures paid tribute to a Jewish composer, Felix Mendelssohn. Hitler, of course, ordered the statue be removed from the roof and destroyed. However, the officers carrying out this task apparently weren't classical music buffs and didn't know what Mendelssohn looked like. Following their own prejudiced beliefs, they simply found the statue with the biggest nose and pushed it off the roof. As it turned out, they'd instead destroyed the statue of Hitler's favorite German composer, Richard Wagner. Throughout World War II and to this day, Felix Mendelssohn remains on the roof of Rudolfinum, a symbol of defiance to the Nazi regime. As we learned the history of Prague Castle, the Old Town Square, and other famous landmarks, the story of Rudolfinum remained my favorite. It embodied the spirit of this resilient city. Prague endured war and political turbulence, yet, just like its people, the buildings and monuments survived.

We took advantage of this rich history in the girls' homeschooling and got them researching the stories behind the places we were visiting. Although, I quickly learned that this educational strategy would need to be monitored very closely.

"Hey, Mama, guess what?" Liv said to me one day from behind my laptop screen. "You know that big fancy clock at the square? The one with all the moving people and stuff?"

"The Astronomical Clock?"

"Yeah, that one. So, you know what they did to the guy who built it?" she asked, a look of amused disgust on her face.

"No . . . " I braced myself.

"They gouged out his eyes with a hot poker!"

"What! Why?" I walked over to look at the web site she'd been reading.

"Because the leaders didn't want him to make another clock as good as that one. Isn't that gross?"

"Good grief," I muttered, scanning the article. "Let's work on your math facts, okay?"

Another time, Emily stared at the computer screen in shock and said, "Um . . . Mom . . . What is this?" While researching Prague Castle, she'd stumbled across a web site showing gratuitous images of the inhumane torture devices once used on the prisoners in its dungeons. I quickly snapped the laptop shut. So much for medieval history lessons in elementary school . . . or ever for that matter!

Perhaps it was this startling exposure to the darkness of the human soul that put the girls in a bit of a mood during our time in Prague, because the kid drama reached an unprecedented level. At any given moment, one of our girls had something to be furious about—a bossy sister, a broken toy, a homework problem. The three of them were a rotating trilogy of emotional turbulence. I imagined them secretly planning their schedule of drama like athletes taking on a rival team.

"Okay, Liv, you head us off with the morning grouch play, and I'll take over at noon with a round of prepubescent moodiness. Then Ali will come in with her overtired preschooler routine. If we haven't broken them by dinner, we can always fall back on the old shrill-screams-of-laughter zone defense until one of them cracks. Got it, team? Okay, *break!*"

The daily dose of tension the girls delivered to our tiny apartment put everyone on edge. One particularly drama-filled morning, Brian and I exchanged exasperated looks as shrieks and accusations spilled from their bedroom.

"Stop taking paper out of my notebook, Emily!" Liv screamed.

"I didn't!" Emily yelled back. "Stop accusing me of something I didn't do! What about Ali? Maybe she took your stupid paper. You never accuse *her* of anything!"

Shaking his head, Brian pulled out a pair of headphones. "Hey, Trace, if you need anything, I'll be wearing these all day." He stuck a headphone into each ear and feigned an exaggerated look of relief and tranquility.

"Yeah, well, if you need me, I won't be here." I grabbed my

jacket and jerked open the door of our apartment, selfishly leaving Brian to play referee on his own.

Walking through the stone plazas of Prague Castle and alongside the immaculate flower beds in the Royal Gardens, I ruminated on our cranky kid situation. By the time I'd wandered down through the city's cobbled streets and into the gardens of Wallenstein Palace, I'd gotten myself pretty worked up over the dysfunctional dynamic our family had fallen into.

This is not acceptable! These children are going to be happy and appreciative and respectful and cooperative, even if it kills all of us!

As I silently rehearsed the lecture I intended to unleash on the girls, I stumbled upon an unusual situation unfolding among some manicured bushes.

The Wallenstein Garden had several resident peacocks, and one of them was apparently walking in an area deemed inappropriate for peafowl strolls. I watched as an angry uniformed woman chased the peacock around the bushes, getting both herself and the bird very riled up. When she started yelling at it, a crowd of onlookers gathered to watch the peculiar scene. The guard flailed her arms and shouted in Czech as the peacock darted out of her reach.

A little British boy standing next to me looked up at his mother and asked, "Why does the peacock live in this big garden if he isn't supposed to be here?"

Good point, kid. If they don't want peacocks in the bushes, why have peacocks at all? The whole place was pretty much a massive collection of decorative shrubbery.

And that's when another parenting epiphany hit me. *Why do kids have all these emotions if we never want them to use them?*

For the last several months, Brian and I had essentially been chasing the girls out of their bad moods. We'd taken a "Be happy or else!"–approach when it came to their fighting and grouchiness. It probably should have come as no surprise that we were getting the same results as this security guard chasing a peacock. The girls kept doing what they were doing, but they were confused and they liked us a lot less.

Watching the wheezing guard, I realized giving the girls yet another lecture was not the answer to our problem. As with the whole stolen wallet fiasco in France, this wasn't about what was happening, but rather how I would choose to react. Instead of viewing the girls' foul moods and melodrama as Machiavellian attempts to turn my hair gray, I suddenly saw it all as preparation for life. This emotional development is a normal process for kids to go through, but as parents, we want them to just *be happy.*

I mulled all this over as I walked back to the apartment, and the moment I opened the door I stepped into another kid battle.

"Mama!" Ali yelled. She rushed to the door and stood in front of me, hands shoved into her armpits and her little face pulled into a scowl. "Emily moved all my stuffed animals to a different shelf! I had that shelf *first* and now she's trying to *steal* it!"

"I'm not stealing it, Alison!" Emily yelled from the girls' bedroom. "It doesn't make sense for you to have the higher shelf and me to have the lower shelf! I'm taller! You're shorter! *Duh!*"

I looked over to the table and saw Brian serenely working at his computer, the headphones clearly serving their intended purpose. Shaking off the rage I felt bubbling up, I squatted down so I could look Ali in the eye. Then I took a deep breath and tried a new tactic.

"I can tell you're really mad over that shelf," I said. She nodded her head slowly. "The shelf is making you all mad and icky inside, isn't it? It's kind of controlling the way you feel right now." Another solemn nod. "What do you think you can do to be in control again? What could you do that would make you happy instead of mad?"

Internally, I rolled my eyes at myself. I sounded like I was trying to be a damn child psychologist. This was so stupid.

But then . . . magic.

Ali pursed her lips and shrugged. She looked back at the bedroom where Emily was arranging her Pooh Bear and some books on the shelf in question. After a moment, Ali turned back to me and said, "Hey, Mama, can we see if that Czech cartoon with the weird little mole is on?"

Drama defused.

I smiled. Apparently, Ali didn't care about that shelf as much as she thought she did. It was time for a happy episode of *Krteček*, the mischievous mole.

◎ ◎ ◎

As the girls' behavior improved, so did nomadic life. They did their schoolwork in the morning while Brian worked, and then we all went out to explore the city together in the afternoon. We volunteered with some local organizations, spending a few days making sandwiches for a homeless shelter and constructing a sensory garden at a school for children with disabilities. Once we got to know them a little, the Czech people were warm, welcoming, and extremely helpful. However, as we'd noticed in Croatia, the culture of the former Soviet Bloc didn't embrace pleasantries much. There were no greetings from passersby or friendly interactions with store clerks. In fact, whenever I smiled at someone they looked at me like I was batshit crazy. This stark cultural difference became a topic of conversation with new friends of ours.

Through some of our volunteer work, we'd gotten to know Linda and Rostislav. Their daughter, Lada, was Liv's age and their son, Sebastian, was just a little older than Ali. Rostislav was an entrepreneur and had a wealth of knowledge about the historical changes his country had experienced since the fall of communism. Linda was a leadership consultant and an adjunct professor at a local university. She loved bringing big philosophical ideas to even the simplest of dinner topics. Our conversations with them always left me feeling inspired and educated.

"The Czech seem rude to you because you are a peach," Linda said as she refilled my wine glass one night. "You are used to everyone being so smiley all the time. But to me, a coconut, friendliness from strangers seems a bit . . . how do you say it? Fake?"

"Peaches and coconuts," Brian said. "Are we talking about dessert now?"

Linda laughed. "You do not know Fons Trompenaars' analogy on international cultures?" she asked.

"No, I think we missed that one," I teased, taking a sip of wine. "Why don't you tell us about it, Linda?"

"Okay, I will," she said with a giggle and leaned back in her chair. "You see, you Westerners are the peaches. You seem really soft and nice on the outside, but in the middle, you are very tough. You have a hard pit. And that pit does not let people in easily. You are friendly to everyone, but you do not consider everyone your friend. It takes a long time for you to really let someone into your inner circle. To be like family to you."

Linda leaned forward and gestured to Rostislav. "But we Czech, we are the coconuts. We have a hard shell on the outside. No smiles on the streets. No talking to people we do not know. We seem very serious, but then, boink." She made a little gesture, like a hammer tapping the air. "One little crack in the shell and you find we are all milk inside. When we talk to you, when we invite you into our homes, it is because you are like *family* to us. That is the difference between the peaches and the coconuts."

Brian nodded thoughtfully. "That makes total sense. We've hardly talked to anyone here, but with the few people we do know, it seems like we've been friends for years."

"The first time I experienced this difference I was very confused," Rostislav said. "This American starts talking to me on a train. I thought it unusual, talking to a stranger like this, but soon I am in a conversation with this man. We tell each other about our families and our work and where we grow up. Very personal things. So, I think he and I are very good friends now, yes? When we come to his stop, the guy takes his bag and says to me, 'Okay, have a good trip' and walks off the train. The end! Have a nice life!" Rostislav laughed and shook his head. "It was so strange to me."

"I've never thought about it before, but it's absolutely true," I said. "I strike up conversations with people all the time, knowing I'll never see them again. I never thought it was weird . . . until now."

"But it is not weird," Linda said, her face lighting up with excitement. "It reflects the history of your country. The United States, it is the melting pot of the world. All these new and different people coming together, meeting each other, working together. This easy connection to new people is a fundamental element of your society. But our Czech history is so different. We had wars and communism and political upheaval. We learn over the centuries to keep our heads down and to be careful who we talk to. It's our history that makes us who we are today. It's fascinating, yes?"

I smiled at her. "Yes, it is. And so are you, Linda." Then I raised my glass and looked around the table. "Here's to drinking the milk of your coconuts." Pause. "Yeah, that didn't come out right."

And then we laughed with our new, old friends.

SHINY HAPPY PEOPLE . . .
DRINKING BEER

Unhealthy calories consumed: All of them

Friendly strangers: All of them

Beers drunk: All of them

Regrets: 0

IRELAND

"**H**elp you with somethin', folks? You're lookin' a bit lost, I'd say."
It was our first day in Ireland, and we were standing in the middle of Dublin's large pedestrian walkway staring at Brian's phone. A tiny woman with pink cheeks and a bright smile appeared next to us, her small frame bringing her barely to Brian's elbow.

"We're just trying to figure out where to go," Brian said, gesturing to the Trip Advisor page open on his phone. "We're only in town for a few days."

"Oh well, in that case, I might have a few suggestions for ya. Those web site things don't know Dublin like they think they do," she said with a conspiratorial wink.

Our friendly stranger proceeded to spend twenty minutes with us, listing off places to eat, pubs with the best music, and scenic drives along the coast. It was a substantial change from our life with the coconuts. In Ireland, we were surrounded by smiley, happy peaches everywhere we went.

We spent a few days in Dublin and then made our way across Ireland's green countryside, stopping to explore the gray, weathered remains of Celtic ruins. After a lunch of fish 'n' chips and a short detour caused by a large herd of sheep, we arrived in Castletownshend, a tiny village sitting on the southwest coast. Row houses lined each side of the main street, the transition from one cottage to the next distinguishable only by a change in paint color. The exterior of our little rental house was bright white, and its quaint Dutch door gleamed electric blue.

We'd just finished hauling in the last of our bags when our neighbor from next door came out to stand on the sidewalk. His stocky frame leaned against the brick wall of his cottage as he puffed on a cigarette in one hand and took swigs from the can of hard cider in the other.

"Evenin'," he called out in a deep, raspy voice. "Need any help thar?"

"Thanks, but that was the last of it," Brian called back before walking over to introduce himself. "I'm Brian. Our family's staying here for a while."

"Yeah, I know. Ever'body knows ever'thin' here. I'm Alan. I told the owner I'd help ya out if ya need it. I do work for folks 'roun town. Ya wanna bitta firewood? I can get ya some if yar planning to make fires in yar fireplace, which ya should best do, by the way, cuz' the heatin' oil's bloody expensive. I got alotto wood out back. Ya wanna cider?"

That's pretty much how all interactions went during our time in the land of green grass and rainbows. We made instantaneous friends who offered their help, advice, and often alcohol in every conversation. Alan and his ciders became a regular part of our life in Castletownshend, as did McCarthy's Pub down the road from our cottage.

The girls quickly met the only other family in the village with young children. Manu, Leo, and Naza were the same ages as the girls, and soon the six of them were running around town, thick as thieves. They played in the woods, collected shells at the beach, and bought sugary treats at Batt's Shop, the only store in town.

The metropolis of Skibbereen—population 2,400—was a ten-minute drive inland, and our family soon became regulars at the public library and Apple Betty's Café. Our first days in Ireland felt like stepping back in time. The girls ran around the village all day and came home dirty, sweaty, and smiling, talking about the new game they'd invented or the fort they'd made from fallen branches. When an afternoon shower rolled in, the kids all ran back to our cottage and piled though the door a wet, laughing, hungry mob. I made hot chocolate and put some snacks on a tray while they pulled out a board game to play in front of the fireplace. Yes, we had a lot of Norman Rockwell moments in our little Irish village.

It was during one of these happy, rainy afternoons that I noticed Ali scratching her head a lot. Upon inspection, I found a series of angry, red bumps running down the middle of her scalp. The next day, I took her to the Skibbereen medical clinic and stood anxiously awaiting a diagnosis from the young doctor examining her head. *Lice? Ringworm? What fun plague of parenthood will I get to deal with?* "Well," the doctor said, poking around in her hair. "Looks like she's got the midges."

My face contorted into a look of shock. After getting our family vaccinated for everything under the sun, I didn't think there could possibly be a disease I didn't know about.

"Ya need not look so horrified, now," he said with a smile. "She won't be dyin' from it."

I relaxed a bit. "That's good to know, but what are the midges?"

He laughed and sat down at the examination room's desk. "They're just wee little bugs that come out near evenin' time. Kids her age often get bites along the parts in their hair, I s'pose 'cause they're about as tall as the midges can fly." He pulled out his prescription pad and began writing. "I'm going to give you an antihistamine spray to help with the scratchin'. It'll take a couple weeks, but her system'll get used to 'em and she won't have such an allergic reaction like she does now."

He tore the paper from his pad and handed it to me as he stood up. "If you don't mind me askin', are you Americans?"

"Yes!" Ali exclaimed, hopping down from the examination table. "We're going all the way around the world. We're homeless!"

"Are you, now?" the doctor said, shooting me a smile as he talked to her. "You sleep outside, now do ya?"

"We do actually have a house," I said. "We're travelling internationally for a while and decided to come to Ireland for about six weeks."

"You don't say! Well, fair to play to ya. What made ya pick Skibbereen? We don't get many American visitors down here in these parts."

"We just wanted to be near the coast and we found a cheap rental out in Castletownshend."

"Oh yeah, nice lil' spot. I've actually got good friends out there near ya. Mark and Anne Townshend." He opened the door to the hallway. "I imagine they'd like to meet this homeless family of yours," he added with a wink.

True to friendly Irish form, a few days later we were sitting at Mark and Anne Townsend's kitchen table drinking wine and sharing stories while the girls watched movies with their daughter in the living room. Their family's English ancestors settled Castletownshend in the seventeenth century, building a stone castle overlooking the harbor and the church of St. Barrahane up on the hill. The castle now served as a bed and breakfast, and the Townshend family lived in a cozy home nearby with a view of the water.

"I've got loads of people I can connect you to for volunteering if you'd like," Anne said. "The most darlin' little woman you'll ever meet organizes Christmas boxes for children in Africa. And we've got a cultural festival comin' up in a couple weeks. You could be our American representatives!"

I laughed. "Wear red, white, and blue and bring apple pie?"

"Exactly!"

"I can use you this weekend for our charity race if you're interested," Mark suggested. "We need people to help work the trail running course. And the best part is, you can come to the party afterwards." He smiled mischievously. "It's a gas. You'll love it."

On the day of the Skibbereen Charity Adventure Race, Brian and I spent the morning standing on a hiking trail directing runners. That night, we went to the event's after party and sat around drinking beer with a table full of fun, welcoming Irish. Needless to say, it was a good time. In fact, a person would have to be just about the biggest stick in the mud on the planet to *not* have fun while sitting around drinking beer with the Irish.

Mark and Anne introduced us to their friends, and everyone who heard about our family's trip had a similar response. "Fair play to ya!"

After hearing it for about the tenth time, I had to know. "What exactly does that mean?" I asked.

The table erupted in laughter. That's what Irish people do— they laugh a lot.

"Yeah, I guess that's probably a new one for ya," Mark said. "Doesn't really make much sense if you've never heard it."

"It just means 'good for you'," Anne explained. "Like 'nice work', something like that."

"If you're going to be here for a while, you'll have to be pickin' up our weird sayings," one woman laughed. "We have a helluva lot of 'em."

That night and in the weeks to come, we learned many of Ireland's idioms. Even though we technically shared the same language with our new Irish friends, it could still be extremely hard to follow a conversation. "Yeah, they were on the tear since it'd been donkey's years. Totally acting the maggot. Got a bad dose, but since it's bucketing down, it's a good day to stay in the scratcher." Try figuring that one out without an Irish slang dictionary floating around in your head.

Thanks to the advice of Mark, Anne, Alan, and our other new friends, we thoroughly explored our little corner of Ireland. We watched rainbows appear in the sky as we picnicked among Celtic ruins, and we hiked through forests overflowing with hemlocks, ferns, and trees glowing fluorescent green with moss. We drove up to the Cliffs of Moher, where the rolling pastures suddenly dropped off hundreds of meters into the sea and created miles of spectacular cliff bands. Ireland was picturesque and friendly and easy.

For some strange reason, the effortlessness of it all made me a little uncomfortable. A restless yearning seemed to follow me around, yet I couldn't understand why. I was living in this unique part of the world, making friends, trying new foods, seeing something new every day. Hell, I was even driving on the other side of the road. *Why do I feel like something's missing from all this?* I wondered.

It finally occurred to me one day where this troublesome feeling was coming from. I'd run into Skibbereen to pick up a few things at the store, and when I pulled up to the house a startling thought hit me.

You don't remember driving home. You're totally doing it again! You're so wrapped up in your own thoughts, you're completely spacing out on the world around you!

Despite five months navigating through foreign countries and meeting people from all walks of life, I was still the same distracted woman I'd always been. Evidently, this life-changing journey wasn't changing me at all.

In the weeks before we left the United States, as we packed boxes and wrapped up our life in Chattanooga, I'd felt a little space open inside me, like a small void in my soul waiting to be filled. It was similar to the feeling I'd had before Ali came along, when Brian and I were debating whether we should have a third child. We'd talked about the costs and risks of another baby, but ultimately, the decision had come down to one simple belief: *Someone isn't here yet.* Deep down inside, I knew our family wasn't complete, that another little person was supposed to be with us.

That's the same feeling I had as I sat in the car and stared out onto Castletownshend's little main street. *A part of me isn't here yet, and I'm supposed to find her on this journey . . . so, where is she?* Ireland, with its gorgeous coastal views and friendly, happy people, seemed to be a little too pleasant for a deep, life-altering search of the soul. Perhaps I needed some uncomfortable drama to push me forward on my spiritual path.

As though the universe had read my mind, the very next day we ran into some uncomfortable drama—as in, we *literally* ran into it.

Exploring Ireland meant braving its narrow, winding roads, which often turned at acute angles around the fields and rock walls of the countryside. Driving was even more challenging for us since we had to maneuver our French right-hand rental car in the left lane of traffic. This meant the driver's seat was positioned on the outer shoulder of the roads, often mere inches from the tall stone walls and thick hedgerows paralleling them. Some sections of road were so tight that the foliage on either side had indentations where the side mirrors of vehicles had slowly chipped away at the leaves and branches.

We were travelling along one of these narrow country byways, surrounded by a tunnel of bushes and overhanging branches, when an ear-splitting crack suddenly shattered through our car.

I screamed from the passenger seat and covered my right ear as a pain erupted inside my head. "WHAT HAPPENED?" I shouted.

Brian rolled the car to a stop and turned to look through our back window. "Someone just blew off our side mirror! When I went by that truck, the car behind it was driving down the middle wah wah wah woe wha whay . . . "

His voice warbled as ringing filled my ears. Brian gave me a concerned look. "War wah wah whay?"

"WHAT?" I yelled back. "YOU SOUND LIKE THE CHARLIE BROWN TEACHER!" The ringing slowly faded to a hollow silence.

"WAH WEE, WAN WOO OKAY? CAN YOU HEAR ME?"

I nodded, not entirely sure this was the truth. My right ear still felt numb and strangely empty.

Brian and I got out and inspected the damage while the girls stayed in the car. The impact had shattered the side mirrors of both vehicles, leaving tiny fragments scattered all over the pavement. A few wires and some shards of plastic stuck out from the hole where our mirror had been, and a long crack ran down the length of the door panel. We spent some time picking up the wreckage and waiting to see if the other driver would show up. When my hearing finally returned to normal, I called our rental car company to find out what we should do next.

"Right lucky, you are," Alan said later that night, taking a swig from his can of cider and swinging his other arm over the back of our couch. "Sounds like they were tryin' to pass." Another swig. "Bloody dodgy drivers kill people on the road ever' day."

"I know there's no way it was my fault," Brian said, throwing a log on the fire. "I was over as far as I could get when I went by the truck."

"Oh, you can be sure tweren't your fault, my friend. That driver would've showed up fer sure if he thinkin' it be your fault. Nah, he knew he were to blame. Prob'ly gettin' in a car all knackered er out on a tear, suckin' diesel an throwin' shapes fer some feek." Alan drained his can and let out a loud burp. "Bloody gobshites."

Maybe I really had lost my hearing.

One afternoon, Brian and I walked down the block to McCarthy's Pub and wound up talking with two locals, Paddy and Moritz. By the end of our first beer, the four of us were laughing like old friends as they gave us advice on things we should do in town.

"Ya can't miss the phosphorescence on Loch Hyne," Paddy said. "You gotta go out there late at night to see it, though."

"What is it?" Brian asked as the bartender slid him another pint.

Paddy and Mortiz exchanged a look. "Ummm . . . well, I can't really describe it," Paddy said with a shrug. "It's a bit mental when you see it. These wee little bugs light up the water."

I'd heard of the bioluminescent phenomenon occurring on beaches around the world, but no one we'd met in town had mentioned one in this area. I looked skeptically between Paddy and Moritz and couldn't help but think they were pulling a prank on us.

"Are you being serious?" I asked.

"Yeah, o'course!" Paddy said. "It's amazin'!"

Brian glanced at me, sharing my skepticism. "So, you're saying we should drag our three young children out to Loch Hyne late at night and show them the little bugs that light up the water?"

"Yeah, they'll love it!" Paddy said, nodding enthusiastically.

I looked past him to Moritz, who'd been quiet on the topic. "Moritz," I said with grave seriousness. "Is this real?"

Paddy threw out his arms. "What? You don't believe me?" he cried, dramatically putting his hand on his chest. "I'm hurt. Truly hurt."

Moritz smiled and shook his head at Paddy. "Yeah, 'tis real, actually. I take me own kids out for it."

"But you know what they say," Paddy interjected, throwing an arm around Brian's shoulders. "Ya did hear it from a guy in a pub!" And then he burst out laughing, making me wish I knew what that Irish saying meant.

Still skeptical, we headed out the next evening and drove to the shore of Loch Hyne. The moonless night left us straining to see, but we could make out the silhouettes of people standing along the retaining wall throwing pebbles into the water. When we joined them, we saw the splashes cascading down like little blue fireworks, leaving glowing circles floating on the surface. Further out in the loch, the iridescent, shimmering trails of kayaks and canoes criss-crossed the still, dark water.

"It's like . . . magic," Liv said in amazement.

"How is this happening?" Emily asked.

"Wee little bugs . . ." I mused, transfixed by the surreal scene in front of us.

"Mama, watch!" Ali called out, and stomped her boot into a puddle, shooting out a blast of blue light around her. "It's like watching a cartoon in real life!"

We spent the night walking through the shallows in our galoshes, never tiring of the blue sparkles we created with each step. It was certainly worth following the advice we'd heard from a guy in a pub.

◎ ◎ ◎

In the midst of our many Irish adventures, I was making plans for our next destination—a continent hop and cultural leap into Africa. I'd been working for several months to line up our time in Addis Ababa, Ethiopia, where we'd be volunteering through a US-based NGO called Cherokee Gives Back. While our family stayed in the organization's guest house for volunteers, local contacts would connect us to schools and community programs in need of assistance. I'd had multiple conversations with Cherokee's in-country director, Amy Vercler, to make the arrangements, and we were excited to experience a place so different from anything we'd ever known.

But then came the African Ebola outbreak of 2014. As we confirmed our housing and researched flight options, the deadly virus waged a microscopic war on the western coast of the continent, killing tens of thousands of people. The crisis created a frenzy of fear around the planet, especially in the United States. Africa, already a mysterious and dangerous place to most Westerners, got a lot scarier.

When our new Irish friends heard it would be the next stop on our journey, we got a lot of raised eyebrows. "Aye, you best be careful down there. Don't be catchin' your death."

Family and friends back home reached out with their own warnings. "I'm assuming you're going to cancel your plans for Africa with everything that's going on," one email read.

Another message included a link to a news clip where commentators argued about travel restrictions and immigration quarantines. "If you have an African country on your passports, you may not be able to get back into the United States!" the email frantically warned.

This was a stark contrast to the information we were getting from Amy and our other contacts in Ethiopia. They'd told us Addis Ababa was in a stable and peaceful region of the country, far from the border conflicts effecting many African nations. As the seat of the African Union, the city had implemented advanced security protocols to respond to major threats. Ethiopia had never had a single case of Ebola, and the World Health Organization reported it was the African nation most equipped to handle the disease. Brian and I felt certain there was no legitimate reason to alter our plans.

And yet . . . I started having second thoughts. I put off buying our plane tickets into Addis as I watched the news clips showing up in my Facebook feed. While I rolled my eyes at all the fearmongering, I had to admit there was a part of me buying into it. After months of work and research to line up this part of our trip, I began to seriously question whether or not we should go.

And why was that, exactly? Did I think our family would somehow defy all the odds and be the first people in the history of Ethiopia to contract Ebola?

No.

Did I suspect our contacts in Addis of being big fat liars and covering up the fact it was a dangerous place where we'd be kidnapped and held for ransom upon arrival?

No.

The only thing leading me to have any doubts about going to Africa was that *other people* thought we shouldn't.

That's when I made an uncomfortable discovery. It was a jagged little pill to swallow since I'd always thought of myself as a strong-willed, free-thinking woman, but the brutal truth was . . . I put a *huge* amount of focus on other people's opinions. Did I really want people thinking we were irresponsible parents, recklessly leading our children into a disease-infested continent, risking health and safety just to have some feel-good experience? Because that's what they'd think, right? If we went to Africa, they'd say we were crazy and naïve and reckless. And I didn't want people to say I was crazy or naïve or reckless . . . so maybe we shouldn't go.

This mode of thinking had influenced pretty much every decision I'd made in my life, both big and small. I was addicted to the approval of others, avoiding any behavior that might result in people worrying about me or judging me or thinking I'm less than perfect. In fact, I could only think of two life choices I'd made that wouldn't qualify for inclusion in my parents' annual Christmas letter.

The first was getting a tattoo. As I'd sat in an old dentist's chair wincing with pain while a guy with four lip rings needled a tiny rose next to my hip bone, I remember thinking, *Yeah, there's a very good chance I'm going to totally regret this.* But I did it anyway. I'd apparently needed some quiet act of rebellion to counter all of my good girl behavior. A hidden tattoo seemed better than wild partying and flunking out of college, I guess.

My second controversial decision was when I moved out to Salt Lake City and "shacked up" with Brian before we got married. This did not go over well with my parents, and yet, amazingly, I'd still done it. That decision made things a little tense for a while, but everyone gets along well enough now, so it's at least been forgiven if not forgotten.

Other than those acts of defiance, I'd been the poster child for the straight and narrow, following the Ten-Step Program to Success for Middle Class Females. It went something like this:

Step 1—Obey your parents
Step 2—Study hard
Step 3—Excel in extracurricular activities
Step 4—Go to a good college
Step 5—Take on leadership roles
Step 6—Land a good-paying job
Step 7—Get married
Step 8—Pop out some grandkids
Step 9—Exceed the expectations of others
Step 10—Refrain from questioning your life

I'd pretty much stuck to the program until Step 10. Brian and I were an over-achieving duo until we'd gone and sold everything we owned to become wandering nomads. Which is why my parents and many of our friends were so shocked when we embarked on this crazy adventure. It ran counter to everything else we'd ever done. And now here we were, not just traveling through civilized Europe, but getting ready to go to Africa? In the middle of a world health crisis? Have we lost our minds?!

I'd been going back and forth on this whole "to go or not to go" decision for a couple weeks on the day I made my periodic check-in call to my mom. I kept the conversation light and breezy, trying to avoid the topic of our plans for Ethiopia, but before long was I listening to a well-intentioned guilt trip.

"It boggles my mind thinking about you taking those beautiful little girls into that mess," my mother said with a sigh. "But if you decide you have to go . . . then we're going to have to figure out a way to keep your grandmother from finding out."

I could picture my mom pacing the tiled floor of their retirement home in Florida, nervously running her fingers along her necklace as she looked for any words that would keep me from doing what she considered to be the unthinkable. *What can I say to keep my baby from taking her babies to that god-awful place?!*

"Tracey, if Grandma finds out you took your family to Africa, she's going to have a stroke. I'm not kidding. I really think she'll stroke out if she finds out you did this."

I squeezed my eyes shut and pinched the bridge of my nose, willing myself not to scream. Behind my closed eyelids, I could see the shaking heads sitting around the table of my mom's weekly card game. I could hear the appalled comments of our friends who would never take their own children into the dangers of a developing country. Was it worth this much scorn and condemnation? Could that approval-seeking side of me handle so much disapproval from the people I loved and respected?

The answer to that question turned out to be a big, fat no. That approval-seeking part of me couldn't handle this controversial decision. So, you know what happened to her? She shriveled up and died. She was the one that stroked out as I politely ended the conversation with my mom and then sat down at my computer to stare at the travel itinerary for the hundredth time. Barcelona to Qatar. Qatar to Addis Ababa. Arrival time 11:51p.m.

You know what you're supposed to do, Observer Tracey whispered in my ear. *The question is whether or not you have the courage to do it. So, what's it gonna be, Goody Two-Shoes?*

I stared at the flight schedule on the screen, feeling goosebumps skip across my arms and legs.

"That's it!" I said emphatically, smacking my hands down on our cottage's rough-hewn dining table. "I'm doing this! I'm buying these tickets today!"

A tidal wave of excitement and relief rushed through me. I'd finally liberated myself from my own guilty conscience, triumphantly gaining my independence from the opinions of others. *We* were the ones who had the facts about Ethiopia. *We* knew it was safe. *We* knew what was best for our family. I wasn't going to cave into the pressure of pleasing other people only to regret the decision later. Our family was meant to volunteer in Addis, and by God, I wasn't going to let my childish obsession with getting approval from everyone else keep us from doing it.

An exhilarating laugh rolled through me, and I looked across the table at Brian with a confident smile. "I'm finally buying these damn tickets!"

He looked up from his computer screen and pulled a headphone out of his ear. "I'm sorry, did you say something, Trace?"

I rolled my eyes, this glorious moment of self-actualization feeling a little less climactic.

"I'm ready to buy these tickets to Addis," I repeated.

"Really? You're ready to do it?" Brian's face brightened.

"Yes. We're taking this family to Africa, babe."

Fifteen minutes later, another wave of excitement coursed through me when I hit the purchase button for our non-refundable tickets on Qatar Airways, flying us into Addis Ababa just two weeks later. As I checked my inbox for the confirmation message from the airline, I noticed another email had recently come through. My stomach dropped when I saw it was a notification from the U.S. State Department's Smart Travel Alert distribution list.

From: STEP-Notifications@state.gov
Date: Sun, Oct 14, 2014 3:14 p.m.
Subject: Ethiopia Travel Warning

US citizens in Addis Ababa, Ethiopia are advised to avoid large crowds and places where both Ethiopians and Westerners frequent due to a credible threat for a potential imminent attack by the al-Shabaab terrorist network.

I stared at the screen and shook my head, dumbfounded by the ridiculous timing of this message.

"Great news," I said to Brian. "We won't get Ebola, but we might get blown up by terrorists."

He looked up and pulled a headphone out of his ear. "Did you say something, babe?"

I paused for a moment. "I said I'm going to get a beer."

Then I stood up, went out the front door, and walked straight to McCarthy's Pub.

A short drive from our cottage sat a quiet peninsula called Toe Head, where the tenacious forces of nature carved away the earth, leaving a tall, narrow strip of land assertively pushing its way out into the sea. Standing on the lush, verdant blanket covering the ground, I could look out over the boulders jutting up from the water and hear the wind whisper through the tall tufts of grass at my feet. I breathed in the sweet, warm, salty scents floating on the air, and then closed my eyes, leaned back, and let myself fall open-armed onto the bouncy nest of thick foilage pillowing the ground. I lay there staring up at the sky and listening to the waves crash below.

And there was no Ebola.

No terror alerts.

No one judging or worrying or thinking we're crazy.

It was just me and Ireland and the sea.

FERENGI

Rooftop mystery animals: 1
Rodents in hair: 1
Rides in blue donkeys: 57
Existential crises: 1

ETHIOPIA

"Excuse me, there seems to be a mistake," I said to the flight attendant as I checked the seat number on my boarding pass again. "We aren't supposed to be in first class."

The pretty young woman with smooth, caramel skin and big brown eyes glanced at my ticket and smiled. "These are the correct seats, madam," she said, a slight Arabic accent softening her words. "It seems your family has been upgraded."

I swear to God, there are no sweeter words you could hear when boarding a five-hour flight with your three children.

Settling into the plush seat, I added first class travel to the growing list of new experiences we'd had over the last few weeks. We said good-bye to our Irish friends over fun dinners where they gave us little parting gifts to remember our time in Castletownshend. Then we took an overnight ferry from Ireland to France during a major windstorm, leaving us all a bit queasy and happy to step back onto dry land. We explored Paris together, taking the stairs up the Eiffel Tower and touring through the tall, crowded corridors of the Louvre. We gazed up at Notre Dame's remarkable flying buttresses and strolled through the immaculate gardens of the Tuileries. I even let a friendly homeless man with a massive following of pigeons place one of those filthy birds into each of my children's cupped hands. (Yeah . . . I'm gonna have to blame the French wine for that last one.)

However, the most surprising new experience of all had been my reaction to the State Department's travel alert for Addis Ababa. Rather than completely freaking out and launching into a stressful period of relentless research and worry, for the first time in my life, I responded to a highly controversial predicament by saying, "Aw, screw it. I'm sure it'll be fine."

And off we went to Africa.

The moment the wheels touched the ground at Addis Ababa International Airport, most of the passengers jumped to their feet and began yanking bags from the overhead storage bins while the plane taxied into the terminal. Flight attendants tried to push through the aisles and direct everyone to sit down, but they were powerless to stop the mayhem. Our family had barely unbuckled our seat belts when a throng of petite, yet bizarrely strong, female passengers pushed their way up through the plane. Brian stood up in the aisle and braced his hands against the seats to hold back the mob.

"This is crazy," he said with amusement, just as a little woman wearing a purple turban attempted to squeeze between him and the seat. "Seriously?" Brian said, shifting his body to block her while the girls and I scrambled into the aisle.

When we walked through the doors of the airport terminal, the reality of where we were smacked us in the face, or rather, passed a red laser across our foreheads. A medical team waited to take a laser digital temperature of every passenger. As soon as we got through the quick medical screening, we moved on to the immigration area where we spotted some cats.

Yes, you read that correctly.

Several feral cats were strolling around in the terminal. Under normal conditions, seeing any animal would elicit a sympathetic, "Aw," from our girls, but the absurdity of seeing cats in a secured border checkpoint was not lost on them. Emily grabbed my arm and said in a stunned voice, "Um . . . Mom, there are *cats* in here."

We discovered that our flight from Qatar had been directed into Addis Ababa's small domestic terminal, a stark contrast from the large international concourses we'd been traveling through over the last six months. The terminal building reminded me of my elementary school, with its low ceilings, fluorescent lights, cement brick walls, and cracked linoleum flooring. When we got to the immigration area, the shoving and jostling began again, but since we were foreign visitors requiring visas, our family was quickly pulled from the line and parked in chairs off to the side. The animated crowd, comprised mostly of women in colorful skirts and head scarves, created a symphony of shouting and singing. I noticed an elderly woman absentmindedly pulling on the loosened, stretched skin of her lower lip, which hung down passed her chin in the absence of the traditional lip plate she'd once worn. A little girl standing in the immigration line tried to wrestle one of the terminal's small cats into the basket at her mother's feet. Many of the travelers stared and pointed at our family, a couple of them reaching out across the crowd control ropes to touch the girls' blonde hair. We could definitely add this bizarre scene to our growing list of new experiences.

While Brian went to retrieve our luggage, I sat with the girls in a row of aging plastic chairs and watched their reactions. Ali had fallen asleep within minutes of sitting down, her little body contorted awkwardly across two chairs. Emily appeared surprisingly at ease having gotten over the initial shock of seeing cats in an airport terminal. She sat with her backpack clutched in her lap, staring straight ahead into the lively crowd.

But then I looked at Liv sitting next to me. Big, silent tears streamed down her smooth, pale cheeks, and her lip quivered with pent up emotion. When I put my arm around her shoulders, she immediately buried her head in my chest and broke into heaving sobs.

"I don't like this," she whimpered. "I want to get back on the plane. I just want to go home."

"Oh, baby, I know," I said, stroking her hair and planting a kiss on the crown of her head. "I know this is so different." I gave her a squeeze and gently placed a hand under her chin so I could look into her big blue eyes. "Listen to me, Liv. We're safe. It's going to be okay. I promise."

I was freaking out a little myself, but managed to feign confidence pretty well. "Come on, kiddo," I said, standing up. "Let's get our family through this."

I held out our stack of five passports to her. Liv blinked a couple times, straightened her shoulders, and took them with the same reverent care she would have given the Sorcerer's Stone. I led her over to an empty immigration desk and we stood together in a line going nowhere, yet the simple act of doing something seemed to immediately calm her down. Soon we were talking to a British photojournalist standing near us, and before long Liv was smiling and laughing again.

It took over an hour, but we eventually got our visas and made our way out into the dark parking lot where Amy from Cherokee Gives Back was supposed to be waiting for us. Under the dim streetlamps, my eyes strained to make out anything, much less a person I'd never met before. After scanning the mass of people milling around outside the terminal, Brian jokingly called out "Aaaaaa-meeeeee, where *are* yooouuu . . . "

And then suddenly there she was, emerging from the crowd like an old friend. "You made it!" she shouted. "Sorry you had to come into the domestic terminal. I'm sure that was kind of a crazy experience your first time here."

Why, yes. Yes, it was.

After getting everything loaded into the van, we did the short drive to the Cherokee Gives Back volunteer house. We bounced down a dark, bumpy dirt road lined with concrete walls and dotted with piles of construction debris, passing several cows and goats along the way. The van turned to stop in front of a solid steel gate. The driver waited for a guard to push the doors open and then pulled forward onto a brick driveway.

"Don't let the security scare you," Amy said. "This is a safe area."

As we climbed out of the van, I couldn't help but notice the height of the property's concrete wall and the three layers of barbed wire running along its top. It occurred to me "safe" might be a relative term in Ethiopia.

Bright flood lights illuminated a beige stucco house with tidy landscaping and a few chairs arranged on the front porch. It resembled a typical suburban home found back in the United States, down to the neat flower beds bordering the front walkway. Inside, a foyer opened up to a large living room filled with an arrangement of well-worn couches and armchairs. The kitchen and a long dining table occupied the back of the house, and clean terra cotta tile ran throughout the first floor. Only some faint cracks in the walls and a few water stains on the ceiling served as evidence of the building's longevity in a developing country.

Amy led us up to the second floor of the house and gestured to two closed doors in the hallway. "Tyson and Reagan stay in these rooms," she said in a hushed voice. "They're the only other volunteers staying in the house right now. You'll meet them tomorrow."

She stopped at a doorway across the hall and looked down at Emily, Liv, and Ali. "You girls will get this room all to yourselves," she said with a smile.

The room was stocked with three metal bunk beds, two nightstands, a tall wicker shelf, and a small weathered desk. Without hesitation, each of the girls walked over to a bed and laid down, exhausted from our long day of travel. After getting them tucked in under the covers, Brian and I followed Amy down the hall to the last door.

"As the only married couple, you guys get the honor of the master suite," she said, opening the door with a flourish to reveal a large room with a queen bed, a private bathroom, and a door leading out to a small balcony overlooking the front yard. "Normally, we'd have four bunk beds squeezed in here, but your family came at the right time. Autumn is pretty quiet as far as volunteers go, so it'll just be the eight of us in the house."

After bringing our bags upstairs, Brian and I finally called it a night around 2:30 a.m. I slipped under the blankets, closed my eyes, and felt the tension of the day melt from my body. A sweet state of semi-consciousness enveloped me, sending a delicious, numb contentment sliding through my limbs. *Our family is living in Africa*, I thought with amazement, and then immediately fell asleep.

What felt like seconds later, I was jolted back to consciousness by a thunderous series of chimes and a booming voice reverberating through the air. My eyes popped open and searched the darkness, trying to figure out what I was hearing.

"What in the hell is that?" Brian asked, sitting up and looking around as though the source of the sound was in our room.

I recalled something I'd read as we prepared for our time in Addis. "It must be one of the calls to prayer," I said. "Both the Orthodox Christian and Muslim religions do them throughout the day."

"At three in the morning?"

"Apparently," I said with a yawn. "It'll be over soon."

The call to prayer rang out for a few minutes and then everything grew quiet again.

Deep sigh.

Eyes closing.

Breath slowing.

Consciousness slipping away . . .

CHIMES!

BOOMING VOICE!

MORE CHIMES!

And so began our sleep torture. Shortly after one round of prayers came to an end, another began. I drifted off to sleep in the brief interludes of silence, only to jerk awake when the next round started up.

"I just want to sleep," I whined quietly into my pillow like a belligerent two-year-old. "Why won't they let me sleep?"

Finally, as the sky began to lighten, the alternating series of booming voices seemed to finally stop. It had been almost half an hour since the last wave of noise, and a hopeful relief settled over me. *Oh, sweet Jesus, please let it be over.*

Silence. The beautiful sound of silence.

And then . . .

THUMP! THUMP! THUMP! Scuffle, scuffle.

Noooooooooooo! I squeezed the sides of my pillow against my ears, hoping my delirium had me imagining things. But then I heard it again.

THUMP! THUMP! THUMP! Scuffle, scuffle. THUMP! THUMP! BANG!

Something was definitely on the roof.

"Oh my god," Brian groaned.

I propped myself up on my elbows and stared at the water-stained ceiling. "What *in the hell* is that?"

A repetitive, guttural noise started. Grrrruh! Ruh! Ruh! Ruh! Ruh! THUMP! THUMP! BANG!

"Do they have monkeys here?" I asked.

"I don't know, but whatever it is, I might have to climb up there and *kill it*," Brian grumbled before slamming his pillow over his face.

Grrrruh! Ruh! Ruh! Ruh! THUMP! THUMP!

After listening to the antics of our rooftop mystery animal for almost an hour, I finally gave up, threw back the covers, and followed the smell of coffee down the stairs. Stepping into the kitchen, I discovered a beautiful woman with umber skin swaying over the stove singing softly to herself, her hair cascading down her back in long, dark waves. The wooden spoon in her hand methodically stirred a pan of coffee beans, the obvious source of the fragrance wafting through the house.

"*Sälam*," she sang, without taking her eyes from the stove. "I am Asni. Coffee ready soon."

Coffee is a big deal in Ethiopia. The country proudly claims discovery of the drink thousands of years ago, when a young farmer investigated the berries making his goats so frisky in the fields. Today, coffee remains an integral part of life for most Ethiopians. The traditional coffee ceremony begins with roasting the beans, crushing them with a pestle, and then brewing them over an open fire in a special clay pot called a *jebena*. The full coffee ceremony wasn't done daily in our house of volunteers like in many Ethiopian homes, but Asni always roasted and crushed the beans herself.

As soon as I'd poured my first cup of genuine Ethiopian coffee, Amy strolled into the kitchen from her bedroom on the first floor. "Did you guys sleep okay?" she asked with an apologetic look. "That was a pretty loud night."

"Yeah, we're kind of tired this morning," I admitted, although the dark circles under my eyes probably spoke for themselves.

"Don't worry," she said, pouring herself some coffee. "That was unusual. The calls to prayer don't usually go through the night like that."

"That's good to know. I know Brian will be relieved to hear it."

Seconds later, he lumbered into the room and leaned against the counter, tousled hair and droopy face serving as solid evidence of his rough night's sleep. Amy, Asni, and I exchanged smiles.

"Tough night?" Amy asked sympathetically.

"You need coffee," Asni insisted, opening a cabinet and grabbing a mug.

"No, that's okay," Brian said with a yawn. "I don't drink coffee."

Asni's eyes grew wide. "What! You come *Etiopia* and no coffee!" She shook her head with disapproval and turned back to the stove, mumbling to herself. "Too bad . . . too bad for tall man."

◎ ◎ ◎

Beniam, a member of the local Cherokee Gives Back staff, helped us get oriented to life in Addis. Our first week proved to be an overwhelming shock to the senses as he took us around the city to the various organizations we'd be working with. A brown haze of pollution blanketed dusty, traffic-choked streets lined with a jumbled mix of modern buildings and dilapidated shacks. Tiny stores patched together with scraps of rusty sheet metal stood next to contemporary offices several stories tall, all of them coated in a thin layer of grime. Abandoned construction projects dotted the city, their stacked, skeletal floors of unfinished rooms curtained with rickety scaffolding and deteriorating sheets of plastic. Smells of animal waste and burning trash alternated through our noses as we walked by streams running toxic shades of green and ancient cars belching out black fumes. Emaciated livestock roamed the dirt roads of our neighborhood, forcing us to dodge piles of cow dung and horse manure as we went to and from the house.

Addis was like nothing we'd ever experienced before.

Emily, Liv, and Ali all adapted surprisingly quickly to the harsh realities of Ethiopia. About a week after we arrived, the four of us were walking to a small shop near the house when we passed the remains of a dead dog baking in the sun, its legs sticking straight up with rigor mortis. Liv and Ali both glanced at it without even flinching, while Emily stopped to give it a curious look.

"That dog must have just died today or else the other dogs would have eaten it by now," she said. "Crazy how fast they bloat up, huh?"

The girls' tolerance for dirty streets and animal tragedies seemed to grow as their young minds processed the human heartbreak so prevalent in Addis. We passed people sitting along the roads begging, their faces etched with hardship and their limbs withered from polio. Young women with sleeping babies tied across their chests stood in the middle of congested intersections begging motorists for help. Children in tattered clothes wandered the streets scrounging for food or discarded items they could sell.

"Why aren't they in school?" Ali asked one day as a group of barefoot boys passed us on the road.

"Their families can't afford to send them," Emily said, looking down at her little sister as she slipped her hand into mine. "They don't get to go to a good school for free like we do."

Our blazing white skin and Western clothes marked us as *ferengi* (foreigners), so we were constantly approached by people with an extended hand, silently asking for money. In the beginning, my sympathies won out. On one of our first days in Addis, I gave a couple Birr to a young boy on the sidewalk, and instantly a dozen more people clamored around me, pleading and tugging on my clothes. Frightened and panicked, I finally exploded and yelled at them to get away.

Later that day, when I told Beniam about the experience, he gave me a fatherly look and shook his head. "I say to you the same I say to Tyson and Reagan and all volunteers who stay with us," he said in a grave tone. "The work you do will help. Giving money only makes things hard for you and for them. You must promise me you do not do this again." I followed his advice, and after that I never had a problem. When I was approached by people begging for money, I subtly shook my head and they immediately backed away. We quickly learned Ethiopia's poverty didn't mean it was a dangerous place.

Transportation was a good example of this. The main mass transit option in Addis was the "blue donkey" passenger van system, named for the vehicles' bright cobalt color. At various locations around the city, a disorderly mass of dilapidated vans gathered at the curb. One person drove while another leaned out the window calling out the destination. Shouts of "Bole, Bole, Bole!" or "Gerji, Gerji, Gerji!" rang out as people pushed and shoved their way through the van doors. Once inside a blue donkey, we were packed in like sardines behind windows caked with dirt. On more than one occasion, I got poked in the butt by a rusty seat cushion spring. Yet, the people we sat next to were friendly and smiling, and we always got to our destination safely.

One day, the girls and I had been waiting for a blue donkey to Bole for almost thirty minutes. When one finally pulled up, an unusually large crowd pushed and shoved its way toward the door. Just as Emily and Liv climbed into the van ahead of me, I felt Ali's hand slip from mine. I spun around and frantically searched the crowd, but I couldn't see her anywhere. I pushed back and tried to stop the momentum of the people behind me, but I found myself inside the van without her and screaming into the noisy crowd. "Stop! Stop! I lost my daughter!" My heart pounded in my chest as I tried to squeeze around a large woman hoisting herself through the door. "Alison! ALISON!" I shrieked at the top of my lungs, sending a painful scratching sensation down my throat.

"No worry, Mama!" a deep voice called back to me. "She coming!" And suddenly there she was, her smiling little face floating above the crowd as a pair of strong hands carried her toward me. I pulled her through the door and squeezed her against my chest protectively as my body unwound with relief.

"That was fun," Ali said cheerfully, before scrambling past me to sit with her sisters.

"Everybody is okay," said the soothing, baritone voice. I turned to find a handsome, ebony face leaning through the van door. The man smiled, flashing impossibly white teeth. "No mama lose a baby in our van," he said before pulling the door closed and walking around to the driver's seat.

Dirty didn't mean dangerous.

In some ways, our time in the volunteer guest house felt like a life of luxury. The twenty-four-hour security guards, cleaning staff, and full-time cook were all firsts for our family. I felt like a total slacker letting other people do our laundry and make our meals, but rules were rules. One morning, Hana, the housekeeper, came into our room as I was making our bed.

"No, no, no, Miss!" she cried as she ran over and yanked the sheet from my hands. "This for me! This work for Hana! You have *your* work. This *my* work."

How can a gal argue with that?

Of course, despite the conveniences of a fully-staffed home, life in the guest house presented new challenges. For instance, all water we consumed had to go through the purification system set up in the kitchen. Even brushing teeth with tap water could result in a mild bout of diarrhea. I would know this, because I frequently forgot and ran my toothbrush under the tap, only to later find myself spending an inordinate amount of time on the toilet. Luckily, the girls adjusted to our new water ritual quickly and were there to remind me.

"Mama!" Ali yelled, her arms flailing in the air with exasperation and then landing firmly on her hips. "You're about to do it *again!* You *cannot* use the faucet! Do you *want* diarrhea?"

The inconsistency of electrical power also served as a daily reminder of how spoiled we'd been when it came to utilities. Frequent blackouts popped up at the most inconvenient times with consequences we didn't anticipate. For instance, water pressure in Ethiopia wasn't strong enough to push the water through the pipes of the house, so an electric pump was used to increase it. It worked so well, we never thought about the importance of that pump . . . until the power went out when I was mid-shower with a head full of shampoo. Then I thought about it *a lot*, and from then on, I learned to rinse very quickly.

Coexistence with rodents was also a little reminder of life's differences. Every day we saw rats running across the yard or scurrying into the tiny holes they'd dug into the security wall. Watching their funny habits, I started to develop a weird affinity toward them.

"Rats are kind of cute, in their own skittering little way," I said to Reagan one day while we sat out in the front yard taking in the sunshine. I'd been watching a dark brown one run along the top of the security wall. "I don't know why I've always been so freaked out by them."

Reagan scrunched up her face in a grimace and looked up from the *People* magazine her mom had sent in her latest care package from home. "You're freaked out by them because they're disgusting, disease-infested vermin, that's why." She followed my gaze up to the rat, now sitting back on his haunches and swiping his paws around his head as he cleaned his ears. She shuddered before turning back to her celebrity sightings. "Blech . . . gross."

"I don't know," I said. "They're just furry little animals. How are they any different from guinea pigs and hamsters?"

But this open-mindedness toward the Rodentia species came to an abrupt halt the night I woke up from a bizarre dream where

Brian was braiding my hair. As I slowly regained consciousness, I felt a strange tickling sensation on the top of my head. My hair had literally become a rat's nest. I bolted upright and I heard the distinct sound of claws scampering across the pillow case.

"OH MY GOD! OH MY GOD! OH MY GOD!" I jumped up and began a frantic running-in-place routine on the mattress. "A rat was in my hair!"

"Wha . . . what's happening?" Brian mumbled and rolled over.

"Wake up, god dammit! There's a rat in our room!"

That got his attention.

Brian popped up and reached for the bedside lamp, but it wouldn't turn on. Apparently, the power was out again. He fumbled around on the nightstand and a moment later the narrow shaft of light from his headlamp scanned back and forth across the room. After inspecting under the bed and looking behind all the furniture, Brian gave me a resigned sigh.

"Trace, you were dreaming. There's nothing in here."

"Um, no. It wasn't a dream," I insisted, still standing on the bed. "I felt it. I *heard* it. A rat was *in my hair.*"

"Yeah, okay. Fine. A rat was in your hair." He turned off the headlamp and climbed back into bed. "But there's nothing we can do about it now, so go back to sleep."

Ha. Fat chance of that.

The next morning all of our housemates heard about my middle-of-the-night freak out from Brian. I felt a little silly and started wondering if maybe he was right and I'd dreamt the whole thing. After dinner that night, we were all sitting in the living room chatting, when suddenly Reagan screamed bloody murder.

"AAHHH!" She jumped onto the couch and started the running-in-place routine I knew so well. "RAT!" she shrieked pointing across the room.

Yes! Vindicated! Standing on furniture and running in place is a totally normal response to this situation.

The first floor erupted into pandemonium. Brian and Tyson wielded brooms and began swinging them around, trying to force the rodent out of its hiding place. Amy, Reagan, and I grabbed couch cushions and attempted to create a barricade, forcing the rat to run toward the back door. Em, Liv, and Ali stood on the dining room table and provided shrill commentary on the animal's erratic movements around house. "He went behind the shelf! Now he's under the table! He's headed for the *kitchen!* EEWWW!"

This ridiculous scene of uncontrolled hysteria went on for about ten minutes, until the security guard came in to see what the ruckus was all about. He found each of us standing on a piece of furniture.

"What is problem?" he asked, looking around with concern.

"There's a rat in here," Amy replied, pointing to the kitchen. "We think it's behind the stove."

The guard's look changed from concern to amusement. "A rat?" He casually walked over to the electric range and gently pulled the unit back from the wall. "This for all the screaming?" The rat scampered out and ran straight through the open back door. The guard shook his head and smiled. "So much fear for little animal. You need some lions in America."

I picked up a large metal pot and gestured to a shelf. The woman's stern face and infuriated posture gave me my answer. She raised her arms in exasperation, and then slammed one hand on her hip while jabbing the other toward a different shelf. *Wrong again, idiot!*

While Brian lent his programming skills to a nonprofit banking cooperative downtown, the girls and I volunteered at a children's home on the outskirts of Addis. As Em, Liv, and Ali helped organize school supplies with a volunteer teacher, I'd wound up playing a game of charades with a rather cranky cook. My lack of pot placement knowledge was clearly ruining her life.

Soon an ally came to my rescue. The other cook in the kitchen saw the frustration unfolding and floated over with a smile. Her bright yellow head scarf and flowy wrap-around skirt matched her cheery disposition. She waved a dismissive hand at her coworker, gently placed an arm around my shoulders, and took me through an unspoken tour of the kitchen's storage shelves.

Don't you worry about her, she wordlessly said. *You're doing fine. Big pots here, pans over here, cooking utensils in this bin, eating utensils in that bin.* She patted my cheek, smiled warmly, and then returned to the *injera* dough she'd been kneading.

As I cleaned, dried, and stored the pots and pans from the day's breakfast preparations, I empathized with the cranky cook's irritation. So many volunteers passed through this kitchen, usually white people from Western countries coming in for a few days to do our bit of sanctimonious service for the impoverished, orphaned children of Ethiopia. Each time we arrived, the cook had to train us, deal with our incompetence, and pantomime instructions since none of us could speak Amharic. I felt self-conscious, sensing I might be more of a hindrance than a help.

After the last pot had been put away, I walked out of the dark kitchen and into the bright sunshine of the courtyard. My eyes were still adjusting to the light when Zelalem, the assistant director of the orphanage, waved to me from the administration office.

"*Sälam,* Tracey!" he called out as he strode toward me. "Tell me, how is your first day with us?"

"Good . . . I think."

Zelalem tilted his head and gave me a knowing smile. "It is Aysha, yes? Do not worry. She is always big grouch. But also, she has big heart. Trust me. You are very big help for us."

As we walked toward the facility's classrooms, Zelalem went on to explain how recent changes in the Ethiopian adoption process had put tremendous strains on their resources.

"The process to get the children into homes is much more difficult now," he sighed, frustration clouding his face. "And not for good reason. Our officials had concern with orphaned children being one of our country's big exports, and so now they block many international adoptions."

We stopped at the door of a large room with colorful concrete walls. A woman was feeding an adolescent girl with severe cerebral palsy. When the girl saw us, she raised her arm in a wave and gave us a big smile. Zelalem walked over to hug her and then exchanged a few words with her caregiver. When he walked back to me, he picked up the conversation where he'd left off.

"You see, officials in the government tell us we should have Ethiopian adoptive parents, but to find a local family able to take these children is . . . " He shrugged. "It almost never happens. We take more and more children, but the process for them to go to adoptive families in other countries is much longer now. Because of this, we need more food, more teachers, more supplies, and especially more dishwashers," he added with a laugh.

Zelalem and I heard a burst of giggles from one of the classrooms. When we got to the door we found Em, Liv, Ali, and a group of children ranging in age from six to sixteen huddled around a table together. Emily was teaching them to make Rainbow Loom jewelry. The children watched intently as she slipped the plastic hook through each rubber band and looped links into place. After a few moments, she handed the loom to the girl sitting next to her and began coaching her through the process. They'd evidently found their way through the language barrier with no problem.

As I put our girls to bed the night of our first day at the orphanage, I had to blink back tears. *What's bedtime like for those boys and girls? Is anyone tucking them in? Reading to them? Telling them they're loved?* The unfairness of life for those children weighed on me as I lay there hugging my sleeping five-year-old.

Before this trip, I'd gotten quite good at ignoring the world's disparity. I could get passionate and involved when it came to a school board vote, but the ills of humanity left me feeling powerless. I pushed them out of my mind, thanked my lucky stars they weren't happening to us, and periodically wrote a check to some organization that was supposed to be helping the world. This emotional distance was a lot easier to maintain when those tragic stories happened in faraway places I knew little about.

While the girls played with the kids at the orphanage, I worked behind the scenes doing dishes, cleaning out closets, and organizing classrooms. As I did, the staff who spoke English told me how some of the children had come to live there. A thirteen-year-old boy witnessed the brutal murder of his entire family during a conflict near the Somali border. One pair of sisters made a daring escape from their kidnappers, after being repeatedly raped and beaten. Other children had lost most of their relatives to AIDS.

Standing so close to these heartbreaking stories made me want to scream. *What in the hell is wrong with us?! How have we let this kind of inequality and unfairness exist? What's the point of cleaning out this stupid closet when our human race is so incredibly screwed up?* I could feel myself turning cynical and morose as we came face to face with the enormity of human tragedy. I wouldn't forget the things we'd seen in Ethiopia, but I couldn't fix the problems either. They were too big. Too complicated. Too painful. A gloomy hopelessness cut into me with each sad story I heard, leaving behind a dark, jaded despondency that started following me around like a shadow. I managed to smile during our days at the orphanage and laugh with our housemates in the evenings, but at night when I lay next to Brian in the darkness, a quiet panic grew inside me, telling me that coming to Ethiopia might have been a horrible mistake.

One afternoon, we were sitting in the back of a taxi cab on our way home from the orphanage. The girls laughed at the herd of goats blocking the intersection and leaned out the windows to watch other drivers chase the confused animals off the road. Ignoring this scene, I let my thoughts hover over the most recent tragic story I'd heard that day. A little girl in the room for children with disabilities had sustained severe brain damage when her little sister stepped on a land mine. They'd been collecting their family's water at a pond and made the tragic mistake of taking a short cut home. Her sister died instantly. The little girl would never walk or talk again.

"What's wrong, Mom?" Emily asked. "You look so sad."

Unable to brush away my depressing thoughts of unfairness and loss, I shrugged and shook my head. "It's just hard to see how unfair life can be," I said quietly. "So many bad things we let happen in the world . . . ." My voice cracked, and my eyes filled with tears. I stopped talking, realizing this wasn't a conversation appropriate for a child.

But then Emily said something wise beyond her years.

"Don't you see all the good in it, though?" she asked. "There are so many people helping each other. Those kids at the orphanage are happy, even though they've been through so much. They have all these people working to give them a better life."

And just like that, it started to happen.

As Emily's words rang through my mind, a flood of relief washed over me, sending a strange, numb sensation trickling down my spine and expanding through my chest. With her pure and innocent view of the world, Emily opened my eyes to the beauty I'd been missing in this country. I'd been focused on dead animals, dirty streets, and heartbreaking stories of loss, but that day, sitting in goat-stopped traffic, Ethiopia changed for me. I'd been overlooking the beauty and tremendous progress in this country, letting my Western perspective blind me to the extraordinary improvements the Ethiopians were creating in their communities.

I suddenly realized, if we want to do something good for the world, then we must put our focus on the good things that are already happening. We need to pay attention to the inspiring stories humans create through their individual acts of kindness. The love and the compassion and the hope we give to each other every day. The disintegrating sidewalks of Addis were filled with people helping their fellow man. I watched a woman leave a bakery and discreetly hand a young beggar a bag of rolls. A man standing in line in front of me at a shop bought two packages of rice and gave one to the disabled, elderly woman sitting outside on the curb. Students walked to school wearing crisp uniforms and carrying backpacks full of books, evidence of the country's slowly increasing literacy and graduation rates.

These inspiring little pieces of Ethiopia had been there all along. I just had to shift my perspective to see them. Remove my cultural blinders. When I stopped to really look at the country's challenges, I inevitably found hope and strength blossoming inside them. When we hear stories focused on what's wrong with the world, we have a choice. We can be overwhelmed and immobilized by the injustice of it all, or we can look for the good miraculously finding its way out from under the rubble. Seeing those rays of light keeps us from turning away from the pain. Instead, we gain the courage to examine it, understand it, and then come together to find the solution to it. The successes of our humanity are often born in the midst of our failures.

One day, Emily and I stood watching Ali and Liv play on the orphanage's little merry-go-round with some other children. As she leaned against the courtyard's wall, Emily said, "You know what I've learned here, Mom?"

"What, sweetie?"

"I've learned you can't find happiness. You just have to choose to be happy."

I turned to look at the profile of my eldest child, this little Buddha in the body of a ten-year-old.

"They've lost everything," she said, her eyes fixed on the blur of giggles and shrieks spinning in front of us. "But they're happier than my friends back home."

She was right. Despite the country's poverty and struggles, Ethiopians held an immense amount of joy in their hearts. People who had so little still showed such extraordinary gratitude for life's little pleasures, proving happiness truly is a choice. Each day these children chose to be grateful. They chose to focus on the good things they had in their lives, instead of the many things they'd lost.

A week later, Zelalem stopped by the kitchen as I finished the pots and plates from breakfast. "Good morning, Tracey," he said before exchanging a few words with the cooks in Amharic. After a moment of conversation, Aysha gestured toward me with the large wooden spoon in her hand. The other cook smiled and nodded, adding something else I couldn't understand.

Zelalem smiled and turned to me. "Aysha wants me to tell you this. She say you wash dishes very well and you are one of best volunteers she ever have in her kitchen."

Aysha gave me a half smile before turning to drop a pot on the stove. A swell of satisfaction filled my chest. Over the course of my illustrious career, I couldn't recall a time I'd felt so much pride in my work.

As a special adventure for our family's last weekend in Ethiopia, Beniam organized a camping trip with the other volunteers and some of our local friends. He coordinated it through a man who lived near Lake Wonchi, a large crater lake to the west of Addis. Beniam had taken some friends out to the area before. He said locals would haul our gear in for a small fee while we hiked down into a river valley. There we'd rent horses from a family for ten Birr a piece and ride them up through the ravine to the lake's shoreline. Then we'd pay another ten Birr per person for a boat ride over to our camp site on the opposite side of the lake. We'd get a tour of the Ethiopian countryside for a great price, and Beniam had been kind enough to serve as our guide.

On the day of the trip, our large group of Ethiopians and Americans loaded up two vans with the camping equipment we'd rented and began the four-hour drive out to the Oromiya Province. For the first part of the trip, we cruised along a paved highway, but soon we turned onto the bumpy, washboard road that would take us up into the hills surrounding the lake. Although the passengers didn't have too much of a problem with the jittery drive, the vehicles revolted. When our van suddenly began an awkward lurching, the driver pulled over and found one of the back tires in shreds, looking like a ferocious wild animal had clawed at the rubber in search of a meal.

While Brian and Beniam helped the driver change the tire, curious locals gathered around us. They approached me with their hands extended at first, but our friend, Yesikor, stepped in.

"No, no, no," he said firmly, and then spoke to the villagers in Amharic. Immediately, the interaction shifted to a friendly, translated conversation.

An older man said something to Yesikor and gestured to me.

"He want to know if you meet Barack Obama," Yesikor said.

I smiled and shook my head.

A little girl spoke to Yesikor quietly, and the rest of the villagers laughed.

"She want to know if everyone in America is as white as you," he said with a smile.

I laughed and shook my head again.

After a few more questions, it was time for us to climb back into the van and resume our journey. Unfortunately, it wasn't long before the other van blew a tire. We had another conversation with curious locals, and soon we were back on the road again, with no spare tires left. As we drove by round, thatched-roofed huts and fields dotted with acacia trees, it occurred to me that our weekend camping trip might take place on the side of the road if we got another flat.

We eventually reached our destination, a tiny village sitting atop a high mountain ridge. A few buildings patched together with plywood and sheet metal stood along the road, framed by a panoramic view of the wide valleys stretching out below. Most of the village's homes hid behind fences constructed from wooden planks and tree branches. Only their thatched roofs peaked out from behind the protective barriers. Our little caravan turned into a driveway and pulled up to a simple house with white clapboard siding. Anywhere else the home might have seemed a little rundown, but set in this tiny, remote village, it looked like a mansion.

Beniam hopped out of the passenger seat and walked up to greet the man leaning against the porch railing. The rest of us came out into the bright sunshine and unloaded our gear, while an audience of village children watched us with amusement. After we'd stacked all the tents and bags into a pile, Beniam came back with a frustrated look on his face.

"It seems they will not haul our camping equipment for the price they gave me on the phone," he said, throwing a disapproving glance at the man he'd been talking to. "I think it might be because half our party is . . . well, you are . . . "

"White?" Amy suggested with a smile.

"I am so sorry," Beniam said apologetically. "They told me 100 Birr, but now the cost is 500."

"How far is it to haul it in ourselves?" Brian asked.

Beniam shook his head. "Almost five miles. It would be very difficult. We do need their help."

"Then we'll just pay it," Brian replied. "I mean, we're not going to turn around and go home, right?"

"I kind of figured this would happen," Amy said. "It's fine, Beniam."

Tyson and Reagan both nodded in agreement. "It's still only $25," Tyson said with a shrug.

"Okay," Beniam said with a sigh. "I will tell them we do it, but I promise they lose my business in the future. This is very embarrassing."

Beniam exchanged a few curt words with the man, and within seconds a group of men and women appeared out of nowhere, lifting our gear onto donkeys, wheelbarrows, and their own heads. They would follow a road leading directly to the camp site while our group took a longer trail through a scenic area.

Soon we were hiking down a steep, rocky path underneath a canopy of trees, passing herds of goats and watching monkeys swing above us. Eventually, the trail popped out onto a flat, broad river gorge. A blanket of bright green grass and colorful flowers covered a valley floor laced with a network of narrow, twisting streams. Tall stone pillars rose up in the middle, some of them reaching almost as high as the canyon's walls. Water gurgled around them, flowing through the tiny canals carved through the thick grass.

"In the wet season this canyon is full of water," Beniam said, as he came up from behind to walk alongside me. "But in the dry season, the grass and flowers come out."

"It's gorgeous," I said, taking in the vibrant shades painted across the ground. "This isn't at all what I expected."

I thought back to the Sally Struthers commercials I'd seen as a kid in the eighties. Naked children with distended bellies stood in dusty fields, and emaciated babies lay limply in their mother's arms. I didn't understand why the people couldn't get food or why they chose to live in such a horrible place. Back then I knew nothing of the advanced civilizations once thriving on the African continent, before the forces of colonization and slavery crumbled them. I was ignorant of the oppressive government programs confiscating the citizen's farmland and leading to violent rebellions. As a happy, middle class American kid, I couldn't begin to fathom the struggles Ethiopians had been forced to overcome. I just thought they didn't have enough rain.

After hiking for another hour through the gorge, we came upon the family renting us the horses. As the local man talked with Beniam, his two children smiled shyly at our girls. The little boy had enormous brown eyes and wore a fraying pair of sweatpants with a gaping hole curiously cut out of the crotch. His older sister pointed at Liv's white blonde hair and giggled. Her apprehensive look and hesitantly reaching hand asked the silent question, *Can I touch your weird-looking hair?* Liv held out a long lock, and the girl smiled with amusement as she held it between her fingers.

"Well, unfortunately, we have the same problem," Beniam said with a sigh as he turned away from the man. "It seems the horse rides are now 100 Birr per person."

"Seriously? That's ten times the original price, isn't it?" Brian said.

"Yes, it is," Beniam said, shaking his head. "Again, I apologize."

"I feel like we're getting taken for a ride while trying to get taken for a ride," Tyson joked.

"You're hilarious," Reagan said, throwing him a sideways glance.

Yesikor sighed and shook his head. "I am sorry to say I can no longer have this friendship with you *ferengi*. It is much too expensive for me." His face broke into laugh. "Hey, Reagan? Am I hilarious now, too?"

"This is just the way it goes here sometimes, guys," Amy said with a shrug.

"It's alright," Brian said. "I don't think I should ride one of those little horses, anyway. I might break its back."

"We'll pay it for the girls, though" I added, glancing over at Ali who was lying on the ground in the late afternoon sun and looking like she might fall asleep.

We paid the family and started off on the second leg of our journey to the lake. The little girl led Ali's horse along the trail, proudly showing us tricks she could do with the end of the rope. Her brother also walked along with us, but he frequently jogged away from the trail to squat behind a bush. It occurred to me that easy access was probably the reason for the large hole in his pants, and I worried for him. Thousands of Ethiopian children died every year from intestinal diseases.

We hiked another hour up through the river valley as the sun slowly disappeared behind the trees sitting atop the canyon walls. When the ravine began to narrow, the owner of the horses called out to Beniam.

"The trail is not good for the horses from here," Beniam translated. "He will take them back now."

The girls climbed down and we waved good-bye to the children as they followed their father back up through the valley. Soon the trail narrowed, forcing us to duck under tall bushes and scraggly trees until the shore of Lake Wonchi spanned out before us. Rolling, forested hills surrounded its blue waters, which lay sparkling with the reflection of late afternoon sunlight. A few islands sat in the distance and dotted the lake with clumps of trees. We followed the trail along the shoreline, passing small, lakeside homesteads with thatched-roof huts, gardens, and pens of goats. Eventually we arrived at a small dock, almost invisible among the tall cattails. A large metal row boat floated next to it, tethered with a rope made from woven reeds.

Nearby, two men stood with their fishing poles cast out into the lake. When they saw us, they reeled in their lines, and Beniam and Yesikor walked over to talk with them. Within moments, Beniam's irritated tone and sharp gestures told us we could anticipate yet another price increase. He stalked back, shaking his head while Yesikor kept walking up the trail past the dock.

"They say 100 Birr again," Beniam said, raising his hands and letting them slap down on his thighs.

"Per person? That's ridiculous!" Amy scoffed. "It's only a ten-minute ride, isn't it?"

"Yes, I know. This is very disappointing," Beniam said, his anger pulling a quick sigh from his chest. "Yesikor is walking to see if we can take the path the rest of the way instead of riding in their boat."

"Do we even know if our equipment made it to the site?" Brian asked. "I'm starting to feel like this whole community is out to screw us over. What if we get out there and we don't have any tents or gear? Then what?"

"I truly do not think that will happen," Beniam said. "They are not thieves. They just—"

"Think we're rich *ferengi*," Amy finished for him.

A swell of frustration sent heat into my cheeks, and I turned to look at the two men. One had a frayed white piece of cloth draped loosely around his head and shoulders. The other wore an old baseball cap and a worn-out leather jacket with sleeves stopping several inches above his wrists. They didn't look like scheming characters taking delight in giving us the run-around, yet I couldn't help but feel angry at them. We were out in the middle of nowhere with three children, and the sun was beginning to set. We had little option but to pay whatever they asked.

"Trail is no good!" Yesikor called out as he walked back to our group. "Grass get very high and the path stop." He said something to the two men, and the one wearing the baseball cap shrugged before muttering a few words. Yesikor sighed and put his hands on his hips. "I say we swim. It is nice day for swimming, yes?"

His humor worked. The cloud of angst that had settled over us began to lift a bit. Tyson shrugged and said, "Let's do it then. A hundred Birr per person it is."

I stepped into the row boat with the others, and we settled onto its wooden benches with our day packs in our laps. Soon we were gliding swiftly across the calm water, moving toward the center of the lake and watching the steep hills of the shoreline shrink as the blue sky expanded above us. The two local men faced us and leaned their backs into each synchronous stroke of the oars. I noticed the man wearing the white shawl had two of his fingers wrapped up in a dirty bandage, and at least a dozen pink scars marked his hands and arms. As I watched him, I wondered about his life. *What happened to his hands? How often does he take tourists across the lake like this? How long will the money last his family?*

Suddenly, I realized how irrationally stingy I'd become in Ethiopia. I'd always thought of myself as a generous person, and yet here, in an impoverished country where I'd expected to feel nothing but gratitude, a financial grudge had snuck up on me. Back when I'd taken Beniam's advice and promised not to give out money on the streets of Addis, I'd felt horrible whenever I rejected someone's plea. A pang of sympathy would hit my heart each time a person approached me with an extended hand. However, as the weeks passed, I found myself developing a bizarre callousness to it all. I started to notice that many of the people asking for money were clean and well-dressed. They'd stand in front of me smiling with their hand out, like it was some game to see if the white lady just blindly doled out bills to anyone who asked. I noticed the "*ferengi* tax" I got charged when I stopped to buy something at one of the small stores near our neighborhood, and after reluctantly paying it,

I'd walk out feeling rage simmering under my skin. Even out here, in the rural beauty of Ethiopia, this aggravation over *ferengi* taxes had followed us.

I looked out across the water and surveyed the wavy reflections of hills dancing along the shoreline. My eyes wandered back to the man with the injured hand, and I watched his scarred arms slowly bend and straighten with the movement of the oar. He turned his face up to the sky and the white shawl slipped off his head, revealing another large, pink scar above his ear. As I again wondered what could have caused all his injuries, I noticed a peaceful smile settle on his lips. I looked up to follow his gaze and saw two large birds gliding directly above us, their graceful paths intertwining in the air, creating invisible figure eights. Over and over they looped together, an elegant dance of wings set against the brilliant blue sky. I tried to imagine their view from up there, looking down on this glassy lake surrounded by forests and our tiny boat cutting a clean line of wake through the water. Just like the man, a peaceful smile settled on my lips. I turned back to him and saw he was looking at me. When our eyes met, he nodded and smiled, an unexpected connection between two strangers living vastly different lives, yet experiencing the same wonder for this small, breathtaking moment in nature.

I finally recognized the stingy attitude I'd acquired in Ethiopia for what it really was: guilt. Each time someone stood in front of me with their hand out, they were a reminder of how much my family benefits from the wealth disparity in the world. They made me question if I was as generous and compassionate as I'd always thought I was. Because when it came down to it, I wasn't willing to make big sacrifices for others. I might be volunteering a little of my time and donating to tax-deductible charities, but I wasn't going to forfeit my family's privileged life. If I wasn't willing to give up all my material possessions to improve the lives of people living in dire circumstances, then was I still a good person?

I wasn't sure anymore.

Seeing extreme poverty up close uncovered things about the world and myself I wasn't very comfortable with. It made me look at my life from a very different perspective, leaving me confused and disturbed, wondering why I'd been handed such an easy, luxurious existence. On our last weekend in Ethiopia, I seemed to be starting yet another existential crisis. My first one led us to this crazy adventure, but this new one made me question if I deserved anything I'd ever achieved or acquired in life.

Our boat bumped against the small dock on the other side of the lake, snapping me from my thoughts. We disembarked and walked through the cattails to emerge in a wide, flat clearing where our gear sat waiting for us, stacked in neat piles. A small brick building sat at the far end of the meadow, and beyond it, fields of golden, waist-high grain swayed along the hills rising up from the lake. We quickly got to work setting up our tents.

That night we sat around a campfire cooking a dinner of roasted vegetables and sausage. The little building turned out to be a small store, which sold us Ethiopia's local Harrar beer and some sweets for dessert. While Yesikor sang Amharic songs at the fire, I walked out into the darkness and sat on a log near the water. The sky slowly turned a deep, impenetrable black, revealing more stars than my eyes had ever seen.

Liv walked out and sat next to me on the log, propping her Pooh Bear up on her knees.

"Hi there," I said. "Is Pooh Bear enjoying the camping trip so far?"

She smiled and shrugged. "This is the first time I've had him out of my backpack," she said. "I didn't want him to get dirty."

I nodded. "Smart move."

"Mom, what's that cloudy thing out there?" She pointed to the hazy cluster of stars spanning across the sky.

"That's the Milky Way, sweetie. It's the galaxy our planet's in."

I waited for the inevitable feeling of idiocy to come when my child asked me about astronomical concepts I knew little about.

"But . . . if we're in it, then how can we see it?"

Yep, there it is.

"Well . . . we're on Earth and we can see Earth, right? We're just looking at the rest of the Milky Way."

Another pause. "I've never seen that in the sky before."

"Out here in the country there aren't other kinds of light to distract our eyes. The sky is darker, so we can see even the small stars we wouldn't notice in the city."

"Oh." She paused and squeezed Pooh Bear to her chest. "So, the stars are always there, we just can't see them?"

I looked at her silhouette for a moment before following her gaze back to the sky. "Yeah. That's a good way to put it."

I thought about everything our family had learned in Ethiopia. The country had shown us so many aspects of life we'd never seen before, giving us insights into our humanity, yet leaving many more questions than answers.

"Things look a lot different when we aren't distracted by all the stuff around us," I said quietly, more to myself than to Liv.

"Yeah," she replied. "It kind of freaks me out seeing something for the first time, and then finding out it's always been there."

I put an arm around her shoulders and looked up to the sky. "You can say that again, kiddo."

SPIRITUAL FAILURE

Temple tours: 11

Attempts at meditating: 27

Declarations that meditation is a bunch of hooey: 27

Homebirths: 1

THAILAND

Our first afternoon in Bangkok, we went out to find some good Thai food, setting off fully awake and alert, thinking we'd managed to sidestep jetlag. By the end of the meal, two of our three children were face down on the table while the third laughed maniacally at absolutely nothing.

Jetlag smacked us in the face.

We pushed through the sleep deprivation as best we could and launched ourselves into a whirlwind tour, using the bright pink taxi cabs and frigidly air-conditioned metro trains to navigate the bustling city. When we arrived at one of the many famous Buddhist temples, we stepped out of the chaos and into the serene calm of immaculate gardens and ornate totems. These relics of ancient traditions were quiet oases in the middle of the metropolitan mayhem. In the evenings, we stumbled upon little hole-in-the-wall cafés and discovered dishes with fun names like Tom Yum and Pad Fuktong and Kai Jeow. Friendly, smiling waiters brought us "mild" dishes that scalded our tongues and brought tears to our eyes.

After nine months of travel, our family was in dire need of a wardrobe update, and conveniently, Bangkok happened to be the shopping mecca of southeast Asia. Given our tight budget, I opted for MBK, an eight-story mammoth of a mall with over two thousand vendor stalls known for bargaining. It was here that I learned I have an incredible knack for price haggling. Although, this had less to do with my shrewd negotiation skills and more with being the mother of three children. A Tracey–Thai business transaction went something like this:

Shop owner: I sell for 200 Baht.

Tracey: Uh . . . (looking around to make sure she can see her children)

Shop owner: Okay, okay, okay. For you, 150.

Emily (from another vendor stall): Mom, can you come here?

Tracey: Just a second, honey!

Shop owner: Okay, okay, for you I do very special price. 100 Baht. No less!

Alison: Mama! Look at this!

Tracey: Okay, in a minute . . .

Shop owner: Okay, okay, okay, 60 Baht! Final price!

Sold! If you want good prices in Thailand, I suggest you take a bunch of kids shopping with you. Seems to work like a charm.

Once we'd seen the temples of Bangkok and stocked up on cheap consumer products, it was time to head down to the apartment we'd rented on Koh Samui, an island in the Gulf of Thailand. As our ferry chugged into Nathon Pier, colorful fishing boats bobbed in the harbor under a backdrop of green, jungle hills and coconut trees. *This is it,* I thought. *We've officially arrived in paradise.*

Within minutes of loading into our taxi, we left behind Nathon's busy streets packed with shops and followed a smooth paved road curving through the jungle. The driver sped by trucks loaded with coconuts and dodged the occasional dog darting into the road. After about twenty minutes, the taxi pulled into a driveway lined with bright pink bougainvillea and stopped in front of a large white plantation-style house.

An older couple came out to greet us. We ran into a significant language barrier at first, but with some repeated words and hand gestures we learned she was Thai and he was Italian. They lived on the third floor of the house and rented out two apartments on the second level. Their Italian restaurant operated out of the first-floor patio, and our rental would come with a complimentary breakfast each morning.

When we took our bags up to our apartment, we discovered that a wide-angle lens had clearly worked its magic on the listing's photos. The place was about half the size we'd expected it to be. The two bedrooms barely fit the double beds in them, and the kitchen could only fit a single person at a time. One of the girls would be sleeping on a narrow pleather futon in the apartment's small entryway, which had looked like a spacious living room on the web site. However, the apartment opened out to a large, covered balcony overlooking a garden of flowering trees, and a quiet beach was just a short walk away through a coconut grove. We settled in and made do with our teeny, tiny apartment in paradise.

We came down for breakfast the next morning, and a table had been set for our family, complete with wedges of dragon fruit, fat slices of pineapple, and a pot of coffee. The owner emerged from the kitchen with a big smile on her face.

"Mor-ning!" she called out, clearly enunciating each syllable.

Maybe the language barrier won't be so bad after all.

"Yo wah eck?" she asked.

Guess again.

This is the part of travel I hate. I hate not knowing the local language and being the asshole American who keeps asking people to repeat themselves. They're the ones who have learned some of *my* language, and yet I wind up making them feel stupid because I can't understand a word they're saying.

"Yo wah eck?" our landlady repeated.

Our family exchanged looks to see if any of us could decipher her words. I gave her an apologetic smile. "I'm sorry. We want . . . what?"

"ECK!"

I shook my head and shrugged apologetically. She smiled and turned around to walk into the kitchen, returning a moment later with an egg between her thumb and forefinger. "Eck."

"Ah, eggs! Yes! Yes!" I said nodding, adding a thumbs-up for good measure. "Yes, we want eggs! *Kop kun kah!*" That last part was my one and only Thai word—thank you.

She smiled and nodded back. "Okay, okay. Fi? Yo wah fi eck?"

Oh brother. And so it went.

Later that day, I was sitting out on the patio off our kitchen when a cheery British voice floated through the air. "Why, hello there!"

I turned to see a very pretty and very pregnant woman standing in the doorway of the apartment next to ours. "I'm Mary," she said, walking over with one hand extended and the other resting on her belly. "You must be our new neighbors."

I smiled as we shook hands. "I'm Tracey. My husband and I are here with our three daughters for the month." Brian, hearing the conversation, came out onto the patio and introduced himself.

"So lovely to meet the both of you," Mary said, then turned her head back toward her apartment. "Arjun, darling! Come out to meet the people next door!"

A tall, handsome Indian man walked out to introduce himself and join our conversation.

"We were really hoping to stay in this flat, but it's reserved for another guest starting next week," Mary told us. "We haven't been able to find another place that will work for the birth."

Arjun nodded and gave Mary a concerned look. "Yes, it is very much a problem. Other apartments are not clean. One was filled with cockroaches!"

"Oh, my goodness," I said with a grimace. "I can understand you wouldn't want to bring your baby home to cockroaches."

"I know," Mary said, shaking her head. "And since we're doing a homebirth, cleanliness is very important."

Brian and I exchanged a quick glance.

"Of course, we're telling the landlords we plan to go to the hospital so they won't freak out," she added with a wink.

"Uh huh . . ." I murmured. *Please tell me you aren't doing this on your own.*

"We had a midwife for a while," Mary said, as though reading my mind. "But she was so rigid and everything had to be her way with all the medical stuff. So, we've decided to just do it ourselves."

"Mhmm," came out of my mouth, but inside my head I was screaming, *Are you fucking crazy?!*

"It's been really difficult finding a new place," she said. "We only have a scooter, so getting around the island to see apartments hasn't been fun when I'm this pregnant." She laughed, rubbing a hand over her belly.

I managed to casually laugh with her. "Oh yeah, that must be super uncomfortable." *You don't have a car in case of emergency?! You don't have a place to live in five days?!*

"And the internet is not very good here," Arjun added. "Researching labor and childbirth has been very much a challenge."

My head kept nodding as my eyes got bigger and shot Brian another glance. *Yes, childbirth is an ideal do-it-yourself home project. All you need is a decent internet connection.*

"So, when are you due?" Brian asked.

"Just three days from now," Arjun said, placing his hand on Mary's belly. "We are so very excited."

"Yeah, I bet," I said. *Due to have a baby in three days. Homeless in five. OMG, so exciting!*

Brian and I both left the conversation stunned, to say the least. I don't want to judge other people's decisions, but . . . Okay, that's a lie. Maybe sometimes I do. But I do recognize it's not my life, and therefore none of my business. To each his own, right? Yet, I had a really hard time wrapping my head around this one. This is your *child*, for god's sake. This is *rural Thailand*. No one's going to whiz up with an ambulance if things don't go as planned. What in the hell were they thinking?

Over the next few days, I took note of the frequent power outages and the fact that the nearest medical facility was thirty minutes away. I kept thinking about Mary and Arjun, the baby and the problems that could arise. Brian and I talked about it a couple times and agreed it was a situation we did not want to get pulled into. So many things could go wrong.

Then, late one night, we heard the cry of a newborn baby. Brian and I exchanged shocked expressions. A child was born on the other side of our wall. In a tiny apartment. In rural Thailand.

I paced around for a little while, half expecting Arjun to come banging on our door in a panic asking for a ride to the hospital. As it turned out, everything went just fine. When we saw Arjun at breakfast the next morning, he was euphoric over the birth of his healthy daughter.

"Mary and the baby are very wonderful," he beamed. "It was so miraculous to watch my child come into this world. I am so very grateful."

Our landlady must have overheard the conversation because she ran out of the kitchen, her eyes wide with shock.

"Wah yo seh? Yo heh beh-bee? Heah?"

"Yes, our baby is here. We have a little girl."

"Oh no! No, no, no, no! I tay yo ospital! No good, no good! No good foh beh-bee!" Our landlady took deep breaths and fluttered her hands at her chest. I thought I might watch the poor woman pass out on the spot.

As Arjun calmly explained to her that Mary and the baby were both fine, his words got me a little choked up, calling to mind those surreal, blissful moments after each of the girls were born. Our landlady, on the other hand, seemed to have more practical matters on her mind. Her eyes kept darting up to the ceiling in the direction of their apartment, as though she was imagining the effect a messy birth would have had on her immaculate rental unit. I had to admit, though, I'd apparently been wrong about this homebirth decision. Clearly, everything had worked out just fine.

Later that night, we heard a knock on our door, and I opened it to find Mary. "I'm so sorry to bother you," she said, her hands clasped at her chest and her eyes filled with worry. "Would you mind coming over to check the baby's breathing? I just don't know if it's normal."

Okay. Let's just pause here for a moment and consider the colossal absurdity of this situation, shall we? I can't even diagnose my kids' ear infections! I was in no way qualified to be doing a pediatric assessment on a newborn baby whose crazy mother refused to have her child examined by a certified medical practitioner!

I looked back at Brian and read his expression. *Say no, Trace. Don't get involved in this.* Yet, I heard myself saying, "Yes, of course. I'll come right over."

I followed Mary into their apartment feeling a mixture of fear and anger churning in my stomach—fear that something could be seriously wrong and anger at their idiotic decisions creating this stressful situation. My head began to pound.

Please let this baby be okay.

I walked in and saw the tiny raven-haired girl in Arjun's arms. At first, she just lay there peacefully.

"She's not doing it now," Mary said. "It comes and goes, but it sounds horrific."

What am I doing here? Why did I let myself get pulled into this? I took note of the baby's pink lips, and then reached down to gently open her tiny fists so I could check the color in her fingers and toes. I watched the even rhythm of her little chest rising and falling with each breath. Looking at this tiny baby, I completely understood what Arjun and Mary were going through. It had been a few years since I'd been the new, worried mom, but it all came rushing back. The fear and uncertainty. The bargaining with God. Please let this be nothing serious and I promise to fill-in-the-blank. I remembered what it was like to be in their shoes.

At that moment, I let go of my judgment. I stopped condemning them for their alternative childbirth choices, and I started empathizing with them. They were doing what they believed to be best for their child. We might have different views on what that means, but we were all parents with the goal of keeping our kids safe. Who was I to judge what they chose for their family? It was time to let go of my own opinions and just help them in any way I could.

Suddenly, the baby began making the gurgling noise Mary had described. A little, wet crackle erupted from her throat on each inhale and continued for about ten seconds until she let out a little cough. When I heard it, I had an immediate flashback to Ali's birth. She'd made the same noise the day she was born, and even for a third-time mom it had freaked me out. The nurse had assured me it was very common in the first day or so, just a little amniotic fluid that had settled in her esophagus and would eventually make its way down.

When I looked up, Mary had tears in eyes and a fist pressed against her lips. I put a gentle hand on her arm. "Mary, I think she's fine."

Her face collapsed with relief and tears spilled down her cheeks. "You do?"

"Yes, I do. Her color is really good. Her breathing is normal. She just seems to have a little fluid caught in her throat. One of my girls made a noise like this for a day or so after she was born."

Mary hugged me tightly. "Oh God, thank you. Thank you so much."

"But listen, I really think both of you should go to a doctor and get checked over," I said, looking down at their tiny girl, now sleeping with her pink, pudgy arms flung out like a little warrior. "I can take you to the clinic tomorrow, just to be on the safe side."

Mary nodded and wiped at her eyes. "Yes, okay, that would be good. Thank you." She smiled and hugged me again. "Thank you so much."

The next day, I drove their family to the clinic on the other side of the island. Mary and Arjun convinced the landlady to set up a small studio apartment in some extra storage space in the building so they could stay there after the new tenant arrived. (I've always wondered if that guy ever found out a child was born on his mattress two days before he moved in.) Since we had a rental car, we helped them out by picking up bulky items at the store that wouldn't fit on their scooter. We gave them rides when they had to take the baby somewhere, and we stored breastmilk for them since they didn't have a refrigerator in their new place. We offered our opinion-free assistance. I must admit, it felt much better to let go of our judgment and just be their friends.

Before we'd come to Thailand, I'd decided this country would be the dawn of my spiritual transformation. In Europe, our family learned about each other and started finding the balance we'd been lacking. Africa taught us new things about the world and left us pondering important questions about happiness, disparity, and social responsibility. Thailand would be the place I'd find answers to the complicated questions our journey had brought to the forefront of my mind. With its ancient Buddhist temples and reverent novice monks, vegetarian cuisine and tranquil beach scenes, I was certain Thailand would bring me inner peace. I'd do yoga religiously and create a daily meditation ritual, cleanse my body of toxins, focus on nutrition, and leave Thailand a different woman than I was when we arrived. I'd be like a young Pema Chödrön, with more hair.

Unfortunately, that turned out to be a big, fat dose of wishful thinking. Thailand was not the find-your-inner-peace place I'd anticipated. For one, we couldn't seem to locate those gorgeous Asiatic beaches we'd seen in travel magazines. Even though it was the dry season, Koh Samui was getting an unusually large number of rain storms, giving us a lot of overcast skies and frighteningly turbulent surf around the island. We did manage to find a quiet, desolate beach with some calm water, but when we waded in, we saw little black specks floating all around us and we wound up with itchy rashes. So, we ventured to the less polluted areas and joined the hordes of tourists sucking down Mai Tais and getting knocked around by the pounding waves.

Shopping in rustic outdoor markets was another exotic Thai travel image I'd conjured up in my head. After the behemoth modern malls of Bangkok, I looked forward to quaint little booths, where I'd pick from among piles of produce and scoop rice from big burlap sacks. However, whenever I asked someone where I could find a local market, they sent me to either a 7-Eleven (which are more abundant in Thailand than they are in the US) or the Tesco Lotus, which is basically the Thai version of Walmart.

Driving was another aspect of life on Koh Samui fraying my nerves a bit. I'd learned how to drive on the left side of the road in Ireland, so operating the vehicle wasn't all that bad. It was the island's crazy traffic that put me on edge. And I don't mean "crazy" as in heavy, slow-moving traffic. I mean "crazy" as in these-people-have-a-death-wish traffic. Drivers in Thailand seriously want to *die*. Scooters swerved between lanes or drove in the shoulder, some of them carrying entire families and a farm animal or two. Cars darted out into oncoming traffic to pass by the smallest margin of error imaginable. The roads were curvy, the directional signs were horribly placed, stray dogs darted into the streets . . . and did I mention the whole death wish thing? Every minute spent behind the wheel was mentally and emotionally exhausting.

And finally, our living quarters seemed to be taking a toll on our family. The frequent rain showers meant we spent a lot of time squeezed up next to each other in our little apartment. The electricity also cut out frequently, making connectivity a daily challenge for Brian's work and the girls' homeschooling. By far, our biggest issue was the toilet. Like many buildings in Thailand, our apartment's plumbing system couldn't handle toilet paper, so it had to go into a trash can. Since dirty toilet paper placed into an open basket creates an immediate olfactory problem, a sprayer hose was conveniently located next to the toilet. This device, appropriately called a "bum gun", was used to rinse things off so that the toilet paper only had to *dry* the area, not *clean* the area, if you catch my drift. Unfortunately, this was a difficult concept to teach young children, and a thirty-eight-year-old man, so I wound up taking the trash out about five times a day. In a word . . . bluh.

So, there you have it. My laundry list of whiny, whiny woo-woos. Scary beaches, boring stores, crazy drivers, a teeny-tiny apartment, bad internet, and baskets full of poopy toilet paper.

Yeah, yeah, I know. Boo-friggin'-hoo. Life isn't perfect for the world-traveling family living on a tropical island. Trust me, I knew this attitude was ridiculous. I kept admonishing myself for the woe-is-me outlook I'd started carting around, but I couldn't help it. I felt myself falling into a funk, and I struggled to get out of it.

I really tried, though. Every day I'd go out onto our patio and force myself to get into the flow of some yoga poses. Yoga had been my go-to mood lifter in the past, but for some reason in Thailand I could never get into the rhythm of it. After a couple sun salutations, I'd be swatting at a persistent bug or wiping sweat from my eyes. I'd try to switch over to meditation, but despite my best efforts, that was mediocre, too. Back straight. Shoulders relaxed. Eyes closed. Pull in a deep, cleansing breath, expanding my lungs until they can't hold another molecule of air, and then . . . *whoosh*. Blow it all out, as though it was possible to just blow away my crappy mood.

Let it all go, Tracey. Release it all. Clear your mind. Just sit here and don't think about anything. Your mind is blank. Totally blank. A blank page. . . . That page of math facts I made for Liv is still blank. She needs to do that. . . . These kids can't get behind in their school work. . . . I wonder if the internet is back up so Emily can watch that Khan Academy video she was trying to stream earlier? This homeschooling thing was so much easier when we had decent internet. I should have researched this apartment more. . . . Hopefully our next place will have better connectivity. . . . Our next place . . . We don't even know where we're going after this. We've got to figure out a plan so I can start looking for housing and I'll be sure to find something better than this place . . . Aww dammit! I'm supposed to be meditating!

And that's pretty much how my spiritual evolution progressed in Thailand. Not very well.

One night, after the girls were asleep, Brian fell onto the bed and heaved out a sigh, his eyes staring up at the ceiling.

"You okay, babe?" I asked.

"Yeah. No. I don't know." He took a breath and blew it out. "Thailand just isn't what I thought it would be."

"I know. Same here."

"It's just . . . the weather hasn't been great and this apartment is too small and I can't keep a decent internet connection when I'm working." He shook his head and sighed again. "Maybe we just picked the wrong area. Everywhere we go is so commercialized and touristy." He rolled onto his side and propped his head on one hand to look up at me. "All the other countries we've been to just felt . . . right. Like we were supposed to be there, you know? It seemed like we were really hitting our stride with this travel thing, but these last couple weeks . . . something's just off."

I lay down and curled in next to him, our bodies fitting like puzzle pieces. "I think I built up Thailand too much," I said. "I expected so much from it, and now almost everything about it annoys me."

"My biggest issue is the internet," he said, running his hand up and down my back. "I can't afford these outages we're always having. I mean, *literally*. We seriously can't afford to travel like this if I can't work."

There was a long pause. Brian took a sharp breath as though he was about to say something, but then he stopped.

"What?" I asked. "What were you going to say?"

He rolled onto his back and stared at the ceiling again. "I'll be honest, Trace . . . I think this whole thing might be starting to wear on me." He turned to look at me, his eyes holding mine for a long moment. "Maybe it's not Thailand. Maybe we're just tired of traveling."

Hearing him say the words made me realize I'd been working hard to keep myself from thinking them. Part of me was so sick of this nomadic life, with its language barriers and unpredictable housing. I missed the familiar and the easy, like going to the store without having to translate labels or convert exchange rates. Dropping the girls off at a real school with certified teachers. Cooking in a kitchen with all the gadgets I needed and all the ingredients I knew how to use. I missed normal roads and watching television and having a wardrobe. And I missed my damn hairdryer! I looked like I'd stuck my finger in light socket most days. Maybe Brian was right. Maybe this funk I'd fallen into was a sign I was sick of traveling, and no matter where we went next, I wouldn't be able to pull myself out of it.

"We shouldn't keep doing this if it's not fun anymore," Brian said quietly. "Maybe we need to think about going home."

I took a deep breath and let the idea swim around in my brain. *Home.* The word put a tight knot in my chest, but I didn't know why.

"You're right. Maybe we should think about it." I leaned over him, our noses almost touching. "But not tonight, okay?"

Sex is such a convenient distraction from the realities we'd rather avoid.

The next day, I sat down to meditate and immediately gave up.

Screw this, I thought. *To hell with clearing my mind and connecting to the divine. I'm just gonna sit here and think. Think, think, think, think, think!*

And so, I did.

I perched myself on the patio with my back straight, eyes closed, and shoulders relaxed. I was the picture of inspired oneness with the universe, except underneath this serene exterior my brain rolled through a dozen topics at Mach 1. I ticked through all the things I hated about Thailand. I worried about the girls and their homeschooling and the possibility of them falling behind academically. I thought about the job I'd walked away from, and what I could do to restart my career once we got back to the United States. As the image of going home formulated in my mind, that uncomfortable tightness gripped my chest again.

How can I be this sick of traveling and not want to go home? Why do I have this burning desire to stick it out with this journey? Is it something I truly want? Or am I just afraid of what people will say when they find out we quit halfway through our around-the-world adventure?

I don't know how long I sat there ruminating, but after a while something unexpected happened. Something I didn't even know was possible. I actually got tired of thinking. My brain just shut down, like a cell phone with a dead battery.

I found myself listening intently to the wind whistling through the palm leaves, my ears tuning into its rhythm as the world fell away. I could almost make out a melody playing on the breeze, like a familiar song weaving its way into nature. I breathed into it, and concentrated on these whispering notes, trying to discern if I was imagining it or if the trees were really singing to me. Suddenly, a clear, lyrical bird song rang through the air, so loud it sounded as though it was right in front of me. I opened my eyes and searched the trees, hoping to see what this bird looked like. After listening to it for several minutes, I heard a response from another bird. One called out and then the other responded, with each round coming quicker than the last. They were talking to each other.

A small bird swooped down onto a branch just a few feet away from me. It had a light brown back and a yellow breast, and when it opened its beak the familiar song came ringing out. This time, the response came almost instantly, and within seconds another bird landed on the branch. The two of them hopped around for a few moments before settling down next to one another. I sat watching them, studying the small differences in their feathers and coloring. The quick movements of their heads. The blinking of their tiny eyes. Everything about them pulled me into trance. It was like being hyp-notized. I couldn't look away. And then, without warning, the two birds flew off together, making a loop around the yard before curv-ing out of sight beyond the roofline.

Their absence brought me back to reality. As I looked around, the world seemed a bit different somehow. The colors of the trees and flowers were a little brighter and crisper. I breathed deeply and took in a potpourri of scents I hadn't noticed before. Everything seemed to have a subtle movement to it, like little vibrations of life emanating from each plant, rock, and tree. I reveled in that moment, gazing around me with a sense of calm, blissful reassurance. It felt like . . . relief. The relief that everything in my life, and in the world, was as it should be.

I tried to hold onto the feeling, pushing my mind to grasp tightly onto this buzzing, transcendent sensation I'd stumbled upon. My eyes filled with tears as the joy grew stronger, radiating from me with an energy that seeped through my skin and floated into the air, connecting me to everything. The sky, the trees, the two little birds out there somewhere. Was this the "connection" they always talked about in meditation? Had I finally found it while watching a couple of birds? Yet, the more I tried to stay in this space, the faster it slipped away.

It's hot out here.

I'm hungry.

I need to pee.

My thinking machine booted back up, and as it did, an unexpected vision drifted into my mind. It was a scene from a documentary I'd watched about an ancient temple in Cambodia. Reenactments depicted a king overlooking his land and workers carving blocks of stone.

Cambodia. Angkor Wat. Why I am thinking about this?

I stood up, stretched, and then walked inside to find Brian on his laptop at our tiny dining table. When I put a hand on his shoulder, he pulled the headphones out of his ears. "How's it going today?" I asked, glancing at his screen.

"Pretty good. The connection's way better than yesterday."

I leaned against the kitchen counter and folded my arms. "So, what do you think of Cambodia? Have you heard anything about it?"

He leaned back and stretched. "Yeah, actually. A few days ago, a college friend messaged me on Facebook and asked if we were going there since we're in this part of Asia. He said it's pretty amazing." Brian raised an eyebrow. "Why? Do you want to try Cambodia next?"

"I don't know," I said noncommittally. "I just started thinking about it today."

"I bet the internet's bad there. I'd probably be battling the same issues I'm having here. Or worse."

"Not necessarily," I said. "Not if we stay in a bigger city. It's easy enough to research."

Forty-eight hours later, we'd committed to a month in Siem Reap, Cambodia, the town just outside the Angkor Wat archeological park. I found a co-working office space for Brian where he could work full-time, and after Skyping with one of the owners, a Brit named Alex, we learned the internet connectivity was strong and consistent. Alex even helped us find housing in the city and put us in touch with the landlord. We'd be staying in the home of an Italian woman who'd lived in Cambodia for years and rented out the second floor of her house. Practically overnight, we'd gone from talking about the possibility of ending our trip to planning our life in another country.

Once we'd set our plan for Cambodia, our experience in Thailand improved by leaps and bounds. One afternoon, a wrong turn led me to a quaint local market tucked away in the forest at the end of a dirt road. Canopy-covered stalls sold fruits and vegetables alongside little food carts serving everything from traditional green curry to fried crickets. Little men and women smiled at me as they proudly held up a myriad of items I might be interested in. Some Thai eggplant perhaps? Some ginger root? How about a bag of dead crickets? "Is good! Is good! For you, 20 Baht." I walked back to the car, loaded with bags of produce and rice, smiling with satisfaction. *No more Tesco Lotus for me!*

Our family also made some local friends, and as we'd learned in other countries, having a few friends can make all the difference. Pim and Steve owned a restaurant near our apartment, and we got to know them one night after dinner while our girls played with their five-year-old daughter, Casey.

We'd been chatting for a while, when a very young Thai woman and a Western gentleman, who looked to be in his sixties, walked in and sat at a table on the other side of the restaurant. Pim rolled her eyes and threw me a smirk. "I am very old to be married to American man, yeah?" she said sarcastically.

I laughed. "You're definitely closer in age than other couples we've seen here."

"I do not understand this," Pim said. "When I was girl, my friends want old Western men like they trophies or something. They want only the money, you know? In America you say . . . gold diggers? Not me. No, thank you." She shook her head disapprovingly, then leaned in and whispered, "I no want a man with a little, wrinkled ding dong!"

Pim threw her head back and let out a quick, devilish laugh. She looked over at her husband, who was standing at the bar talking with Brian. "But then, I meet Steve. And I really love him. I say to myself, it okay, because he may be Western . . . but he no have a little, wrinkled ding dong!"

I decided I was going to like Pim's candid sense of humor a lot. We met up with Casey, Steve, and Pim regularly. They told us about quiet, hidden beaches and good restaurants around the island. With Pim's directions, I found a couple more local markets far away from the box stores and tourist traps. Their family even celebrated Emily's eleventh birthday with us, and Pim had the cook at their café make an American-style birthday cake for her.

Pim also connected us to the Koh Samui Dog Rescue Center so we could start volunteering again. The organization helped address the island's stray dog problem by picking the animals up and bringing them to a facility where they could be vaccinated and sterilized. Once deemed healthy, the dogs were taken back to their home territories so they could continue their lives less reproductively.

On our first day at the center, we stood in the courtyard amid the loud, incessant barking reverberating from large, chain-link pens. A few dogs roamed freely around the grounds, many of them missing a leg, an ear, or an eye. One even rolled up to us with its back legs secured in a little two-wheeled cart.

"Oh, my goodness, look at you," Emily said adoringly as she squatted down to pet its blonde fur. "They made you a little wheelchair."

"That's Kira," a cheery voice said. One of the center's American staff members had walked out to greet us. The young woman's happy face and animated voice reminded me of a Disney princess. "Kira's one of our permanent residents. Isn't she precious?"

After introductions and a quick tour, we were ready to get started. "I'm *so* excited to have you girls here today! Can you guess why?" the happy staffer said, her eyes round with excitement. The girls all shook their heads and smiled. "We just got two new litters of *puppies!*" she shrieked, with a level of enthusiasm so over-the-top it made me wince. The staffer clasped her hands together. "How fun, right? Do you think you girls can help us with them?!"

The girls' eyes lit up and they bounced with anticipation. What better way for a kid to volunteer? Playing with cute, little puppies.

But then we saw the puppies. The lethargic, emaciated, disease-ridden puppies. Raw, bald patches speckled their fur, and distended bellies protruded from their skinny bodies. One was missing most of an ear, and another had a severed tail. The sight of them sent my protective maternal instincts into hyperdrive. *Oh, dear god. Scarring, traumatic childhood experience headed right for us.*

"What happened to them?" Emily asked, looking like she was on the verge of tears.

Liv held her hands over her mouth. "Are they okay?" she mumbled from behind her fingers.

"Is that one *dead!?*" Ali asked in horror, pointing to a seemingly lifeless little pup in the corner of the room.

"Don't worry!" Sally Sunshine chimed in, her ponytail bouncing merrily in the midst of this morbid scene. "They'll be just fine with your help!"

The girls all looked at her in disbelief.

The staff member gave us flea powder and showed us how to pull ticks out of the puppies' delicate skin with tweezers. After she left, I leaned down and looked at the girls. I could tell they'd rather be scooping up dog poop.

"We don't have to do this," I said. "We can ask them to give us another job if it's too much for you."

Liv was the first to speak up. "No. These dogs need our help. I'll do it."

"Me too," Emily added quickly.

Ali hesitated as she eyed the puppies. "Okay . . . I'll do it," she said with a sigh, and then added, "But if one of them is dead, I'm seriously going to *freak out.*"

Luckily, none of them were dead, although a few seemed frighteningly close to it. We set to work picking off ticks and giving each puppy a flea bath. The poor things seemed to become more lethargic as the afternoon wore on, and by the time we left them, I was doubtful they'd all survive the night. The girls had worked so hard and spent so much time helping those pitiful little creatures.

I could envision the traumatic scene that would unfold if we came back and learned only a few of them had made it.

When we returned the next day, we couldn't believe the difference. The same puppies barely able to lift their heads were now playing and yapping. As we examined them again for any ticks we'd missed, we had squirming little balls of energy in our hands. The girls beamed with pride as they saw the dramatic effects of their time and effort firsthand, and I breathed a maternal sigh of relief. We'd miraculously managed to sidestep months of childhood nightmares about dead puppies.

Leaning against the back railing of the ferry, I watched Koh Samui grow smaller in the distance. As the engines below me churned out a triangle of white wake, I stared back at the island, thinking about how expectation can influence the experience.

I'd arrived in Thailand with very clear ideas on what this country would be like. They were images perpetuated by the Travel Channel and backpacker blogs. Deserted beaches canopied by curved palm trees. Lagoons surrounded with jungle foliage and rocky cliffs. An archipelago of tiny islands dotting jade blue water. There might have even been a young Leonardo DiCaprio (circa his appearance in *The Beach*) somewhere in my envisioned montage.

But that wasn't what we'd found. Those classic images of Asiatic paradise surely exist somewhere in Thailand, but they weren't really options for a family of five with the financial requirement of staying connected to the internet. So, we wound up with a less bohemian and more commercialized version of the country.

Had I come to Thailand without my romantic notions of exotic beach scenes and spiritual revelations, perhaps I would have had a completely different experience. Instead of spending most of my time seeing all the ways the reality wasn't living up to the pipedream, I might have just accepted Thailand for what it was and focused on the things I liked about it. Sometimes happiness is as simple as letting go of our expectations and just accepting the world as it comes.

SPIRITUAL SUCCESS

Rides in tuk-tuks: 87
Ancient temples: 18
Murdered mosquitos: Too many to count
Spiritual revelations: 1

CAMBODIA

was eight months pregnant with Ali when I came across an article talking about car seat expiration dates.

"Did you know car seats expire?" I said to Brian. He sat next to me on the couch, scrolling through the recordings on our DVR. "Did you delete last week's episode of *The Office*?"

I glanced up. "Keep scrolling down. Did you hear me? This article says we'll have to get a new infant seat for the baby because the one we used for Emily and Liv expired."

He took his eyes off the screen for a moment to shoot me a skeptical look. "So, car seats are like milk? That's ridiculous."

"That's was it says," I defended, holding up my *Parents* magazine like it was the holy grail of truth in automobile safety. "It says the plastic gets hot and cold sitting in the car, so it can become brittle and it won't be safe in a crash."

"And what does that say about the rest of the plastic in the car? Is the whole thing going to shatter on impact because it's too *brittle?*" He started up the episode and stretched out, dropping his long legs onto what was left of my lap. "Give me a break, Trace. They're just trying to sell more car seats."

Yes, he was probably right. Nevertheless, guess what I went out and bought the next day? That's right! A new car seat, even though we had a perfectly good one sitting in our basement. I was not the kind of mother who was going to take *any* chances with my children's safety in a moving vehicle.

Fast-forward a few years, and the same child for whom I bought the brand new, non-brittle car seat was now bouncing around on the bench of our open air tuk-tuk as the motorcycle driver swerved our carriage through heavy nighttime traffic.

Oh, how my parenting style has changed!

The girls loved the tuk-tuks of Cambodia. Every time we went somewhere, they acted like they were on an amusement park ride, and just like any amusement park ride, they had fun while I got nauseous. After a few white-knuckle trips through town, during which I envisioned every bump of a pothole catapulting my kids into oncoming traffic, I was finally able to reach for my newfound aw-screw-it-I'm-sure-everything-will-be-fine attitude and enjoy these rides a little. The wind whipped our hair around our heads as the sights and smells of the city swept by us. The girls giggled with each bump in the road. Despite my safety concerns, I couldn't help but smile at the memories we were making in this unique country.

We settled into our new temporary home and got to know our landlady, Valentina. She was a funny, lively, platinum-blonde Italian who talked with her hands and loved gardening. She gave us two chicly-decorated bedrooms on the second story of her home, each with its own adjoining bathroom. The bedrooms opened to a large balcony set up as an outdoor living room, which overlooked a big yard lined with mango and banana trees. Going down the stairs on the side of the house led to our outdoor kitchen, complete with a toaster oven, small refrigerator, and a two-burner stove. This whole outdoor cooking setup was a bit of an adjustment at first, since meal preparation was accompanied by an elaborate insect extermination ritual. However, I quickly mastered the tennis racket-shaped bug zapper Valentina had given us. I could make breakfast while simultaneously murdering dozens of mosquitos.

Brian's co-working space provided perfect internet connectivity and a quiet place for him to focus. He rented a bicycle for our month in Cambodia and each morning rode out to face rush-hour traffic, comprised mostly of bicycles, mopeds, and tuk-tuks. He quickly became friends with the other ex-pats working at his office, so he even gained a social life with some new lunch buddies.

The girls and I fell into a routine of homeschool work in the morning and then exploring the area in the afternoon. We flagged down tuk-tuks in town and rode out under a canopy of banyan trees to one of the many Khmer temples. At the most popular complexes, vendors milled through the crowds selling fresh cut fruit, guide books, and cheap clothing. Tiny women sang out in high-pitched voices, "Madam yo wah some paaants! Yo wah scaaarf, Madaaam!" We walked through these sprawling, ancient shrines alongside hundreds of other visitors, all of us staring up at the ornate stone statues and snapping photos of massive tree roots converging into the crumbling buildings.

But my favorite days were the ones we spent off the beaten path. A tuk-tuk driver would take the four of us out of the city, passing miles of rice paddies dotted with palm trees. Soon, dense foliage swallowed the flat farmlands, and we were zipping through the tiny villages nestled within Cambodia's rain forests. We saw homes built on stilts, shops run out of bamboo shacks, and chickens roaming everywhere. Turning off the paved lanes, our tuk-tuk rumbled along dirt tracks cut through the jungle, tree branches scraping the roof of the carriage as our driver maneuvered around ruts and logs in the path.

Eventually, we'd emerge into a clearing where a quiet, ancient ruin stood waiting to be seen. No fences or directional signs or ladies trying to sell me a pair of "paaants." Just a lonely stone building, blackened and weathered with age, some pieces resolutely standing tall through the march of time, while others disintegrated under nature's unrelenting forces.

While the girls studied the statues or played games of follow the leader, I sat and tried to imagine these structures as they'd been hundreds of years ago. Surrounded by bustling towns, these stone temples had served as quiet places for religious retreat and contemplation. They'd been gifts from the Khmer kings to both the gods and their loyal subjects. Places where people would come to find peace and certainty in their lives. Sitting among those ruins, I listened to the birds in the trees or watched bugs march across the dirt, and eventually I'd be doing it without even trying—in the moment, completely present, with zero thought for the past or the future.

At some point during our time in Cambodia, this easy centeredness slipped into my life. It no longer felt forced, like an antidote periodically applied to my frazzled nerves. Somewhere along the way, mindfulness became a habit. It felt familiar and comfortable. Watching my daughters play, I knew this fully present state of mind was how I'd spent my childhood, before the goals and to-do lists of adult life leached it out of me, pulling me away from "the now" and into my thinking head. Sitting in those tranquil Khmer temples, the child in me reawakened, and often I'd get up and join the girls' in their game of follow-the-leader over ancient stones.

In Siem Reap, Brian and I began to fully appreciate the tremendous value of traveling with our children. Navigating this adventure with them slowed down our pace and made us look at the world through a much younger set of eyes. They noticed the gorgeous patch of violets growing out of a temple wall. They stopped to examine the details of a mural and interpret the story etched into the stone. They showed us the beauty and the little miracles our adult eyes would have missed.

One afternoon, as I sat watching the girls swing on a thick, wooden vine hanging down from the branches of a tree, I found myself thinking back to the day I'd learned I was pregnant with Emily. I recalled that calm inner voice convincing me it was all part of a plan, and now I understood. This journey was the reason our life needed to take an unexpected turn into parenthood. We were meant to see this world as a family. If Brian and I had traveled together as young twentysomethings, I doubt we would have wound up on a global, nomadic adventure with our kids. Sometimes our unfulfilled desires turn out to be life's greatest gifts. Through the girls' innocent observations, I began walking toward the spiritual revelation I'd tried but failed to find in Thailand.

It began on the day our family took a long tuk-tuk ride out to visit Banteay Srei, a tenth-century temple dedicated to the Hindu god Shiva. After wandering around the moat-enclosed structures for several hours, we were making our way back to the main entrance when I realized Liv was no longer walking with us. I turned around to find her a hundred paces back, staring up into the trees.

"Liv!" I yelled. "Keep up! It's time to go!"

She pointed above her. "But look!"

I rolled my eyes and groaned. I was not amused. I was hot and thirsty, and I'd had enough of the temples for one day. "It's a tree, dear! I've seen trees! Come on!" My irritation was obvious, but she persisted.

"But you guys have gotta see this!"

"Liv, come on!" Brian pulled out his commanding baritone. "We're leaving *now!*"

Not even the annoyed Daddy voice could get her moving, "Seriously, you'll *really* want to see this!" she shouted back.

Brian and I exchanged exasperated looks. "I'll go," I said resignedly.

When I walked back to her, Liv pointed up again. "Do you see it?" I looked up and saw nothing but leaves. "Um . . . no. Seriously, Liv, did I come all the way back here to look at a bunch of branches?"

"No, Mama, *look*. It's right there."

I looked again and, among the shadowed shades of green, something unusual caught my eye. I adjusted my focus to try to make sense of it. "What *is* that?"

Camouflaged among its surroundings was a volleyball-shaped basket made from leaves, each one cut and folded into a precise, symmetric design. "Did someone throw it up there?" I asked.

"The ants are doing it," Liv said from the side of the path. I walked over and saw hundreds of ants swarming around a branch, working in teams to move leaves into position and fold each one into the basket. I'd never seen anything like it in my life.

Liv grinned at me. "Kind of worth stopping for, right?" she said.

"Yes, kiddo. Definitely worth stopping for. Nice work."

Our family found more of those curious little baskets in the foliage alongside the trail, and we stood there for a while watching armies of ants in their meticulous work.

Later, as our tuk-tuk rumbled along the road back to Siem Reap, I kept thinking about the unseen force responsible for the ant baskets and the bee hives and all the everyday miracles on this planet. I'd never given much thought to it before, but something about seeing the ants' intelligent cooperation in the middle of an ancient, spiritual place left me marveling at it all. We call it instinct or God or Mother Nature, but what does that really mean? What's the connection giving simple insects the complex blueprint and collaborative abilities to build something so intricate and beautiful?

I remembered a day years before when Liv and I had been in our yard together. While I yanked weeds out from among the petunias, she dug in the dirt looking for worms. Suddenly, my quiet little Liv spoke out in an unusually loud, strong voice.

"This worm has no idea we're here," she said. I looked up and found her leaning over, her face just inches away from the little creature squirming along the ground. "He doesn't know this is our yard. Or that our house is right here. Or what a car is. Or what a grocery store is. Or Legos. Or M&Ms. Or Pooh Bear."

As I chuckled at her amusing list, Liv sat up and looked at me, an expression of grave seriousness furrowing her little brow. "He doesn't know anything about the world," she said.

I smiled. "Well, he's just a little worm, sweetie. He can't even see."

She tilted her head back to look up at the sky, her eyes squinting with scrutiny. "Yeah, but . . . what if we're like this worm? What if there's a bunch of stuff around us, and we don't even know it's there."

Bouncing along in our tuk-tuk, I felt the same overwhelming rush of awareness I'd experienced that day after hearing Liv's words. There really is a bunch of stuff around us that we don't know is here. We can't see it or measure it, but that doesn't mean it doesn't exist. It's a cosmic connection beyond our understanding. Scientists call it dark matter. Some call it spirit or prana or life force. We try to explain it and label it, attribute it to something we can define in our rather primitive minds. But it's undefinable. Beyond words and reason.

A familiar tingly numbness rushed over my skin, a flash of the buzzing, transcendent sensation I'd felt while hypnotized by the little birds in Thailand. After the feeling passed, I closed my eyes, focused my thoughts, and felt the buzz course through me again . . . and again . . . and again. It was like giving myself goosebumps on command. I kept closing my eyes and grabbing onto the feeling, guiding the rush of energy across my arms, down my legs, and up the back of my neck. My body felt expansive and connected, woven into the space around me. No beginning or end. No thinking or judging or wanting. Just being. Dissolving into a place of complete and total contentment.

"What in the heck are you doing?"

Emily's voice jerked me back to reality. She and Liv were staring up at me, while Brian and Ali dozed on the opposite bench of the carriage.

"I . . . um . . . I was . . . "

"You looked weird," Liv said with suspicion. "You kept opening and closing your eyes. And you had this freaky smile."

"Are you okay, Mom?" Emily asked with genuine concern.

A bubble of laughter floated up through my throat. "Yes, I'm fine," I said, as tears welled up in my eyes. The two of them exchanged wary looks. This was probably why I'd never heard of a spiritual guru reaching enlightenment while raising young children. They had to tone it down so their kids wouldn't think they'd gone nuts.

I wiped the tears away and put an arm around each of the girls. "Ladies, I couldn't be better," I said, barely able to contain the joyful, blissful discovery I'd stumbled upon. We bounced along the dirt road, its dusty surface dappled with the sunlight filtering through the trees. As I breathed in the warm, humid air laced with the earthy smells of the countryside, I felt something precious blossoming inside me. Something that just might change me forever.

Who knew ants could be so damn enlightening?

I don't know if it was this natural high I'd found or the genuinely joyful culture of Cambodia, but I loved *everything* about this country. The people, the landscape, the streets, the shopping. The Old Market in the heart of Siem Reap put me in my happy place, making me feel like a true world traveler as I walked its labyrinthine maze of stalls piled to the ceiling with everything from fresh fish and fruit to knock-off Crocs and Ray-Bans. For less than five bucks, I could buy more healthy food than I could comfortably carry home, and everywhere I went I met smiley, happy, grateful people.

Within our first week in Siem Reap, I'd developed a weird affinity for the fish foot massages offered by the beauty parlors found on every block. The first time I lowered my feet into the tank of hungry little fish, I squealed as dozens of mouths began chomping on my heels and toes. However, once I got used to it, I found it surprisingly relaxing, and the results were amazing! My feet were baby smooth with no callouses, and that was saying a lot given they'd been tromping around in Tevas for the last five months.

The girls loved these fish pedicures, too, but I learned to be careful which salons I let them go in. One day, we were letting fish have a buffet on our feet when I noticed a prominent sign on the wall directly in front of us.

NO SEX IN SHOP

Liv saw the sign first and elbowed Emily, nodding to it with a questioning look. Emily read it, shrugged, and turned to me.

"Mom, why does that sign—"

"*Nope!*" I blurted out.

She gave me a confused look before continuing. "But, we just wondered—"

"Sorry. Huh-uh. Not going there. Ask me in a few years." I spewed the words out like Rain Man, avoiding eye contact and shaking my head.

The girls exchanged another look, but thankfully let it drop. I simply wasn't ready to explain to my young daughters the concepts of sexual intercourse, prostitution, and the nefarious activities sometimes associated with Cambodian beauty parlors.

A young woman working at the salon gave me a friendly smile and said, "You no worry, madam. No naughty-naughty in my shop!" Then she very proudly pointed to the sign I was trying so desperately to get my kids to ignore.

This joyful friendliness we found among the Cambodian people made it easy to forget the country's tragic history. We knew nothing about the Khmer Rouge before coming to Cambodia, but I quickly learned about it reading the books sold by disabled vendors on the streets of Siem Reap. A man missing an arm or a leg would slowly make his way down the sidewalk carrying a small display of books with titles like *First They Killed My Father* and *When Broken Glass Floats*. These tragic memoirs gave me a glimpse into the horrors the Cambodian people endured in the 1970s at the hands of their fellow countrymen. In a backward attempt to completely restructure the country's society, Pol Pot and other Khmer Rouge leaders began a campaign of mass murder, executing anyone with an education. The oppressive government abolished free commerce and forced urban residents out of their homes to live in the countryside as farmers. It's estimated almost a quarter of Cambodia's population died during the Khmer Rouge era either by execution, disease, or starvation.

The people continue to struggle back from the economic and psychological damage caused by this dark period. Most of the population still lives in extreme poverty, with a typical family making less than $2 a day. As our tuk-tuks drove us around town, we passed shanty houses built from patchworks of bamboo and plywood. Children played naked on the littered shoreline of the Siem Reap River while their mothers washed clothing and dishes in its murky, polluted waters. Amputees, the victims of landmines left behind after decades of war, wheeled themselves along the streets in rickety homemade carts. Everywhere we looked, we saw people struggling to survive from one day to the next.

And yet, we also saw the ingenuity and perseverance of the Cambodians. Always smiling as they worked and finding reasons to laugh, the Khmer people possessed something special. A remarkably unshakable spirit borne from their unimaginable tragedy. The Cambodians' outlook on life underscored a fundamental truth we'd seen in Africa: happiness is based on your state of mind, not the estate you live in.

The spirit of this country seeped into the core of my being, bringing me a centeredness I'd never before experienced. I found myself flowing through yoga poses with unusual grace and slipping into a surreal, tranquil state of consciousness. This newfound serenity was a bit surprising at first, since my pursuit of yoga had initially stemmed from my obsession with losing baby weight rather than any desire to connect to my inner spirit. For years, I'd marched into Power Yoga classes determined to burn off as many calories as humanly possible. It wasn't until my panic attack over pinot noir that yoga really changed for me. I began appreciating the mindfulness of it all, the way it would switch off my brain and give me a more balanced and peaceful place to put my focus. I stopped turning it into a calorie-burning marathon and instead made it a retreat from my overscheduled life, a place where my only obligation was the one I'd made to myself.

Once our world trip began, I'd been determined to take yoga with me, but uncertain how I'd do it without a certified instructor directing my every move. I muddled through in the beginning, but eventually I began seeing steady improvements in my practice. Before I knew it, I was contorting myself into poses I'd once deemed physically impossible.

Cambodia brought a profound spiritual centeredness to my yoga sessions. Some days, when I let myself fall into it, my inward focus became so intense I seemed to lose contact with the physical world. A detached, floating sensation overwhelmed my senses and a hazy light appeared behind my closed eyelids. And then . . . it was like being pulled through the doorway of perception into a room with no walls, everything blending together until I couldn't tell where my body ended and the rest of the world began. The filter of logic and reason melted away, and an underlying unity with nature consumed me. Little whispering thoughts seeped in now and then, but they were like thin trails of smoke floating away with the slightest breath. I'd discovered a connection to something much bigger than myself.

It was always temporary, though. Every time I reached this transcendent state, my ego pulled me back. *Good for you,* it would say. *Look how enlightened you are, Tracey!* And then the blissful connection drifted away, like a feather on the wind, and I'd be back in the real world. Back to the place where each thing has its own beginning and end, where we're separated by the space between us and oblivious to all the stuff around us that we don't even know is there.

"Mama!" Ali yelled. I looked up from the flower bed I'd been weeding to find her standing at the top of the slide and pointing to the little girl standing next to her. "This is Akara! Can she come play at our house?" Before I could answer, the two of them giggled and slid down together.

That morning, Emily, Liv, Ali, and I had served the students at a village school their breakfast of rice porridge. While I spent the rest of the day tackling landscaping work with another volunteer, the girls climbed on the playground equipment in the sunny courtyard. The school's bright yellow buildings, tucked among shady trees and bordered with blooming flower beds, stood in stark contrast to the rundown shacks and littered dirt roads just outside the facility's gate.

This was one of twenty-one schools supported by an organization called Caring for Cambodia. Over the course of ten years, the efforts of the local staff and volunteers had transformed a one-room shack with a part-time teacher into a thriving school serving hundreds of students. It was an enormous improvement for the children of this tight-knit community on the outskirts of Siem Reap, but there was still much to be done to improve the quality of life for its residents. The school uniforms, donated from private schools overseas, were often the only clothes the children owned, and many students wore them several sizes too big for their undernourished bodies. When they left class each day, the boys and girls walked to homes with no electricity or running water, no screens in the windows or pantries full of food. The time they spent at school was the most stable, healthy part of their lives.

Despite the spiritual centeredness I'd found in Cambodia, the tragedy plaguing this country sent a weight of sadness creeping onto my shoulders. I could hear Observer Tracey's comments popping up again.

Think of all the meals you could buy for those students with the money you spent on that crazy expensive jar of peanut butter you found at the western market the other day. Eight dollars, was it?

My first-world guilt had returned with a vengeance.

I decided to tackle these repentant thoughts during my daily meditation and yoga sessions. Surely my new one-with-the-earth superpowers could cure my privileged white girl remorse, right?

Nope.

Apparently, it doesn't work that way. I could let go of the self-admonishment while sitting on my mat and meditating, but as soon as I opened my eyes and remembered the poverty around me, the shaming started up again. I pushed against it, trying to focus on the joy and hope we saw in Cambodia, but that little nagging feeling remained.

Can I be a good person when I'm living a life so much more fortunate than others? Do I really deserve the easy existence I was born into?

One morning, I woke up before dawn, my brain wide-awake the moment I opened my eyes. As I lay there letting my pupils adjust to the darkness, an idea popped into my head.

I should go to the temples alone today.

Without putting any more thought into it, I rolled over and put a hand on Brian's chest. "Brian," I whispered. "Babe, wake up."

"Mmmm," he groaned and murmured something in his sleep.

"I'm leaving," I said quietly. "I'm going to the temples."

Brian opened one eye. "What . . . what's wrong? You okay?"

"Yeah, I just want to go to the temples today. Can you work from here and stay with the girls?"

"Sure . . . yeah . . . temples . . . "

Uncertain he'd remember our conversation, I took a piece of paper into the bathroom and scribbled out a note. Then I threw on a sundress, brushed my teeth, grabbed my bag, and tiptoed out of our room. Within five minutes of waking up, I was walking down our dark, quiet road in search of a tuk-tuk.

It took a while to find a driver at such an early hour, but as the sky began to lighten in the east I was finally able to flag one down.

"Bayon," I said to the driver as I climbed into the carriage.

Until the word came out of my mouth, I hadn't known Bayon Temple was the one I wanted to visit. I'd been there before with Brian and the girls, but I felt the need to see it again on my own.

As my tuk-tuk driver sped along quiet roads, the invigorating morning air hit my cheeks. We zipped by the throng of people gathered to watch the sunrise over Angkor Wat and then passed a group of elephants lumbering along the road with their *mahouts*. By the time we crossed the south bridge leading into the ancient city of Angkor Thom, the world had brightened around us. Trees glistened with morning dew and birds fluttered among the branches. Macaque monkeys climbed down to the ground, yawning and stretching as they watched my tuk-tuk rumble by them.

When we pulled up to Bayon Temple, the famous complex was practically deserted. Only a few vendors milled around, setting up their stalls and calling out greetings to one another. I walked through the entrance and explored the quiet pathways and corridors alone. As I wandered through the rooms and stared up at the large, square pillars of stone faces, this ancient place felt completely different without the hordes of tourists around me. The temple seemed to be awakening, drawing in her first breaths of the morning and pulling the fine mist of evaporating dew into her lungs.

I sat down and tried to meditate in this peaceful space, but my mind had no interest in turning inward. Instead, I watched the rays of the sun rise slowly from behind a tree, sliding light across the ground like a blanket and casting dark shadows on the temple's walls. After a while, I stood up and decided to leave Bayon, so I could make my way to another temple before the crowds began congregating. I looked around to regain my sense of direction and walked briskly toward the entrance.

But then, something made me pause. It was a long corridor I hadn't noticed before. The walls glowed with warm, pink tones as the morning sunlight streamed through the windows. I stepped into the passageway and walked slowly through a series of simple, stone rooms, each one separated by a large rectangular doorway. When I stepped over the threshold into the last room, I was startled to find I was no longer alone. A Buddhist nun, dressed in a flowing white robe, sat at the base of a large Buddha statue. An orange cloth was draped around the Buddha's broad shoulders and necklaces of beads adorned its chest. A vase of fresh flowers and a decorative pot filled with sand sat on a low stone platform. The nun bowed her shaved head, and between her wrinkled hands sprung a cluster of incense sticks. She gently extended them toward me, offering me to take one.

I'd come across nuns in the temples with these prayer offerings before, but being totally ignorant of the ritual involved, I'd always politely declined. On this day, at this moment, with this nun, something compelled me to accept her offering. I stepped forward, and when I bent down to pull an incense stick from the woman's hands, my gaze locked onto hers. The skin of her temples crinkled into little lines and her eyes almost disappeared behind plump, round cheeks. Tiny lights deep within her pupils twinkled out at me, holding me there, captivated and motionless, as a soothing sensation coursed through me. It was a feeling I knew, but couldn't quite define. The nun watched me expectantly. She didn't move. She didn't even blink. She simply stared into my eyes until I could finally discern what I was feeling.

It was recognition. The comforting peace that comes with seeing something deeply familiar. Something loved and cherished. *I feel like I know this woman.*

As soon as the thought formulated in my mind, the nun began nodding, and when she smiled, the sparkle in her eyes grew brighter until her face seemed to illuminate the room.

Suddenly, a tidal wave of emotion came flooding up from deep inside me, an unrelenting force pushing up through my chest and rushing out in a gasp. Tears sprung to my eyes and spilled down my cheeks as a racking sob escaped from me. Embarrassed and confused, I shoved one hand over my face and let the other hang at my side, clutching the incense stick with an intensity that shook my entire arm.

Oh my god, what's happening to me?

I felt the nun's fingers wrap around mine, and the tension in my trembling arm vanished as she gently pulled me down to kneel with her. Sucking in erratic breaths, I pressed my hand against my eyes, but when her fingers touched my wrist, once again the muscles relaxed. My hand fell into my lap, revealing a blubbering mess. Salty tears ran down my lips and dripped off my chin. A stream of snot leaked from my nose, and I hiccupped through uncontrollable sobs. I tried to smile through my tears, shrugging my shoulders and shaking my head.

I'm so sorry. I don't know what's come over me.

A pensive expression came across the nun's face as she watched me, and then she smiled and slowly nodded. Gathering my hands together, she pressed them tightly between her thin, soft fingers. A powerful heat radiated from her skin, sending cascades of warmth up my arms. She leaned toward me until our bowed heads almost touched.

"We all have journey," she said in a quiet, raspy voice. "Be proud of yours."

I gasped at her words and pulled back so I could look into her familiar eyes. "No shame," she said firmly. "Only joy."

A surreal understanding passed between us, and I burst into a bizarre mixture of laughing and sobbing. Relief shot through me as my guilt collapsed into nothingness. The shame I carried for my privileged life. The remorse I felt for not doing enough. Not helping enough. Not serving an important purpose. It all vanished in an explosion of divine awareness.

Only joy will guide me in this life.

Not guilt.

Not shame.

Not fear.

Only joy.

The turbulent emotions gradually calmed, leaving a soothing serenity flowing through every cell of my body, purifying me from the inside out until my lungs finally pulled in a deep, cleansing breath. I looked around the room, absorbing the details of the moment. A bird landed on the nose of the large stone face outside the window. A breeze drifted through the room, rustling the cloth wrapped around the Buddha's shoulders. The scent from the fresh flowers caressed the air.

When I wiped my eyes and turned back to the nun, she smiled and gestured to the candle next to her. I lit my incense stick against the flame, then gently pushed it into the pot of sand on the stone platform. Together, we sat watching it slowly burn, its trail of smoke curling and twisting in a floating dance. The higher the smoke rose, the lighter I felt, like a physical weight being lifted from my shoulders.

After a few minutes, I took a deep breath and looked back at the nun, hoping to memorize her peaceful face. I brought my hands together and gave her a deep, grateful namaste bow. Then I stood up, feeling lighter than air, and walked out of that temple room . . . forever changed.

DRUG DRAMA

Psychedelic episodes: 1

Drug deals: 1

Thai police officers: 2

Frantic text messages: 5

CAMBODIA ◎ THAILAND

On one of our last days in Cambodia, Brian staggered into our room and collapsed in a heap on the bed.

"Babe, are you okay?"

He groaned a pained, "Nooo," into the pillow.

"Are you sick?"

I rubbed my hand over his back and felt anxiety rising in my chest. *Our whole family has been so healthy on this trip, please don't tell me we were dealing with a major illness now.* I had no interest in seeing the inside of the Siem Reap hospital.

Brian groaned miserably and brought his legs up into the fetal position.

"Okay, you're kind of scaring me here," I said. "I don't know what to do for you. What's wrong?"

With his face still smashed into the pillow, all I got was a muffled, unintelligible response.

"What? I can't understand you. Brian, you need to tell me what's going on."

He turned his head away from the pillow. "I don't want to tell you," he said quietly.

I paused. "What does *that* mean?"

He rolled onto his back and brought his hands over his eyes. "I ate a happy pizza."

I sat there for a moment, confused. "Happy pizza? What are you talking about?"

He groaned again. "This friend of mine . . . he said to go to this pizza place . . . and tell them to make it . . . happy."

He looked up at me with a combination of regret, fear, and wild-eyed giddiness. And then it clicked.

"Wait a minute, you mean 'happy' as in they put *marijuana* on it?"

Brian stifled a laugh and then gagged a little. "Oh god." He sat up and gripped the edge of the bed. "I think I'm gonna throw up."

A torrent of sympathy flooded my heart for my beloved husband. "Oh, honey, I'm so sorry. What can I do to help you?"

Hahaha!

Just kidding. No, that's definitely *not* what happened next. Despite my flash of spiritual insight with the Buddhist nun, I didn't have that much kindness and understanding in me.

What really happened was this: I shoved Brian so hard he almost fell off the bed, and then I screamed in his high-as-a-kite, on-the-verge-of-puking face. "YOU ATE A PIZZA LOADED WITH CAMBODIAN HASH?! ARE YOU CRAZY?"

He put his hands over his ears. "Please . . . not so loud, Trace . . ."

"Oh, I'm so sorry, honey," I said, sweetly at first. "Am I hurting YOUR POOR LITTLE EARS!"

I got up and paced the room. "What the hell, Brian! You're not some twenty-year-old stoner! You have no tolerance for that stuff! You can't go off and eat an entire pizza full of it! What were you thinking?"

More groaning. "I wasn't . . . it was so dumb."

"Uh, ya think? You could've been arrested and thrown into a Cambodian prison!"

"Actually it's . . . kind of . . . legal . . . here," he said between moans.

"Kind of? KIND OF! There's no 'kind of' legal, Brian! It's either legal or it's not! God! I can't believe you!" I stomped over to the desk, grabbed my purse, and headed for the door.

"You're leaving?" he asked pathetically.

"Yes, I'm taking the girls out for the rest of the day. I don't want them seeing you like this."

"Trace, wait!"

I stopped with my hand on the doorknob. "What?!"

"Can you at least get me some water? Please?"

I shook my head and laughed. "You're on your own, Cheech."

Cue the dramatic door slam.

I took the girls to the Old Market area of town and found the only thing I thought might have a chance of calming me down in this situation—a fish pedicure. As the four of us soaked our feet in a tank next to the sidewalk, I people-watched to take my mind off this whole happy pizza business. Scanning the crowds, I noticed three young Cambodian men standing across the street from us. Two backpackers walked up the sidewalk toward them and when they passed by, one of the Cambodians said something that made the backpackers stop and turn around. A few words were exchanged, some cash and a plastic bag changed hands, and the backpackers continued walking up the street while the Cambodians went back to chatting.

My mouth dropped open.

Oh my god. I just watched a drug deal go down right in front of me.

Had Brian been approached like this? Had he bought weed from random guys on the street? Was a happy pizza just the tip of a deep, dark iceberg of lies? My mind reeled as I conjured up my husband's secret drug habit, complete with images of him sneaking off to roll joints in dirty, sinister alleys.

By the time the girls and I returned to the house that night, I was practically envisioning Brian's rehab program. I opened the door to our room and found him sitting on the bed propped up on pillows.

"Hey," he said, his voice heavy with regret. "I'm so sorry, Trace. That was *really* stupid of me."

I folded my arms across my chest. "You're feeling better, I see."

"Yes, but I promise I won't be doing that again. It was a total nightmare." He looked at me, closely gauging my reaction. "You have every right to be mad. I'm really, really sorry."

I stared at him for a moment, trying to read his face for lies. "Is this something you've done before?"

Brian threw his head back with a laugh. "Oh my god! No!" He stood up and walked across the room to put his hands on my shoulders. "Tracey, I clearly have no tolerance for the stuff. This is not a habit for me."

I eyed him suspiciously. "You promise?"

"I promise." I let him pull me into a hug and breathed a sigh of relief. Then he added, "There's one problem, though." I pulled back and looked at him suspiciously. His face scrunched into an apologetic grimace. "I have no idea what I did with my phone. I think I might have left it by the river when I was all high and shit."

Cue the dramatic eye roll.

Thanks to the modern miracle of GPS locator apps, we recovered the phone Brian lost during his happy pizza stupor, and a few days later we were packing our bags again. We would have stayed in Cambodia longer, but our tourist visas were running out, so we decided to give Thailand another chance. This time we'd be visiting the northern part of the country, flying into Chiang Mai after a layover in Bangkok.

As we made our way up to the carry-on X-ray machine at the Siem Reap airport, Brian froze and stared ahead of us. "Oh crap, Trace. Your name's on that list."

"What list?" I looked around to see what he was talking about.

"*That* one." He nodded toward a clipboard sitting on top of the X-ray box, too high for me to read. I watched as the security guard who'd just checked my boarding pass grabbed the clipboard, scanned the names, and then looked at me.

"Excuse me. Tacey Cah-weesh?"

Great. I reluctantly admitted that I was, in fact, Tacey Cah-weesh.

"We have problem with your bag. You come with me." The fearful and confused look on my face was apparently obvious, because he quickly smiled and added reassuringly, "Is no big problem. No need to worry."

As Brian went through security with the girls, I followed the guard through a set of double doors. In the middle of a large room, one of our checked bags sat on a table. When we walked over to it, the guard gestured to the bag's security lock. I rotated the dials to our code and popped the latches. He opened the bag to reveal the bug zapper Valentina had insisted we bring with us, telling us we'd need it for the mosquitos in rural Thailand.

The guard picked it up. "Not okay to fly. Cannot be on plane."

Is that all? The relief rushing through me made me realize how nervous I'd been. The guard kept the bug zapper, and within a few minutes I'd joined my family at our gate.

When I told Brian the reason for all the drama, he laughed and said, "At least they didn't find drugs in our bag."

"What's that supposed mean?" I asked accusingly. "Why would they find drugs in our bag?"

"Oh my god, calm down." He rolled his eyes. "I'm just kidding, babe."

While we waited for our flight, my mind rolled over the crazy stories I'd heard about drugs getting planted on tourists. I began imagining corrupt baggage handlers being bribed by Cambodian cartel bosses and sneaking bricks of opium into the luggage of unsuspecting travelers. I'd seen *Brokedown Palace* and the sequel to *Bridget Jones' Diary*, so I was practically an expert on Southeast Asian drug smuggling tactics.

Suddenly, a frightening thought popped into my head.

Did I relock our bag after he took the bug zapper out of it?

Of course, I did.

Wait. Did I?

I worried about the security of our suitcase during our flight to Bangkok, but by the time we were walking through the crowded terminal to the gate of our connecting flight, I'd forgotten all about it.

That is, I forgot all about it until a tiny Thai woman was standing over me saying, "Cah-weesh? Are you Tacey Cah-weesh?"

I nodded and exchanged a look with Emily and Liv who were sitting next to me.

"We have problem with your bag," the woman said.

Oh. My. God. Not again.

"He escort you to baggage area." She gestured to a young man in a security uniform standing behind me.

"But my husband isn't here," I said, reaching into my backpack and digging for my phone. "He's somewhere in the terminal with my other daughter. I can't leave my kids alone. He'll have to come back before I can go anywhere."

The woman shook her head. "No, you need to go now," she said firmly. "I can be here with your children until your husband return."

I looked down the concourse, but Brian and Ali were nowhere to be seen. Kneeling down in front of Emily and Liv, I could see they both looked scared out of their wits.

"I'll be right back," I said. "I'll text Dad and he'll be here soon." They nodded wordlessly.

"Take your passport please," the woman said from above me. My heart hammered against my chest as I followed the guard and punched out text messages to Brian.

Get back to gate!
Problem with bag!
Again!
Had to leave with guard.
E and L w/ woman from airline.

"Can you tell me what this is about?" I asked the security guard as we turned down a hallway. He grimaced and shook his head. No friendly smile, no reassuring words. Just a serious face and brisk steps.

How can this be happening for a second time in one day? Unless . . .

The guard led me into a room and gestured to a seat next to a desk, where two women in red blazers shuffled through papers. The moment I sat down, an older gentleman in a dark suit walked into the room, thumbs jabbing at his phone. After a few minutes, he slipped the phone into his jacket pocket, and looked down at me with a long, appraising stare.

"Passport please," he finally said, holding out his hand.

I gave it to him, and he thumbed through it quickly before handing it to one of the women. He exchanged a few Thai words with her, and then quickly left the room. The security guard walked over to plant himself in front of my chair, as though expecting me to make a break for it. I started to type another text message, but the guard cleared his throat and shook his head sternly.

Searching the room's sterile grey walls for a distraction, my eyes settled on a large picture window cutting through to a concourse hallway. Travelers rushed by with carry-ons slung over their shoulders and suitcases rolling at their heels, all of them oblivious to the predicament I'd found myself in. My knees bounced nervously, sending an incessant cacophony of squeaks out from under my chair. When the woman returned my passport to me, I sat staring at the United States seal on the cover, tracing the eagle's wings with my finger.

After what felt like an eternity, the man in the suit finally returned, this time with two Thai police officers.

"You follow them," the man in the suit said.

Oh my god. This is the beginning of my worst nightmare.

My mouth went dry and I heard the blood rushing through my ears. Standing up, I thought my legs might buckle, but I took a deep breath and managed to propel myself into motion. I followed the men through a series of secured doors and brightly lit hallways, and at one point caught a glimpse of my reflection in a glass wall. The two police officers were in front of me, the security guard walked behind me, and the man in the suit trailed all of us.

This is all just a mix-up. Someone else's bag. Stay calm. Everything will be fine.

Thinking the words to myself did little to convince me.

One of the officers pushed open a door, and a nauseating mixture of steamy air and jet fuel hit my nostrils as we walked out onto a staircase attached to the side of the building. The roar of aircraft engines and the clanging of our footsteps on the metal stairs competed against the panic-stricken thoughts screaming through my head.

Holy shit, why are we going outside?! Where are they taking me?!

When we reached the pavement, a man in a yellow vest stood waiting for us. He directed our group to follow him under the wing of an airplane and into a baggage area beneath the terminal. After passing busy workers with clipboards and carts piled high with luggage, our group walked into a small room with steel mesh walls. Sitting on a table in the middle of this cage was our black Samsonite hard shell suitcase, covered in a collage of colorful stickers from countries we'd visited. It was the same one I'd had to open in Siem Reap.

My heart sank and bile stung the back of my throat as the bag's presence eliminated the possibility this had all been a mistake. I hadn't walked down here to breathe a sigh of relief. Whatever this was, it was actually happening. And it was happening to me.

A stocky man in plain, blue coveralls hoisted himself out of a chair and gestured wordlessly at the bag's lock. I stepped forward and, with trembling hands, turned the dials to pop open the latches. I watched him through a fog as he pulled out clothes and tossed them onto the table. My brain desperately wanted to reject this reality—the caged room, the police officers, the roar of plane engines filling my ears. Quentin Tarantino couldn't have crafted a more ominous scene.

This is just a bad dream. Wake up, Tracey. Wake up, goddammit!

Suddenly, the man searching my bag cleared his throat loudly, and I realized he was standing in front of me, holding a small object in each of his hands. They were black rectangular boxes that looked vaguely familiar. He thrust them into my palms, and then crossed his arms over his chest.

I stood there, completely confused. "I don't know what these are," I said, looking around the room.

No one responded.

I turned to the security guard who'd escorted me from the gate. "What does he want? What am I supposed to do with these?"

He exchanged a few words with the man, and then said, "Not okay to fly in check bag. Keep with you."

I blinked several times as his words sank in.

I'm sorry, come again?! All of this— the police escorts and the heart palpitations and standing around in a cage with half a dozen Thai men—was because of these two little plastic cubes? Was this some kind of sick, twisted joke?

"Are you serious?" I said incredulously. "That's all?"

As though he understood my words, the man in the blue coveralls waved his hands at me and then walked back to plop himself onto the chair.

Still stunned, I just stood there. No drug smuggling. No Thai prison. No beginning of my worst nightmare. I took a deep breath and shook my head as the tension melted from my body.

Everything's going to be okay. Thank god.

"Excuse me, madam," the security guard said as he gestured to the disorganized mess of clothing strewn across the table. "You need to pack bag now."

When I was allowed to return to our gate, I marched up to Brian and practically threw those little black boxes at him. "What in the hell are these things?" I hissed.

"They're just battery chargers. That was the problem?" He shrugged and laughed. "That's kind of weird."

Rage coursed through me like an electric charge. "Kind of weird?! You think what just happened to me was just *kind of weird?!* That was the scariest goddamn thing I've ever been through, Brian!"

He held up his hands defensively. "Are you mad at me?"

"Uh, yeah!"

"How is any of this *my* fault? I didn't know they were going to make us pull those from a checked bag."

"Yeah, obviously! But you *should've* known! You're in charge of all the technology shit! You're supposed to know this stuff! And it should've been *you* going down there and dealing with it, but you weren't even here because you had to go wander off and walk around the terminal for no good goddamn reason! You were out there looking at stupid souvenir stores while *I* was practically going into cardiac arrest, thinking they'd found drugs in our bag!"

He gave me a confused look. "Why on earth would they find drugs in our bag? Come on, Trace, that's ridiculous."

"*You* were the one that said it!"

"Oh my god, I was *joking!*"

"And you had to go and eat that stupid happy pizza and get all *high!* So, I'm down there thinking, what if he bought something else in Cambodia and forgot about it and now it's in this bag and *I'm* going to be the one to rot in a Thai prison!"

"Tracey, come on. I would *never* do that."

"How am I supposed to know that? I never thought you'd eat a happy pizza but you fucking did that, didn't you!"

My dramatic arm flailing and spewing of curse words left me a little winded, forcing me to pause my diatribe and take a breath.

Brian rubbed his hands over his face before speaking in a quiet, even tone. "Okay. Look. I'm sorry for whatever I did that led you to have to deal with this. And I'm sorry you freaked out because you thought they'd found drugs in our luggage." He put an arm around my shoulders. "But can you please calm down? Everything is fine, Trace."

"Easy for you to say! You didn't just have the shit scared out of you!"

I stalked off to a chair further down the row and proceeded to spend the next half hour rationalizing how wrong Brian was and how right I was and how I was totally justified in yelling at him over this situation because he should have known and he should have been here and—

You know this isn't Brian's fault.

And she was back. Observer Tracey showed up to spoil my temper tantrum.

You aren't mad at him. You're stressed out because that situation scared you and now you've decided to take it out on him. But he had nothing to do with it.

I rolled my eyes and sighed. As much as I hated to admit it, Observer Tracey was right. Brian hadn't done anything to cause this whole baggage debacle. It was completely illogical to blame it on him.

And then a piercing moment of clarity flipped a switch in my brain.

Oh my god. I'm a blamer.

In an instant, I saw my behavior from a new perspective. Situations from the past ran across my mind's eye as though projected onto a movie screen. Silly fights with Brian, feeling annoyed with family and friends, silently getting angry at strangers. Almost all of it came back to my habit of looking for blame. Big stuff. Little stuff. It didn't matter the situation, I could always pick out the person who'd done something wrong. Just that morning, we'd been in our usual frantic rush to get to the airport, and I stubbed my toe on a suitcase. I'd silently blamed Brian for putting the luggage too close to the door. It was a completely irrational response, but I was stressed at the time and so it became his fault.

The more I thought about it, the more I realized that blaming seemed to be the way I handled stressful situations. If I was late for a meeting, it was because city engineers needed to time the traffic lights better. If I couldn't find a file on my computer, it was because said computer was a piece of junk. There always needed to be someone or something at fault. And it was rarely me.

When the gate agent started the boarding call for our flight to

Chiang Mai, I walked over and stood in front of Brian as he tapped the keys on his laptop.

"Hey," I said quietly.

"Hey, babe. What's up?" he said, giving me a quick smile. "I just want to finish up this section of code before we board."

I took a deep breath. "So . . . I'm sorry I freaked out on you," I mumbled. As good as I was at blaming, I was horrible at apologies. "That situation wasn't your fault at all. I shouldn't have yelled at you like that."

"No worries," he said without looking up from his screen. "You were just stressed out."

My eyes welled with tears. This man knew me so well and tolerated so much. I silently vowed to never play this stupid blame game again.

SECOND CHANCES

Elephant rides: 15

Monk chats: 1

Not-so-noble truths: 4

Sex in shop: 1

THAILAND (AGAIN)

Kai's shoulders rolled under my legs with each long, slow stride, moving me back and forth in a hypnotic, rocking motion. I ran my hands across the leathery folds of skin creasing her neck and then up over the top of her head, feeling the prickle of her stiff, wiry hairs against my palm.

"Hold tight," Kai's *mahout* called out as he walked alongside me. "It get steep."

I grabbed onto the tops of Kai's ears and leaned forward as she lumbered steadily up through the foliage. When we reached the top of the hill, I turned to watch Brian and Ali emerge over the crest, the two of them riding an enormous bull elephant named Big Daddy. Brian ducked to avoid a low-hanging branch just as Emily and Liv came up behind him, each on their own young elephant. I smiled and shook my head in amazement.

Holy moly. We're riding elephants.

Our time in northern Thailand alternated between the quiet jungles of the rural areas and the bustling streets of Chiang Mai. After spending a week exploring the city and wandering through its Buddhist temples, we'd head out into the countryside for a couple days to visit one of the elephant parks in the region. We helped care for the animals, throwing out bales of fresh hay and loading huge balls of pachyderm poop into sacks. But most of the time was spent just watching them roam the grounds or splash together in a river.

On this day, we were given the unique experience of riding the elephants bareback. The *mahouts* had led our group out of the park's open meadows and onto a narrow trail cutting through dense rainforest. After an hour of riding up and down hills and across gurgling streams, we stopped in a clearing surrounded by a thick grove of bamboo. The elephants slowly kneeled to the ground so we could slide off their shoulders. As the *mahouts* led them into the trees to graze, I sat watching the four elephants, mesmerized by their slow, graceful movements and the quiet grunts they exchanged. "Mama! Look what he did!" Ali yelled. She was standing a few feet from Big Daddy. The massive elephant towered over her, almost three times as tall as her little body. She pointed to the two broken stalks of bamboo Big Daddy had tucked between his cheeks and his colossal tusks. "He's saving them for later," she giggled. I laughed and watched as Big Daddy's massive trunk began roaming over her, sniffing at her hair and rubbing along her neck and shoulders. Ali burst into hysterics. "Big Daddy! Stop! That tickles!"

I'd evidently lost all my maternal instincts. As a parent, wasn't I supposed to keep my children far away from potentially lethal animals weighing more than two thousand pounds? The elephants' calm disposition and intelligent eyes seemed to put me at ease.

Sadly, each of these animals had experienced a treacherous training process called *phajaan*, or "the crush." As young elephants, they were taken from their mothers and trapped inside tiny cages, where they were beaten around the clock until they became totally submissive. Once trained, the elephants usually worked in the logging or tourism industries, spending their days dragging tree trunks or carrying two-person bench seats. Some wound up as spectacles on the streets of Bangkok, where their owners led them through heavy traffic and sold bananas to the tourists willing to pay a few Baht to feed them. While many of Thailand's elephants lived exhausting, unhealthy, and dangerous lives, some of them were eventually sold to parks and sanctuaries. In these havens, the animals spent their days roaming with other elephants and grazing in meadows, their workloads limited to the occasional bareback trail ride.

Perhaps the difficulties they'd overcome in life had given these elephants the wise, calming demeanor they seemed to possess. There was just something about them. A tranquil, meditative presence that seeped into my consciousness and magically drained all the worries out of me as I watched them munch on their lunch of bamboo just a few feet from my six-year-old.

In Chiang Mai, we lived in a modern high-rise apartment building with a balcony overlooking the skyline. Some days, the sun glowed red through the haze of smoke floating over the city, an effect of the slash-and-burn season during which farmers around the region cut small fields into the forest for a few years of cultivation. Brian found a co-working space in town and rented a moped to get him to and from the office. Each morning, he set out to navigate the river of cars, tuk-tuks, and motorbikes swarming Chiang Mai's streets.

An open-air market sat across the street from our apartment, giving me my daily dose of Southeast Asian life. Every day I shopped among rows of tables filled with fresh produce, blooming flowers, household goods, and steaming bins of Thai dishes. Everything under the sun was just steps away, stacked into neat piles and offered by a friendly vendor. Some dragon fruit, some green curry, toothpaste, pickled quail eggs, or a new pair of underwear perhaps? How about a teeny, tiny trash can to hold the toilet paper you can't flush down the toilet? Our neighborhood market was a chaotic mosaic of colors, aromas, and smiling faces.

The girls and I often flagged down a tuk-tuk and went into the moat-enclosed Old City. During its construction in the thirteenth century, Chiang Mai had been fortified with a stone wall and a wide protective canal. Most of the wall had succumbed to the forces of nature, but the rectangular waterway remained, with bridges connecting the ancient parts of the city to the new ones. Inside the moat, we found little cafés with cheap, delicious food. We wandered through historic temples, learning a little more about Buddhism's sacred traditions. On the weekends, we visited the eclectic Sunday Night Market, where over a mile of booths lined the streets of the Old City, and traditional Thai bands created a walking music festival for shoppers.

One day, we happened to be at a large Buddhist temple called Wat Chedi Luang during Monk Chat. This weekly event gave locals and tourists the opportunity to sit down and talk with one of the temple's monks. Throughout our time in Thailand and Cambodia, we'd seen Buddhist monks daily, their heads shaved and their simple orange robes intricately folded and twisted around one shoulder. They were usually working on the temple grounds or sitting in meditation, but sometimes we saw them doing things as normal as chatting on their cell phones or eating at cafés. They'd become a notable part of our time in Southeast Asia, so talking to one of them about his daily life sounded intriguing. Plus, Monk Chat gave out free popcorn and lemonade, so the girls were fully on board.

"As monk we make merit," the young monk at our table explained, smiling shyly and bowing his head frequently. "Because I monk, I bring merit to my family."

Making merit is a significant aspect of spiritual development in Thai culture. A person earns it by doing good deeds, carrying out Buddhist rituals, and giving alms to spiritual figures. The most honorable way to make merit is to become an ordained monk or to be the mother or father of one. Therefore, most Thai men became monks at some point in their lives, bringing merit to both themselves and their parents. Some served for just a few months as part of a personal spiritual retreat, while others committed their entire lives to the monkhood. Once ordained, they spent their days meditating, studying, and working in the temple facility.

"I choose to be monk for five year," the monk explained to us. "For five year, I honor my family and learn to be good man."

"And what does that mean to you?" I asked him. "What does it mean to be a good man?"

He thought for a long moment before speaking. "I must know *my* joy to show others *their* joy." He paused again to search for his words. "Not have joy some of time. I must have joy *all* of time. This my most important work. This how I help world. I help world when I have joy inside me, in good times and also bad times." He leaned forward, looking me steadily in the eye. "When I have true happiness in me, then I help others know true happiness in them."

Hearing the monk's words, I was reminded that Buddhism had always seemed a bit beyond my intellectual and spiritual capabilities. I'd had the opportunity to hear the Dalai Lama speak when I was in my twenties and living in Salt Lake City. A friend invited me to use her extra ticket, so I went with her having no idea what to expect.

That evening, the Dalai Lama walked out to a packed auditorium and sat down on a platform covered in pillows. He intently scanned his eyes over the audience for a long time, as though expecting one of us to start talking. After adjusting his robe and arranging the pillows a bit, he finally spoke. His words were direct and powerful.

"The purpose of all major religious traditions is the same. They carry the same message. That is love, compassion, and forgiveness. What is most important is these things are part of daily life. Do not hear my words tonight and think you should become a Buddhist. You need not change your religious beliefs. Buddhism need not be your religion for you to learn from it."

That night, the Dalai Lama's open-minded, accepting beliefs pulled me in, and for the next two hours I sat in rapt attention, absorbing every word of his talk. The next day, I felt compelled to learn more about this wise man's philosophy. So, I went out and bought a book on the basics of Buddhism, convinced that learning the tenants of this faith would be life-changing for me.

But then I started reading the book.

Within just a few pages, I was already struggling to comprehend the Four Noble Truths, the fundamental concepts Buddha had shared with his students after he found enlightenment.

The Four Noble Truths of Buddhism
1. Life is full of suffering.
2. Suffering arises from attachment to desires.
3. Suffering ceases when attachment to desires ceases.
4. Freedom from suffering is possible by following the Eightfold Path.

I couldn't understand all this suffering stuff. It just didn't make sense to me. My life wasn't full of suffering, was it? I wasn't in pain or starving or grieving. That cushy dual-income-no-kids lifestyle I was enjoying during our years in Salt Lake City definitely didn't feel like suffering of any kind. If you recall, I was hosting Pampered Chef parties that turned into wild drunkfests.

And the next part about how suffering arises from "attachment to desires?" What did that even mean? I could see suffering arising from an illness or an injury. Or losing a loved one. Or even getting dumped by a boyfriend. But attachment to desires? I'm suffering because I desire a piece of chocolate cake? Or a Kate Spade purse? How is that suffering?

Back then, I couldn't relate to any of it. My mind simply wasn't ready yet. In fact, the Buddhists say that bringing the philosophy of their religion into a new culture can be like trying to plant a flower on a rock. A disconcerted mind must first be cultivated into fertile ground so it can let wisdom and clarity blossom. In Chiang Mai, after months of meditating and learning how to sit peacefully in the present moment, my mind was finally ready. There were apparently fewer rocks in there and more fertile earth. In the days after our conversation with the young monk, I slowly began seeing the relevance of the Four Noble Truths in my own life.

During our talk, the young monk had said, "We lose our joy when we let the actions of others control our happiness." As we walked among the city's ornate, gilded temples, I began to understand the truth of his statement. For most of my life, that's exactly what I'd been doing. I'd been letting the actions of everyone around me determine my happiness. Good things lifted me up, and bad things brought me down. If someone cut me off in traffic, I'd be annoyed. If I made it through the green light, I'd be happy. When someone hit the brakes and turned without signaling, then I'd be annoyed again. I could bounce my way through an obstacle course of vacillating emotions in the time it took to drive across town. But that's just how it works, right? Humans are hardwired to feel good when good things happen, and bad when bad things happen. We're simply responding to life. We don't have a choice in how we feel from moment to moment because we're forced to deal with the reality in front of us. If we can't control the world, then we can't control our happiness.

Or so we think.

As my mind marinated on the young monk's words, I finally began to see the truth. The truth that we always have control. We always have a choice. Just like Emily had said in Ethiopia, we can't find happiness, we have to *choose* to be happy. I alone determine how the world will affect me.

Pema Chödrön, a world-renowned Buddhist nun and author, explains how we humans look at everything in the framework of duality. We judge each experience and try to avoid one thing while seeking out another. We want pleasure, so we avoid pain. We want to be praised, not blamed. We want victory, not defeat. Everything in our lives gets slapped with a judgment of either good or bad, and then our emotions respond accordingly. Judging the world in this way is like sitting on a teeter-totter and letting the rider on the other side choose whether we're going to be up or down at any given moment. It's this judgment we must release if we want control over our own happiness. When we replace those verdicts of "good" or "bad" with a neutral acceptance of the world as it is, we start to realize that happiness isn't based on the events or people we encounter. Happiness is based on how we react to the unfolding of it all. The most powerful skill we can acquire in life is the ability to connect to our inner happiness, regardless of what's happening around us.

Even attributing joy to positive experiences has a downside, because the happiness they create in us is fleeting. If someone compliments me and I let their praise contribute to my happiness, then I'm going to live my life looking for approval. (Been there, done that.) If a new purse or dress or set of Tupperware gives me a jolt of happiness in the moment I buy it, then I'm going to keep buying stuff I don't need. (Yep, been there, too.) When we look for happiness outside of ourselves, we're likely to lose our way and end up with the opposite of what we were searching for.

We can't *find* happiness. We must simply *choose* to be happy.

Those Four Nobel Truths of Buddhism hadn't resonated with me at first because the semantics of them didn't fit my cultural perspective. Words like "suffering" and "attachment" and "desires" seemed a little obscure and severe for my Midwestern sensibilities. However, after our little monk chat, I began to understand them. Suffering doesn't require a severe condition, like starvation, physical pain, or intense grief. Suffering is simply any emotion not rooted in joy and love. Fear, guilt, frustration, irritation, stress, jealousy, hate. We suffer through these emotions. No matter what kind of life we have, we can always let go of some of our suffering.

To help me integrate the Buddhist philosophy into my daily life, I came up with my own version of the Four Noble Truths, one which put these concepts into simple terms my foul-mouthed brain would always remember.

The Four Not-so-Noble Truths of Tracey

1. Life is full of frustrating bullshit.
2. Frustrating bullshit arises when we insist the world should be the way we want it to be.
3. Frustrating bullshit ceases when we let go of expectations and accept the world as it is.
4. Freedom from frustrating bullshit is possible when we stop judging and instead open ourselves to the lessons, joy, and opportunities rooted in every situation we encounter in life . . . even the ones that seem like total bullshit.

I highly doubt the Dalai Lama would approve of this modified version of the Noble Truths, but they worked for me. I began testing them out during our last days in Thailand, and each time I did they helped me let go of my own little bits of suffering. They turned me inward toward my own happiness whenever I found myself judging a situation and letting the teeter-totter plop me down on the ground. I imagined each moment as a single thread in the intricate tapestry of my life. I couldn't make judgements about the colors and designs around me because I had no way of knowing how they fit into the rich artistry of the fabric as a whole. I just had to have some faith I was creating something beautiful, something crafted with the talented hands of my soul. Only she knew how to weave each moment of my life perfectly into place. Following this new perspective, I began to see the world very differently, and when I encountered a frustrating situation I was able to take a more enlightened, accepting approach.

The philosopher Eckhart Tolle wrote about the three choices we have any time we're faced with something we don't like: We can take action to change it; we can walk away from it; or, if we're not willing to do either of those, then we must accept it and let go of our judgment. Years after reading Eckhart's words, I finally learned how to use his wisdom.

When a man cut in front of me at the pot sticker cart, I asked myself if I was willing to take action to change the situation.

Not really. I'm not in a hurry and don't feel like starting a squabble in a language I can't speak.

Could I walk away from the it?

Heck no! I want some pot stickers!

Then it's time to accept what's happened and let go of any judgment toward this guy. Maybe he's in a huge rush. Maybe he didn't see me standing here. In the end, who cares? I'll have my pot stickers eventually.

My ultimate test with this newfound inner peace came on our last night in Thailand. After we'd packed our bags in preparation for the thirty-six-hour journey to our next destination, I decided the girls and I should have one last cheap pedicure in Southeast Asia. We settled into the salon's cushy armchairs and had our feet soaking in pans of warm, soapy water when . . . there it was. The sign I'd been dodging since Cambodia.

NO SEX IN SHOP

I sighed and waited for the question I knew was coming.

"Mom, seriously," Emily whispered determinedly. "What does that sign mean?"

So, Tracey, can you change this situation?

Nope.

Can you walk away from it?

Not without making a huge mess and pissing off the entire pedicure staff.

Then it looks like it's going to have to be acceptance this time. I took a deep breath and prepared for an awkward conversation with my eldest child. *Here goes a big boatload of accepting the world as it is.*

BULA! BULA!

Islands in paradise: 1
Treasured friends: 4
Bilibili rafts: 3
Shark encounters: 27

FIJI

After a grueling day and a half of travel, including three flights, two long layovers, and a four-hour drive on dark, bumpy roads, our taxi pulled into a gated driveway just after midnight. Bright flood lights illuminated a white two-story house bordered with lush, tropical landscaping. As the five of us climbed out of the van into the warm, humid night air, the home's front door opened to reveal my smiling, beautiful friend.

"Oh, my goodness!" Diana cried as she walked out with her arms open wide. "I can't believe you're really here! Welcome to Fiji!"

She hadn't changed a bit. A hint of Diana's Mexican roots accented her words, and her long, black hair fell across her shoulders as she gave us big hugs and kissed our cheeks.

"Come in! Come in! Come in!" she said excitedly, leading us into the house. "We're so excited to see you!"

Her husband, Reuben, greeted us in the foyer. "Well, if it ain't the world-travelin' Carisches," he said in his southern drawl, hugging me with one arm and taking the suitcase from my hand with the other.

We followed our friends up the stairs to the main living room of the house. "I bet you're exhausted," Diana said to the girls. "Leah and Ike went to bed a little while ago because they have school tomorrow. Do you want to get into bed, too?" Em, Liv, and Ali nodded, their bleary eyes already half-closed.

As we got the girls tucked in for the night, Diana's effervescent personality lifted me out of my travel stupor. *We're in Fiji! We're staying with the Summerlins! This month is going to be amazing!*

We'd met Diana and Reuben soon after we moved to Chattanooga, and throughout our friendship we'd loved hearing about their travels around the world. Reuben had spent his career combatting poverty, working in places like Kyrgyzstan, Haiti, and East Timor while earning a respected expertise in the microcredit industry. When he took a job with the United Nations, the Summerlin family moved to Suva, Fiji where his regional office was headquartered.

"So, lady," Diana said after the kids were in bed and Brian had excused himself to take a shower. "Do you need to call it a night or can I pour you a glass of wine?"

I smiled at my old friend. "Wine, please."

Life with the Summerlins was like taking a break from our travels, yet still living in a foreign country. Their home's big, airy rooms and expansive view over Suva's forested hills were welcome changes from the cramped apartments we'd been renting. The Carisch and Summerlin kids struck up their friendship again, and as soon as Leah and Ike got home from school each day, they were all laughing and splashing in the backyard pool together. Reuben was still a big personality in a medium-sized frame. His funny, authentic, generous nature meant he could command a room, yet make everyone in it feel like the center of attention. During my morning yoga sessions, I'd hear him come in from his sunrise bike ride, singing an old country song in his clear tenor voice, and then splash into the pool for his cool-down swim.

Diana and I instantly slipped back into our easy friendship. She minimized the learning curve by showing me the best markets around town and teaching me a few Fijian phrases. When Reuben went on a work trip to Papua New Guinea, she served as our personal tour guide, taking our family to nearby beach resorts and introducing us to her favorite restaurants.

One day, she and I were walking in downtown Suva when we passed a storefront with a display of Indian saris in its window. "Why do they sell so many saris here?" I asked. "I see them everywhere. Is there a large Indian population on the island?"

"Oh, definitely," Diana said. "Their ancestors came in the 1800s to work on the sugar plantations and then they stayed, passing down their traditions through the generations. Almost half of Fijian citizens are of Indian descent. The tensions between the Fijians and Indo-Fijians can actually get a little rough at times, especially around elections."

"Wow, I didn't realize that," I said. "I guess I need to bone up on my Fijian history."

"Yes, this country has a fascinating story. You know about the cannibalism, right?"

I gave her a sideways glance. "Fijians were cannibals?"

"Oh yeah, big time," Diana said. "These were called the Cannibal Isles, you know. Technically, the practice was banned over a hundred years ago, but there are some who say it still happens today."

I grimaced. "Okay, maybe I don't need to study Fijian history after all."

She laughed and gave me an ornery grin. "You know, there's a little souvenir shop up the street that sells replicas of cannibal forks."

I rolled my eyes. "Dee, stop. Seriously."

"The forks they used were so weird, not like the forks we use. The prongs were in a circle because they would stick it in and then twist it to get the meat—"

"Diana!"

She let out a devilish laugh. "Come on, I know a great place for lunch."

I shook my head. "You're sick."

One afternoon, Reuben got home from work early and suggested he and I take the kids to one of the nearby rain forest parks. He said we could drive to a trailhead and do a short walk to the swimming holes and waterfalls created by Waisila Creek. Soon, we'd piled into their family's SUV with the kids and were driving to the outskirts of Suva.

When we arrived at the visitor entrance, the guard told us he'd be closing the gates and our car would be locked in. However, not ones to be deterred, we decided to walk a couple extra miles. We parked outside the gate, grabbed the towels and water bottles, and made our way down the park's dirt road until we arrived at a trailhead leading into the forest. We trekked through the thick, humid jungle, our sandals leaving footprints in the damp earth as we passed enormous plants dripping with flowers.

Within ten minutes, we reached the first pool and found a rowdy group of Fijian men swinging into the water on a rope tied high up in a tree. Like most Fijians, the men were impressively strong, all over six feet tall with arm muscles as big as an average person's leg. They swung out from the cliff and threw back flips off the rope before blasting giant splashes around the pool. A couple of them started scaling the tree, climbing past the branch where the rope was tied. The higher they went, the more the tree swayed under their weight.

"Oh my god, what are they doing?" I said, my eyes wide and my hands on my cheeks. "They aren't going to jump from up there, are they?"

Reuben grinned and put a hand up to shield his eyes from the sun rays streaming through the leaves. "Yes, ma'am," he said, exaggerating his Southern accent. "I sure do believe that's what they're gonna do."

I watched, stunned, as these massive Fijian men launched themselves out of the tree and dropped four stories into the water. In between their death-defying jumps, they smiled and laughed with us, helping our kids onto the rope and cheering for them as they splashed down a few feet into the pool.

After a couple hours, we had to start the hike back to the car or risk doing it in the dark. Reuben and I walked together, chatting about life, while the kids ran ahead of us. I learned more about his work with the United Nations and the other countries his family might move to when his project in Fiji wrapped up. At one point, we got onto the topic of our marriages.

"When I think back on how much Brian and I have both changed since we met in college, it's kind of surprising we're still compatible," I said. "We've seen some of our other friends grow apart as they've gotten older, but Brian and I got lucky, I guess. We seem to have changed in the same direction."

"Well, there's probably more to it than luck," Reuben said. "I mean, give yourself a little credit. It's obvious you guys are really honest with each other, and that's a big part of it." He paused for a moment, a serious, thoughtful look softening his face. "You know, Trace, I think happiness in life really just boils down to being honest.

That's pretty much it. Be honest with ourselves and with others. Honest about what we want and what we think. It sounds easy, but it can be the most challenging thing in the world. Sometimes people work so damn hard trying to be something they're not, and then everything falls apart."

I looked at him and grinned. "Honesty is the best policy, huh?" "Yes, ma'am," he nodded. "It sure is."

It occurred to me that the tightly-wound, Type A personality I'd once been might have been lying to herself for the first twenty years of life. Perhaps falling in love with my wakeboard-toting Brian was the first brutally honest thing I'd ever done.

"Hey, Trace!" Brian called to me from the living room couch. "What's the name of the volcano in Chile we'll be living next to?"

"Uh, Villarrica, I think," I called back from the deck as I hacked away at a coconut with a machete. "Why?"

"Well . . . it just erupted."

I walked over to stand in the doorway. "You've got to be kidding me."

We hadn't planned much of this trip in advance. Usually we were booking plane tickets and housing just a few weeks out. However, we'd made one major commitment many months ahead of time. And that was living in Pucón, Chile, a small town near the base of the Villarrica volcano. Figuring that a Spanish course would be a good way to start our time in South America, we'd decided to sign up for a language immersion program. We had to book it months ahead of time to guarantee our spots, so back when we were in Cambodia, I'd paid for our classes and put a hefty deposit on a two-bedroom cabin near the school. Unfortunately, just ten miles away from Pucón, the Villarrica volcano was erupting for the first time in over forty years.

"It doesn't look like they had to evacuate," Brian said, his eyes scanning his computer screen. "Scientists were expecting it and the only evacuations happened in other towns where winds blew most of the ash."

"Well, that's good no one was hurt," I said, looking over his shoulder at the article.

"Will we still do the course?" he asked.

I sighed. "I don't know. I'll get in touch with them and find out." Diana's fluent Spanish helped me navigate the process of telephoning the school and learning the status of things after the eruption. Apparently, the effects of it had been minimal in Pucón. There didn't seem to be any reason to change our plans, so after a few hours of intense travel stress, I happily went back to my worry-free life in paradise.

The following weekend, Reuben and Diana set our families up at a posh resort. Using their local discount during the off-season, we stayed at a seaside hotel we never could have afforded at the standard prices. The sun shined brightly in a clear, blue sky for our drive along Fiji's curvy roads. Green, thick jungle foliage blooming with flowers edged up against the pavement, and smiling Fijians waved at us when we passed through villages.

We arrived at Volivoli Beach Resort to find luxurious thatched-roof bungalows overlooking an unobstructed view of aquamarine coastline. It looked like something out of a travel magazine. Our first night at the hotel restaurant, a Fijian music troupe performed, and by the end of the evening our families were dancing around the tables. Reuben, whose eclectic collection of life experiences included being the lead singer of a band, showed us some impressive moves.

The next afternoon, the four adults went out for a sunset cruise while the kids watched a movie in a bungalow. As we sipped champagne and ate appetizers, the captain cruised through an archipelago of tiny islands.

"Man," Brian said with a sigh, stretching his arms out along the boat's railing. "This is the life. You guys seriously found paradise."

"Yes, we love it here," Diana said, looking out across the water to the setting sun. She tucked her feet underneath her and leaned into the crook of Reuben's shoulder. "It was an adjustment at first, though. Fijian culture is so different from the States. It kind of drove me crazy how everyone operates on island time here. But now . . ." She winked and held up her glass of champagne. "Now, I think I get it."

"Fijians have it figured out, that's for sure," Reuben said. "They work to live, instead of the other way around. We Americans seem like crazy workaholics to them."

"It makes sense, I guess," Brian said. "I mean, they've never had to work all that hard to survive here, right? The food practically falls off the trees."

"Exactly," Reuben said, taking a piece of shrimp off the platter in front of him. "Climate and food sources shape cultures. I mean, think about our European ancestors. For centuries, surviving the winter months was a constant struggle. If you worked hard, you lived. If you were lazy, you died. Simple as that. Environmental factors led to a society valuing a strong work ethic above all else. But here in Fiji? Life is so much easier. If you aren't going to starve or freeze to death, why bust your ass?"

"All play, almost no work," Diana said. "It makes sense they're the happiest people on the planet."

Over the next couple days, our families relaxed on the beach, collected seashells, and paddled kayaks out into the bay. Brian tried to talk me into going scuba diving with him and Reuben, but I opted for piña coladas in a lounge chair with Diana. Even though I was a certified diver, I hadn't gone in several years and had no interest in ruining paradise with a scuba accident of my own making.

On our last day at the resort, we were hanging out at the pool when Brian and I struck up a conversation with a family from New Zealand. It turned out that the Adams weren't a typical family on a tropical vacation. Two months prior, Jeremy and Truus had moved with their three children to rural Fiji so they could bring assistance to a tiny village in the interior hills of the island, where the residents still lived without electricity and indoor plumbing. The Adams children attended the village school while Jeremy and Truus worked with locals on community projects. They'd walked away from their life in Christchurch to make a difference in a remote part of the world very few people knew about. The Adams had been offered a weekend at Volivoli by the resort's Kiwi owners so they could come recharge their batteries (both literally and figuratively) and use the internet to connect with family back home. The more we talked with

Jeremy and Truus, the more we wanted to find a way to visit their village and help them with their work there.

Apparently, for a group of pragmatic Americans and New Zealanders, there's no time like the present. The next day, instead of going back to Suva with the Summerlins, our family piled into the Adams' SUV and set out for the village of Sawanivo. It was the sweet irony of life that our weekend at an extravagant beach resort led us to volunteering in the middle of Fiji's primitive hill country. After a quick stop in the big town of Rakiraki for supplies, Jeremy turned the truck off the main highway and onto a gravel road climbing up into the hills. He drove slowly, steering carefully around large potholes and wide sections washed out by the rains.

After an hour of bouncing around in the truck, we came to a stop above the village. Tucked among the palm trees and flowering shrubs, sat a tidy collection of homes built from wood and sheet metal. A gentle sloping hill behind the village led down to a wide, lazy river.

As we climbed out of the truck, a dozen locals greeted us. One smiled and opened his arms wide to gesture at our group. "Look at this!" he said with a laugh. "The white people have multiplied!"

The Adams children introduced our girls to their friends, and soon the kids had run off to play. Brian and Jeremy joined some men working on a new concrete walkway through the village. Once completed, the project would make it easier for the residents to get around Sawanivo during the rainy season, when the sloping paths became saturated and slippery. As the men dug out the soil and began setting boards for the frame, Truus led me down to the house of a village elder where women were preparing the large evening meal. As they laughed and chatted in Fijian, I learned how to peel cassava root and make *lolo*, a dish of raw fish marinated in coconut milk and lime juice.

With the sun beginning to set, our families got ready to attend a combined service of Sawanivo's three churches. Periodically, the members of the congregations came together for a community-wide worship, leaving behind the differences of their religious beliefs and sharing in an evening of prayer and song. Jeremy loaned Brian a traditional *sulu*, the long wrap-around skirt commonly worn by the men of Fiji. As darkness settled on the village, our large group walked into the church and sat on the floor of the small sanctuary. A few solar lanterns dangled from the ceiling on ropes made of braided palm fronds, casting a dancing line of shadows over the light-blue concrete walls. A small stage at the end of the room held a wooden pulpit and two folding chairs.

The building's tiny rectangular windows did little to circulate the humid air, and within minutes, the body heat of the congregation had raised the room's temperature to a stifling heat. By the time the service started, I was soaked with sweat. Glancing over at Truus, I saw she looked just as miserable as I was, which made me feel a little better. At least I wasn't just being a candy ass. She gave me a sympathetic look and whispered, "Try to think of something cold."

A minister walked up to the pulpit, and I recognized him as the smiling, grandfatherly man who'd been leading the concrete path project. Earlier, he'd joked that Brian's height made him look like "a very pale Fijian." As I smiled at the memory, the man took a deep breath and looked around at the congregation.

Then suddenly, his fist slammed down onto the wooden podium with a loud *CRACK!* I about jumped out of my skin. The minister began yelling, accentuating his words by punching his fist in the air. The steamy, crowded room became even more oppressively hot as he bellowed at us in a language I couldn't understand. Sweat dripped from every inch of my body, making me look and feel like I'd just taken a hot shower and then stepped into a sauna. I seriously doubted I could make it through this onslaught of religious pontification without running outside and hurling myself into the river.

When his sermon finally ended, I breathed a sigh of relief, but then braced myself for another dose of the wrath of God as a second minister came to the pulpit. However, instead of yelling at us, this man sent a calm, strong voice out over the crowd. I couldn't understand his words, but I found them soothing and captivating. After a few minutes, he finished his remarks and gestured toward the audience. That's when the congregation began singing the first hymn of the evening.

The song began quietly, with soft voices floating on the air, but by the end of the first verse the notes began to crescendo, splitting into different harmonies. An intense vibration filled the room, sending a numb sensation over my skin. I got lost in the notes, each separate harmony ringing out clear and distinct, yet blending seamlessly with the others to create a human symphony. When I closed my eyes, the music created waves of color swirling and dancing around me, pulling me from my physical body to a detached, ethereal space. The room even seemed to cool. The sweat trickling down my back evaporated, and all the discomfort melted away as my heart and mind focused on the simple perfection of the music. For the rest of the service, I sat motionless and mesmerized. Each time the congregation began to sing, I closed my eyes and felt the buzzing vibration of the harmonies course through me.

"Tracey, it's over."

My eyes popped open, and I realized everyone was standing and making their way to the door. Truus stood looking down at me with her hand on my shoulder. "Get lost in it for bit?" she asked with a knowing smile. "It can be powerful, eh?"

"Yes," I said, still blinking back to reality. "Yes, that was . . . surreal."

The next day began with a breakfast of jam and homemade *roti*, a tortilla-like local bread. While the sun burned off the morning fog, Brian worked with Jeremy and a few other men to prepare a field for planting. A team of oxen dragged a plow through the soil, followed closely by chickens pecking through the freshly-turned earth for insects. The locals lived off the land, cutting cassava roots out of the ground, pulling fish from the river, plucking bananas off the trees, and using long stalks of bamboo to knock down coconuts. They didn't need trash pickup, because everything they ate came in its own biodegradable packaging. They didn't run errands because whatever they might need in life was within easy reach of their front doors. By ten o'clock, when the sun's intense rays beat down on the village, work came to an end and the socializing began.

As we sat in the shade and relaxed together, I thought about my daily activities back home through the eyes of a Fijian. It brought a smile to my face to imagine the reactions our new friends would have if they saw some of the things we do in the United States.

"You buy clothes that can't get wet, and then pay money to have them cleaned in special machines with no water?"

"You dig holes to grow plants you can't even eat, but then you dig out other plants because you don't like the way they look?"

"You have two toilets? In one house?!"

The stifling heat of Fiji's interior region meant the cool river water played a central role in the lives of the villagers. Several locals decided our family needed to experience a *bilibili* rafting tour, so our new friends, Millie, Wise, and Chavvy, set off into the jungle to harvest the two materials needed to build them: bamboo and palm fronds. About two hours later, Jeremy drove us a few miles up the road. We arrived at a bridge to find three long, narrow bamboo rafts waiting for us, complete with raised benches and long oars for steering. We spent the afternoon floating under the shade of the rain forest with Millie, Wise, and Chavvy serving as our guides. They showed us their favorite swimming spots and pulled fruit from the trees hanging out over the water. Our family took the oars for a while and practiced maneuvering the rafts around boulders and little islands in the river. When we got close to Sawanivo, some of the children ran along the shoreline waving at us, and by the time we floated into town it seemed half the village had come out to welcome us back.

Early evening turned into a village swimming party. The children used the *bilibili* rafts as jumping platforms and took turns launching into the river, seeing who could make the biggest splash. I sat on the bank, wet and cool from swimming, and watched our girls invent games with their new friends. As they constructed little dams across the shallows and built makeshift forts from bamboo stalks, I thought about our busy life before this trip. All those activities we'd signed the girls up for back home. In our effort to enrich their little brains and bodies with everything from organized sports to music lessons, Brian and I had allowed less and less time for this—the sheer joy of playing in nature.

After a couple days, it was time for us to head back to Suva. Our stay in Sawanivo came to an end as we drove away from a waving, smiling crowd of Fijians and New Zealanders, all gathered on the road to send us off. The drive out to the main highway was slow-going. A heavy overnight rain forced Jeremy to maneuver the truck through monstrous puddles and muddy stretches of road. Just as he pulled up to the main highway, the Suva bus we were trying to catch went flying by.

"Aw cripes, there goes your ride," Jeremy said.

I shrugged. "The next one is in two hours. We'll just wait in town until it leaves."

"S'all good, mates. We can catch her," he said, before giving me a wink and hitting the gas. The truck accelerated onto the highway, its back wheels fishtailing onto the pavement. The engine roared and soon the bus was right in front of us. Jeremy swerved into the opposite lane to speed passed it, honking and waving one hand out his window.

"Uh, this seems illegal," Brian said.

Jeremy just laughed and laid on the horn.

After a couple minutes of highway mayhem, the bus slowed down and pulled over onto the side of the road. Jeremy skidded to a stop in front of it and then jumped out shouting "Go! Go! Go!"

We scrambled out, giving Jeremy quick hugs. I ran to the door of the bus holding Ali's hand and smiled up at the driver apologetically. He grinned, shook his head, and waved me in. When I reached the top of the steps, I stood awkwardly at the front of the aisle, looking down at the rows of Fijian faces staring back at me. From their astonished expressions, it became very clear that trucks running busses onto the roadside was not a normal occurrence, even in Fiji.

"Uh . . . *bula, bula* . . . " I said, greeting the passengers with a small wave.

Every face split into a smile. "BULA, BULA!" they shouted back.

Yes, these were definitely the happiest people on the planet.

Shortly after we arrived in Fiji, Reuben told us about the shark diving trip he'd gone on several times. He said it was run by a reputable team of shark researchers and master divers through a scuba shop less than an hour from their house.

"By 'reputable' do you mean none of their clients have been eaten?" I said with a smirk as the four of us sipped Diana's margaritas and finished our dinner of spicy shrimp cocktail.

"Only one or two," Reuben replied, licking hot sauce from his fingers. "Seriously, though, you guys have to do it. You'll love it." I shook my head and leaned back in my chair. "Absolutely not. You can spend your energy convincing him." I pointed across the table at Brian. "You're wasting it on me."

Brian, of course, was immediately on board, and a couple weeks later he and Reuben headed out for their trip with Beqa Adventure Divers in Pacific Harbour. They set out on a beautiful Saturday morning and came back with not only all their limbs, but also some big smiles and incredible videos. Reuben hooked up his underwater camera to the television and we gathered in the living room to watch their dive with the sharks.

"Wow, that's unbelievable," I said, mesmerized. A dozen sharks swam gracefully in front of the lens, their sleek grey bodies consuming the entire screen. I sat and watched it in amazement, surprised at the thought popping into my head. "I think I want to go," I said.

Brian turned to me with a shocked look. "Shark diving? Are you serious?"

"Yes! You should!" Reuben shouted from the couch, clapping his hands together a couple times in approval. "You'll love it!"

"That's awesome, Trace," Brian said. "I thought you might not dive at all in Fiji."

"I wasn't going to . . . I don't know . . . " I tried to understand why shark diving had suddenly become something I wanted to do. "This just seems like one of those things I'll really regret not doing. So, yeah . . . I think I want to go shark diving."

A week later, I was the only woman on a boat speeding toward a reef off Beqa Island. Surrounded by six other divers and the Fijian crew, I sat there sucking in deep breaths and attempting to look calm and casual about the whole thing. When the boat came to a stop and the other divers began organizing their equipment, I focused my nervous energy on recalling critical scuba procedures I hadn't used in three years.

Okay, regulator's connected correctly, gauge is clipped onto my vest, defogger is on my mask . . . ohmygodohmygodmygod . . . what in the hell am I doing here?! Have I completely lost my mind?!

I clasped my hands together so no one would see them trembling.

You can do this, Tracey.

I closed my eyes and took a deep breath.

You're not going to be eaten today. There will be no headline FAMILY TRAVELS END TRAGICALLY WHEN MOTHER DEVOURED BY SHARK.

I smiled to myself and released the death grip of my clenched hands.

There you go, just calm down. You can't be freaked out when you're diving. That's when it gets dangerous.

I took another deep breath and let the smooth exhale slip through my lips.

Now put on the mask.

I slid the mask down over my forehead and pressed it into place, then put the regulator in my mouth and bit down on the mouthpiece.

Hold on to that regulator and take one more big step. You've got this . . . go!

SPLASH . . . a wall of bubbles . . . fins kicking above me . . . gurgling noises . . . wavy vision of the boat . . . *Kick up, kick up . . .*

When I broke through the surface of the water, the anxiety I'd felt just moments before had vanished. Floating alongside the other divers, I'd magically regained my confidence.

Buckle up, Buttercup. You're about to dive with sharks.

Moments later, we were following the lead dive master down into the depths of the ocean. I watched in awe as the blue silhouettes of sharks appeared before my eyes, the details materializing as we swam toward them. Their fins had different shapes and angles. Unique patterns of white scars marked their grey skin. One had a large fish hook embedded in the corner of its mouth. When we reached a flat rock platform on the ocean floor, we laid down on our stomachs while several dive masters stood behind us, armed with long metal rods designed to keep the massive fish at bay. Dozens of bull sharks, up to ten feet in length, swam by us, so close I could have reached out and touched them. Their enormous tails gracefully propelled them forward, scattering the schools of small, colorful fish swimming around them. Watching the sharks cut agile turns around each other, I realized what fascinating and beautiful creatures they were.

I'd never really given them much thought before. Grey color, scraggly teeth, big slits in their necks. Meh. But here, seeing sharks up close in their natural environment, they were gorgeous and graceful, even a little miraculous. Their eyes were the most intriguing part of them. Big, black, shiny balls stuck into the sides of their heads. When they swam by, it felt like they were zeroed in on me, scrutinizing my every move. At one point, I reached up to adjust my regulator, and the shark swimming by me jerked his head slightly in my direction. When his big, black ball eye stared at me, I about peed my pants. (Actually, I probably did pee my pants, but it's kind of hard to tell when you're wearing a wet suit.)

I'd heard one of my favorite comedians, Tina Fey, make fun of herself by saying her irises were so dark they made her look like she had "dead shark eyes." Watching dozens of sharks swim by me at such close range, I have to say . . . I kind of agree with her. (By the way, Tina, if you should ever read this, please know I mean that in the most flattering way possible. Because remember, I think sharks are beautiful and gorgeous and graceful and miraculous.)

Checking my air gauge, I knew our time with the sharks would be ending soon, so I tried to be in the moment and focus on the experience. I looked out across the sandy ocean floor and took in the dozens of sharks gliding around us. My eyes followed their movements intently, and I tried to imagine what those slick, grey bodies would feel like if I'd had the guts to reach out and touch one of them.

Suddenly, I felt a pressure on the top of my head, as though someone was pushing me down. I immediately turned, expecting to see one of the dive masters, but instead I stared at a ceiling of white and the vertical fin of a tail.

Holy shit! My head was rubbing against the underbelly of a bull shark! I shifted to my right so the tail fin wouldn't hit me in the face and watched in fascinated horror as the rest of its massive body slipped by just an inch above me.

So, I guess now I know what it feels like to touch a bull shark. It feels like you're about to shit your pants.

With our time in Fiji quickly coming to an end, we took advantage of every moment with our friends. Some nights, the kids stayed at the house with pizza and a movie, while the adults went out for dinner together. The four of us had long conversations over good bottles of wine, talking about everything from poverty to SNL sketches to Reuben's interest in "non-hominid homo sapiens."

We were at a boathouse restaurant in the harbor one evening when Reuben told a hilarious story from his Peace Corp days. He had me laughing so hard I literally fell out of my chair. Tears streamed down my cheeks and my face muscles ached as I climbed back into my seat, with little care for the fact that I'd just fallen to the floor in the middle of an upscale restaurant.

"We'll just chalk that up to this boat a-rocking a little bit, okay darlin'," Reuben said, helping me back into my seat.

"It's a good thing we're leaving in few days, Reuben," Brian said with a grin. "Tracey might wind up breaking a bone if she hangs with you too much."

"Yes, I'm quite the comedic threat to safety, aren't I?"

I looked across the table and exchanged smiles with Diana. *This is what friendship is about. This. Right here, right now.* It was one of those rare occasions when I knew I was making a lifelong memory in the very moment it was happening. *I will never forget this night.*

Despite our laughter, a tiny needle of sadness pricked my heart. We were really going to miss our friends when we left this beautiful island.

RETURN TO THE FIRST WORLD

New friends: 7
Obscenely gorgeous views: Stopped counting
Earthquakes: 2
Dog-Pig home invasion teams: 1

NEW ZEALAND

After six months in developing nations, I was a little surprised how quickly our family slipped back into a first-world mentality. Once we landed in Christchurch, New Zealand and picked up our rental car, we immediately recalibrated to the easy comforts of westernized society. The contrast of life in these two very different worlds yielded strikingly different reactions in me.

Walking in Cambodia: Girls, get over! Watch where you're going! That tuk tuk could have killed you!

Walking in New Zealand: Don't worry, that driver will certainly slam on the brakes for us as we step out into this crosswalk.

Grocery shopping in Fiji: Hmm, I'm not sure what this is or if the kids will eat it, but I'm going to just buy it and see how it goes.

Grocery shopping in New Zealand: Dammit, this store doesn't have the peanut butter with no added sugar that doesn't have to be refrigerated or stirred.

Driving in Thailand: Watch out for the pot hole! Dog in the road! Pothole. Dog. Pothole. Oh, dear god, family on a scooter with a pig!

Driving in New Zealand: Can you please change the album on our Bluetooth-enabled car stereo? We've been listening to Katy Perry for like an hour.

Utilities in Ethiopia: Sweet! The power's back on!

Utilities in New Zealand: Dammit. I only have a 3G signal here. It's taking forever to load this cat video.

The conveniences of a modern society eroded my gratitude for the little things. I had to keep reminding myself to let go of the grouchiness popping up more frequently now that day-to-day life felt so safe and easy again. But the sheer beauty of New Zealand helped me do that. I was in a constant state of awestruck appreciation for the magnificent scenery throughout the country's South Island. Snow-capped mountains rose from behind glassy lakes, creating mirrored images so clear it was hard to tell the reflection from the reality. Scenic canyon roads curved around each turn in the ice-blue rivers they followed. Trails wandered through lush, tropical forests and then opened to wide, stark glaciers set under an intensely blue sky. The splendor of it all was almost too much to believe, as though my brain had the latest version of Photoshop.

Brian, who'd always been a vocal admirer of the natural world, shouted "Beautiful!" no less than thirty times a day. While we hiked around the base of Mount Cook and drove through the Crown Range, the girls and I heard this word over and over again. "You guys, look at this! It's beautiful! Absolutely beautiful!"

We'd been staying in the "beautiful" lakeside community of Wanaka for a couple days when my thirty-ninth birthday rolled around. The first day of my last year as a thirty-something. It felt a little momentous for some reason, so I decided to kick it off with a solo sunrise hike. I tiptoed out of our little cottage on the outskirts of town and drove to the lake, starting my walk in almost complete darkness. As the world lightened to a hazy grey, I climbed onto a boulder and waited for the sun to rise over the water. Wispy clouds streaked the sky, their hues slowly sliding from indigo to rosy pink, leaving brushstrokes across the enormous canvas above me. The lake was so still it created a perfect mirror, reflecting a stunning visual representation of the phrase "heaven on earth." I sat there quiet and reverent as the colors slowly faded and the sun rose from behind the hills, gently brightening the landscape.

Thirty-nine years old. Holy moly.

Just a couple weeks after my thirty-seventh birthday, I'd had my life-altering meltdown during girls' night out. Two years later, almost everything in our family's life had changed, down to the hemisphere we were living in. Yet, the most profound difference for me was the new relationship I'd forged with myself.

Maitri is a Sanskrit word translating as "an unconditional friendship with oneself." It means accepting ourselves for who we are, acknowledging every piece of us and creating an internal dialogue embodying the same love and respect we'd give to one of our closest friends. When I'd first heard about this concept in one my new age, find-yourself books, I'd thought I was a pretty good friend to myself. I could give yours truly a nice pat on the back when I'd accomplished something (e.g. cleaned out a closet) or improved our family life (e.g. signed up one of my kids for yet another enriching afterschool activity.)

Maitri? Absolutely, I've got maitri! I'm evolved and self-aware and all that stuff, right?

However, during this journey, I'd come to realize that for most of my life I'd actually been my biggest enemy. My own expectations left me running myself ragged, trying to prove to my ego I'd reached some acceptable level of success. Nothing was ever quite good enough. On any given day, I'd reprimand myself for an endless list of transgressions—a messy house, a disorganized desk, a forgotten errand, a weedy flower bed. Anything and everything could be cause for self-admonishment. *What in the hell is wrong with you,* a little voice in my head would whisper. *Get your act together, for cryin' out loud.* If one of my girlfriends had talked to me the way I talked to myself, I would have written her off as a psycho bitch and cut her out of my life. And yet, I'd tolerated incessant self-criticism for years.

I'm not quite sure where or how it happened, but I'd somehow stumbled upon true maitri. If something got forgotten or didn't turn out as planned, it wasn't cause for scathing internal criticism, it was just the way things had worked out. *Learn a lesson, my dear, and move on.* I began to see the value in those personal characteristics I'd once criticized so much. The lazy side of me created fun, laid back afternoons with the girls, and my sporadic, obsessive cleaning neuroses meant we had some stellar reviews from our Airbnb hosts. I could see how all the pieces of me, even the ones I'd been condemning for so long, actually benefited my life in their own little ways. When I stopped criticizing myself all the time, I could finally appreciate the true worth of all my traits, even those I'd always considered to be the "bad" ones. As soon as I accepted them in myself, I could accept them in others, too. Pet peeves and frustrations seemed to melt away, giving me a more understanding perspective toward everyone I met. It turns out, choosing to be a friend to yourself is the seed from which authentic happiness grows.

I smiled as I thought back to the woman I used to be. I didn't judge her for being uptight and overscheduled. There were no regrets for getting pulled into the rat race she'd been running back then. She was just a woman finding her way, walking up and down the hills of life to get to the place she was supposed to be—which was sitting on this boulder in Wanaka, New Zealand, ready to start her 40th year of life.

In Wanaka, we made our first set of local friends. We'd been watching the girls burn off some energy at a playground when we started chatting with another set of parents. Rob was a native New Zealander and his wife, Natalie, grew up in France. After talking for a while, they invited us to their house for dinner. Back at their place, we opened a bottle of wine and threw together a simple meal while our girls ran around the yard with their two boys and little girl. Rob and Natalie told us about their favorite hikes and restaurants, and they gave us advice on things to see when we left Wanaka and headed further south. They even offered their home to us when they left for vacation a couple weeks later.

"Yeah, you're welcome to it if you want it," Rob said. "You could feed the cat for us."

"That might be the wine talking," I said with a smile, but I gave Brian a quick hopeful glance. Given the prices we were paying for rentals in New Zealand, getting a housesitting gig could do very good things for our budget.

"You guys just met us," Brian said. "You really want us staying in your home?"

Rob grinned across the table at his wife. "I don't think they look like criminals, do you Nat?"

"I don't know . . . It's hard to tell with Americans." Natalie crossed her arms and gave us an exaggerated suspicious look. Then

she laughed and added, "But I am French, after all. I am a little cynical about everything."

"Well, it's not like we have heaps worth stealing, anyway," Rob
said. "Seriously, we'd be happy to have you here while we're gone, if
you decide you want to come back up this way."

"If you're sure, we might take you up on it," Brian said. "We
don't really have solid plans yet."

"That's an understatement," I added with a laugh. "I have reser-
vations lined up for the next five nights, and after that we're homeless."

Rob raised his glass in a toast. "Well then, here's to housing the
homeless in a couple weeks."

A few days later, we were down to just two days of booked
housing as we continued down the South Island to the town of Te
Anau with plans to see the famous glacial fiord Milford Sound.
On the day of our tour, we woke up at sunrise and drove two
hours through Fiordland National Park, during which time I
think I counted seventeen "beautifuls" out of Brian's mouth—a
new record.

We bought tickets, boarded a large tour boat, and were soon
cruising between the dramatic, sheer rock walls of the fiord. The
girls squealed and ran when mist from the waterfalls sprayed the
boat's deck, and giggled as they watched seals playing on boulders. In Norway, we'd looked down into a fiord from two thousand
feet up, but in New Zealand, we floated through the middle of it
all, staring up at the steep cliff bands and snow-capped mountain
peaks surrounding us. It was the same geological phenomenon,
but we were experiencing it from a very different viewpoint.

This could certainly be said for our family's perspective on
each other, too. In that first country of our journey, we'd been driving one another crazy, and I was nervous we weren't going to survive
the constant togetherness of nomadic life. Yet, by the time the five of
us were cruising through Milford Sound, we'd fallen into a family
dynamic more peaceful and understanding than any other time in
our life together. There were fewer fights and more discussions, less
frustration and more empathy. I'm not sure if we'd truly changed, or
if it was like Reuben had said on that walk back from the rain forest
pools. Perhaps this journey had given us the constant togetherness

we needed to finally get really honest. Honest with who we were, what we wanted, and how much we needed each other.

Before we started this trip, I thought I knew everything there was to know about Brian and the girls, but as the months went by, I uncovered a new understanding of each of them. It turned out, Liv was a classic introvert and needed time alone each day to decompress. Emily loved writing poetry, but had been too embarrassed to show us. Ali, interestingly, had a passionate interest in the Great Pacific Garbage Patch after learning about it in a preschool circle time lesson. The most surprising discovery was Brian's secret OCD behavior when it came to his desk and email inbox. As I learned more about these people I thought I knew so well, I began to see how the same situation could affect each of us in very different ways.

Don Miguel Ruiz, a descendent of the ancient Toltec culture and author of several books sharing its philosophy, offers an enlightening analogy on the unique realities each of us live in. He uses the concept of a movie theater to explain the Toltec beliefs on how humans see the world. According to Ruiz, our Carisch Family Cineplex would feature a lineup of five very different films. One would star me, and the plotline would unfold from my perspective, with every scene and every line of dialogue depicting how I interpret the events and people in my life. In another theater, the audience could watch a film with Brian in the leading role. The same set of characters play out the same events, but the plot line would completely change when it followed Brian's point of view. And so it goes for each person in our family, and every member of the human race. We all see the world through our personalized lens, creating a distorted reality only we can see. Over the course of our trip, I'd begun imagining the movies Brian and the girls starred in, and how our experiences together could feel completely different to each of us.

After our boat ride up through Milford Sound, we piled into the car for the drive back to Te Anau. Brian and I decided to stop at a popular trailhead and take the girls for a hike up to a viewpoint. As the rest of us pulled on backpacks and changed into hiking boots, Liv sat in the back of the car, engrossed in her book.

"Liv!" Brian called, knocking on the window. "We're heading out, kiddo! Come on! Let's go!"

From the other side of the car, I watched Liv's reaction. A scowl darkened her face as she slammed the book closed and threw it against the backseat. After silently climbing out of the car, she stood with her arms crossed and her chin tucked into her chest.

There was a time when her angry reaction would have elicited an equally angry response from me. *What's the problem, Liv! Stop acting like this! We're going out to go enjoy nature, for cryin' out loud!* But now, as I thought about our family's day together, the movie starring Liv Carisch played across my mind's eye.

INT. BEDROOM—SUNRISE
Young girl sleeps in bottom bunk of the small room she shares with two sisters. Her mother enters the room and switches on a bedside lamp.

              MOM
     Girls, it's time to get up. We're going on
     the boat ride today.

Silence.

             MOM (CONT'D)
     Girls, come on. We have to leave early or
     we'll miss it.

Mom moves to the bottom bunk and leans over her daughter.

             MOM (CONT'D)
     Come on, Liv. I need you out of bed right
     now.

             LIV
     (Groaning and stretching)
     Why do we have to go so early? Why can't
     this be an afternoon boat ride?

MOM

Because it's not. Now get up.
(She pulls the covers off her daughter
and exits.)

INT. FAMILY CAR
Liv is reading, but stops to look out the window
with a sour look on her face.

LIV

(mumbling)
How much longer? I don't feel good.

MOM

(from front seat)
Then you need to stop reading, Liv. This
road is too curvy for that. You're making
yourself carsick.

LIV

(exasperated)
But this is the really good part!

Frustrated, Liv closes the book and stares out
the window with a scowl.

EXT. MILFORD SOUND HARBOR
Family walks up the ramp to a large tour boat.
Suddenly, Liv stops.

LIV

Wait! I forgot my book in the car! I need
to go back and get it!

> MOM
> There's no time to go back to the parking
> lot, Liv. Besides, this is going to be
> beautiful. You don't want to have your
> nose stuck in a book for this.

Disappointed, Liv grudgingly follows her family
onto the boat.

INT. FAMILY CAR
Liv climbs back into the car and immediately
picks up her book to begin reading. As the car
pulls out of the parking lot, Liv's eyes widen
in suspense. Images of knights, flying dragons,
and a young heroine float around Liv's head as
she turns the pages.

> DADDY
> (knocking on the car window from exterior)
> Liv! We're heading out, kiddo! Come on!
> Let's go!

By imagining our day through Liv's eight-year-old eyes, I could understand her reaction. Instead of getting mad at her, I opened the car door and grabbed her book. Making eye contact with Brian, I nodded in her direction. *Kid drama brewing.* He nodded back with understanding.

"Hey, Liv," I said, walking over to her. "How about I put your book in my backpack and you can read it when we get to the top?"

She nodded, her mouth breaking out of its hard grimace.

"Girls, here's a challenge for you," Brian called over his shoulder as he jogged to the trailhead. "Anyone who beats me to the top gets five bucks!"

The girls let out a cheer and ran past him up the trail.

When you're a little kid, sometimes you just need a little empathy. We all need that, don't we? Someone to see our point of view when we're having a hard time. To give us the benefit of the doubt and help us find an alternative to our destructive moodiness. By taking a moment to imagine the movies others starred in, I began creating a much more peaceful life for myself.

We were as close to familial bliss as we could get as we made our way around the southern end of New Zealand, staying a few days here, a few days there, and sometimes figuring out housing just a few hours before our heads hit the pillows. We returned to Wanaka and took Natalie and Rob up on their offer to stay in their home while they were on vacation. During our weeklong housesitting stint, we made friends in the neighborhood, frequented our favorite spots around town, and continued our newfound addiction to Kiwi television.

Yes, after months in foreign countries with no access to it, we rejoiced in the wonder that is English-speaking reality TV. Our favorite show was a home makeover competition called *Our First House*, where three young couples each paired up with their parents to purchase, renovate, and sell a home. The team to make the most profit would win something, money probably. Honestly, I didn't really care what they won because I was essentially watching the show just so I could giggle whenever they talked about their decks. When the New Zealand accent turned the short "E" sound into a short "I" sound, I turned into a silly, prepubescent girl.

"We're quite jealous Danny and Sara have such a big dick."

"We want a big dick out front, so we're working on figuring a way to attach one."

"I love the dick. It came out so well. I just want to sit on it all the time."

You have to admit, it's pretty funny, right? Or am I just that immature? Maybe a little of both.

One day, I was checking my email while sitting out on Rob and Natalie's patio (no big dick), when I noticed a message from the owner of a house we'd rented for a few days on the southern coast. Fearing we'd accidentally broken something and they were contacting us to complain, I quickly opened the message.

From: Bev McKenny
Date: Mon, Apr 13, 2015 8:27 a.m.
Subject: Re: Bluff Cottage Rental

Hello Tracey,

Thank you for staying at our cottage in Bluff. My husband and I just took the time to read some of your family's web site about your travels. Wow! We want to extend an invitation to come and stay with us if you are heading north at all. We are on the Kapiti Coast and have a big enough house to accommodate you. In fact, we actually had a bit of a wild thought. We're going away for a week and are arranging care for our animals. You wouldn't be interested in house/pet sitting, would you? Please feel free to say no if too weird or doesn't suit. Would love to meet your family if you come this way, be it for a night or longer.

Cheers,
Bev and Blane McKenny

A year prior to this, the idea of staying in the home of total strangers would have seemed downright crazy. *What if they're psychos luring us into a hostage situation or a satanic cult? How do we know their house will be safe for the kids?* Back then, we would have politely declined Bev's offer after suspecting the worst. After all, the world is a dangerous place, and you can never assume people have good intentions, right?

Twelve months of global travel had shown us a world very different from the one we'd learned about on the twenty-four-hour news networks, where fear and controversy apparently sell more advertising than heartwarming stories about random acts of kindness. Call it naïve or imprudent, but our new worldview had changed us into people who accepted invitations from complete strangers. After a few email exchanges with Bev, we were set to meet her and her husband in Raumati Beach and take care of their cat, two dogs, three chickens, and kunekune pig.

To get there, we left Rob and Natalie's home in Wanaka and began a road trip up the western side of the South Island. The highway hugged the rocky coastline as we passed by the extraordinary geologic phenomena of the Pancake Rocks (which really do look like stacks of pancakes) and the bizarre water shows created by The Blowholes (which really are big holes in the ground blowing water). After a serious financial discussion, Brian and I forked over the money for our family to take an extremely expensive, but extremely worth-it, helicopter ride over the Southern Alps mountain range. We stopped at a couple vineyards in Marlborough's wine country, and then walked along the stark, marshy beaches of Abel Tasman National Park. By the time we caught a ferry to the port city of Wellington on the North Island, our family had experienced our most diverse and beautiful week of travel yet.

Our first day in Wellington, we were driving up to an overlook at the top of Mt. Victoria when the fast-moving traffic suddenly slowed to crawl. We expected to see an accident but never passed one, so we were left wondering what had happened. As we drove the curvy road to the top of the hill, a radio DJ gave us our answer.

"I'm sure most of you throughout our listening area felt that one. Our local quake web site is reporting it as about a five on the scale. Bit of a shake, that was. Hope you don't have too many broken dishes, mates. And now we'll get back to the music here on The Rock 96.5 FM."

Brian and I exchanged a look.

"Wait a minute," Emily said, leaning up from the back seat. "Did he say there was an earthquake here?"

"I didn't feel anything," Liv added.

"I guess our tires cushioned it or something," I said with a shrug.

The next day, however, we definitely felt it. We were sitting in the high-rise apartment we'd rented for a few days when the building suddenly began rumbling, like an engine revving up deep within the structure. The vibration lasted several seconds, rattling pictures on the walls and creating little waves in the glass of water sitting next to me. When it was over, the five of us looked around at each other.

"Was that an earthquake?" Ali asked, her eyes wide.

"Yes, that was definitely an earthquake," Brian replied, giving me an amused look. Neither of us had ever experienced one before.

"So, is the building going to fall down now?" Ali asked, curiously looking around the room.

"No, honey," I said with a laugh. "They have little earthquakes a lot here in Wellington. Big earthquakes that would make buildings fall down are very, very rare. They hardly ever happen."

Then, two days later, a massive earthquake hit Nepal, killing thousands and decimating entire villages. I sat at my computer, absorbed in an article about the heroic efforts of rescuers working to free victims from the rubble.

"Did the earthquake do that?"

Startled, I turned to find Ali standing next to me, a look of fear etched on her face as she stared at my computer screen's large image of a collapsed building in Kathmandu.

"This happened because of *an* earthquake, but it wasn't the one we felt the other day, sweetie. This was a much stronger earthquake and it happened really, really far away from here in a different country."

Still looking at the photo, she quietly asked, "Did people die?"

"Yes. People died. And some people got hurt." I put a hand on her cheek. "But millions and millions of people lived through this earthquake and they're fine."

She looked closely at the photo of rescue workers crouched over the building's rubble. "They're the helpers, aren't they? The people who lived are there to help."

I smiled and nodded. "Yeah, baby. They're the helpers."

With seismic activity still very much on my mind, the next day I received an email from the director of our language school in Pucón, Chile.

From: admin@languagepucon.com
Date: Sun, Apr 26, 2015 6:37 a.m.
Subject: Re: Down Payment Received

Quierda Tracey,

I am sure you have heard of the Calbuco volcano erupting in southern Chile. This volcano is three hours south of us. We do not have damage, but much ash drifted north and covers Pucón. We hope for rain before you arrive to wash away the ash. Please do not worry. Everyone is safe here. We look forward to meeting your family.

Cariñosos saludos,
Karin Malonnek

Karin's message was the first I'd heard about this latest eruption in Patagonia, and for the first time in my life I started researching our planet's geologic activity. The more I learned, the less thrilled I was to be taking my family to Chile.

It had been a busy time for our earth's crust, apparently. When we were in Fiji, the Villarrica volcano near Pucón erupted for the first time since 1971. A couple months later, the small quake we'd felt in Wellington happened less than an hour after Calbuco erupted. The massive earthquake in the Himalayas happened just two days after that eruption, and while rescuers worked to save the Nepalese victims, Calbuco erupted for a second and then a third time over the course of two days. Being a geological novice, all of this freaked me out, to say the least. *Is it normal to have so many eruptions and earthquakes within such a short period of time? Is some cataclysmic environmental nightmare brewing within our planet? Will we arrive in Chile just as the whole damn country crumbles into the ocean?*

As we ended our time in Wellington and made our way up to Bev and Blane's home on the Kapiti Coast, I tried with all my might to reach for my aw-screw-it-I'm-sure-everything-will-be-fine attitude. Unfortunately, it was a lot harder to do with visions of scalding lava and collapsed buildings flashing through my mind.

We arrived in the town of Raumati Beach in time to watch the sun dip below the ocean. Pulling up to the address Bev had given me, we found a latched wooden gate spanning the driveway and thick clusters of overgrown bushes hiding the house from view.

"Is this it?" Brian asked.

"I guess," I said with a shrug. "This is the right address."

"Did she say anything about a gate?"

"No."

"So . . . should we just open it and go up to the house?"

"Well, yeah. We kind of have to if we're going to knock on the door."

A few minutes later, after knocking on the front door several times and getting no response, we returned to the car. Taking our family to the home of complete strangers suddenly felt very weird and awkward. Perhaps our new open-minded worldview was a little idiotic, after all.

Brian looked at me from the driver's seat. "Now what?"

"I don't know. Let's go get some dinner and then try again, I guess."

After a meal and a quick tour around town, we returned to the house. Brian knocked loudly, and this time the door swung open almost immediately, revealing a handsome middle-aged man in a thick wool cardigan with two excited dogs scrambling around his feet.

"Hello, world travelers!" Blane said with a smile. "Welcome, welcome! So glad you made it!" He reached down to calm the dogs as they jumped around us. "Yes, yes, I know, it's all very exciting. This is Niko, our good old boy, and this is Pippen. She's six months old, so still very much a puppy." The girls laughed as the dogs licked them.

"Come on in," Blane said. "Let me help with your bags."

The girls played with Niko and Pippen while Brian and I followed Blane through the house. It had a bit of a rustic, cobbled-together feel, with hallways and steps leading off to annexes, which seemed to be additions to the original home. A patchwork of carpets covered the floors of the rooms, each one filled with an eclectic mix of furniture. Big potted plants, rock gardens and small fountains brought in the feel of the outdoors. One hallway floor had even been painted with a detailed mural of a rocky stream.

"Bev won't be back for a while," Blane explained as we sat down on the benches running along either side of the long, rough-hewn kitchen table. "She's helping with a Shamanic healing workshop tonight. She'll be sad to have missed so much of your time with us. We have to leave before dawn tomorrow to catch our ferry down to the South Island."

"You're staying in New Zealand for your vacation?" Brian asked.

"Well, it's not really a vacation, per say," Blane replied. "We've organized a tantric sex workshop at a resort near Abel Tasman Park."

"Oh, okay . . . " I said, after an awkward pause. I glanced over at Brian and saw him nodding casually, as though tantric sex workshops were a common topic for us.

"We went to this great session in Australia last year," Blane continued. "This guy is absolutely amazing! It was incredible how much energy he helped us create. We've helped him put together another workshop over here, so we had to set things up for it. Researched the hotels a bit, if you know what I mean," he said with wink. "Made sure the mattresses were in good working order, you know?"

Brian and I both let out a burst of nervous laughter. *Yes, indeed, I would imagine good mattresses are a very important aspect of an effective tantric sex workshop.* As we sat there chatting with Blane and getting used to his candid conversation style, I decided he and Bev might turn out to be the most fascinating people we'd met on this journey.

A couple hours later, we heard the front door open. "Hello!" a light voice called through the house. "I'm home!"

"Darling, we're in the kitchen," Blane called back.

Moments later a woman like none I'd ever met in my life appeared in the doorway. Her salt and pepper hair ran down her back in long dreadlocks. On her tall frame she wore casual, flowing clothes, with bracelets running up her arms and Birkenstocks on her feet. Her face, illuminated with bright eyes and glowing skin, radiated a confident, easy connection to everything around her.

"Oh, it's so lovely to see you in person," she said, flashing a smile and flipping a dreadlock over her shoulder. "I want to hear all about your family's adventures. But first," she looked over to Blane, "Darling, have you seen any cobwebs in the house?" She held out her hand and pointed to her index finger. "I seem to have a bit of a wound. I think I nicked it cutting vegetables tonight."

Blane thought for a moment and then said, "I believe I saw one on the stairs going up to the back bedrooms."

"Oh good," Bev said, disappearing from the kitchen and returning a minute later with bits of cobweb wrapped around her injured forefinger. "It's a natural bandage," she explained after noticing my confused expression.

As we chatted with Bev and Blane, I found myself more and more captivated by their homeopathic, one-with-the-earth lifestyle.

I'd never met two people more frank, forthcoming, and comfortable in their skin.

"Where are you headed off to when you leave New Zealand?" Bev asked.

"Well, we're signed up to take a language course in Chile," Brian said, shooting me a glance. "It's down in Patagonia."

Bev gave me a long, contemplative look. "I sense some concerns." I hesitated and shrugged, slightly embarrassed to share my worrywart neuroses on the subject. "There's just been a lot of volcanic activity near Pucón lately," I explained. "I've been a little . . . I don't know . . . anxious about it, I guess. I'm not used to living around volcanoes, much less ones that have just recently erupted."

"I'd say this is probably the best time to go, don't you think?" Blane added with a laugh. "Little chance it'll happen again any time soon, right?"

I hadn't looked at it that way, but he did have a point.

"Oh, you needn't be putting your thoughts on destructive volcanoes and such," Bev said, her bracelets jingling as she waved a hand dismissively. "Your family isn't attracting that kind of energy, dear. Look at what you've created in your life. Only good is flowing around you."

"I know, it's silly," I conceded. "It's just weird hearing about volcanoes erupting in the place I'm about to take my children."

A calm, serious look came over Bev's face, and she gently placed her hand on my arm. Looking me straight in the eye, she said, "It's time for you to let go of that fear and focus on the good things coming to you."

As the words floated out of her mouth, I seemed to hear them from inside my head rather than through my ears. A strange warmth radiated from her hand, traveling up my arm and across my shoulders. Her simple statement had an unexpectedly powerful impact on me. Suddenly the idea of our family being trapped in the middle of a planet-altering geologic disaster seemed utterly preposterous. Looking at Bev, I laughed at the ridiculousness of it.

"You're right," I said, shaking my head. "It's so dumb. Why would I be worried about that?"

"That's the spirit," she said, giving my hand a couple pats. "Okay, shall we give you all the info on the pets?"

Blane and Bev walked us through the house, showing us the bucket for the food scraps we'd feed to the chickens and the bags of store bought food we'd give to the pig, dogs, and cat.

"Oh, and do you think you could keep my bug alive?" Bev asked, walking over to the refrigerator and yanking it open.

"Um . . . I can try," I said, with an uncertain smile. "If you tell me what bug you're talking about."

She pulled a mason jar containing a white substance from the top shelf. "My yogurt bug. Don't worry, it's a piece-of-piss."

"It's a *what?*" I asked.

She laughed. "I mean, it's easy to do, sorry. Kiwi slang. Anyway, if you could make another batch of yogurt so the bacterial culture won't die that would be brilliant. You just bring the milk to a boil and let it cool down to about, oh, 45 or 46 degrees or so, and then you add some of the old yogurt and whisk it up, and then you'll pour it all into the jar and put the jar in this." She placed her hand on a large thermos sitting on the counter. "There's nothing to it," she said with a smile.

"Okay," I said slowly, feeling a bit overwhelmed.

"Oh, and one other thing," Blane said. "Niko knows how to open the kitchen door to let himself out. Which is fine, except sometimes Cecilia gets into the house."

"Who's Cecilia?" Brian asked.

"The pig," Blane said. "She's quite easy to lead out, though. Just grab an apple or something and she'll follow you."

"Oh, your girls will *love* Cecilia," Bev added warmly. "She's such a sweetheart."

"RUN!" Ali screamed. "IT'LL SLIME YOU!"

Her little legs carved a path through the yard's tall grass before she scrambled up onto the trampoline. Looking down at the wet, snotty nose marks on my pants, I had to agree with Ali's word choice. Yes, I'd definitely been slimed by Cecilia. The black, hairy pig grunted at me, nodding her head in the direction of the food bowl she'd just gulped down. The long, furry tassels hanging from her jowls swung back and forth as she tried to convince me to give her a refill.

"You can't bully me, Cecilia," I said sternly, putting my hands on my hips. "I'm not going to give you what you want when you get snot all over my pants." Seeming to comprehend my words, she grunted and lumbered off around the corner of the house.

The second morning of our stay, I woke up to the sound of Cecilia's loud snorts. I launched out of a semi-conscience state, bolting upright and belligerently shouting, "THE PIG IS IN HERE! THE PIG IS IN HERE!"

"What?! In our room?" Brian sat up and blinked against the bright morning light.

I listened intently for a few moments. "Oh sorry. I think she's just outside our window."

"Dammit, Trace! Don't do that," he grumbled, falling back onto the pillow and throwing the blanket over his head.

To alleviate my pig paranoia, I spent the morning constructing an elaborate barricade to keep Cecilia from getting onto the deck and exploiting Niko as her home invasion accomplice. Once the house was secured, our family settled into the routines of Bev and Blane's home. The large yard and open land beyond it gave the girls lots of areas to explore, and they always came back to the house with some new leaf or flower to examine. On the cold mornings and evenings, Brian heated the house by building fires in the cast iron kitchen stove. Most afternoons, we pulled on our coats and took Niko and Pippen for walks on the beach trails nearby, breathing in the clean, salty air while we watched the dogs chase seagulls. I managed to keep the bug alive and made my first batch of homemade yogurt. We fed our food scraps to the chickens, watered the plants with rainwater collected in barrels, and used Bev's homemade, vinegar-based concoctions to clean the house. We fully embraced our new organic lifestyle.

On our last evening in their home, Brian and I went for a long walk on the beach and let Niko and Pippen dodge in and out of the waves. While heavy clouds glowed pink and lavender above the setting sun, we talked about our favorite places in New Zealand. There were a lot of them.

"Every time we've left a country, I've been excited to see something new. But it's different this time," Brian said, staring at the horizon as the last sliver of sun disappeared from view. "I'm too sad to be leaving this place to be excited for Chile."

"Me, too. I thought six weeks would be enough, but it's like we've barely scratched the surface. I wish we were staying another month."

"I wish we were staying forever," he said pensively, his furrowed brow revealing his contemplative mood.

I smiled and wrapped my arms around his waist. "Oh, come on now. We're Americans, baby. We'd miss our big box stores and polarized politics too much."

"Yeah, and our parents would kill us for moving their grandkids to the other side of the planet." He put his arms around me and kissed the top of my head.

We stood there for a while watching the sky's brilliant colors fade to gray. Then we called the dogs, went back to the house, and started packing our suitcases again. It was time to turn the page on New Zealand's beautiful chapter in our journey.

BREAKING THE LANGUAGE BARRIER

Active volcanoes: 5

Accidental house fires: 1

Lucille Ball impressions: 1

Moments of humiliation in front of millions of Chileans: 1

CHILE

"*Hoy vamos a hablar de las experiencias de su familia durante sus viajes. Esta bien? Ahora, hábleme de su país preferido.*" The words spilled from Filipe's mouth in a blurry rush, and he gave me an expectant smile.

"Um . . . something about my family and a country?" I said with an apologetic grimace.

Filipe smiled and repeated himself slowly. "*Escucha*, Tracey. *Hoy . . . vamos . . . a hablar . . . de las experiencias . . . de su familia . . .*"

It was day three with my one-on-one Spanish tutor and we were still off to a very slow, repetitive start.

Travel never ceases to be a humbling experience. By the time we arrived in Chile, we'd considered ourselves seasoned world travelers. We'd navigated confusing visa procedures, adapted to new cultures, and learned bits of the local languages. Yet, we hadn't fully appreciated how much English was used in other countries. Within a few hours of landing in Santiago, we fully understood what it meant to encounter a true language barrier. Arriving at our hotel, bleary-eyed and jetlagged from the thirteen-hour time change, we were confronted with the mind-numbing challenge of exchanging simple information with the front desk staff.

At first, I thought my years of high school Spanish might help us a bit. I could carefully construct sentences, but then I'd be bombarded with a tongue-twisting stream of noises I couldn't begin to understand. As a result, we depended on our translation app a lot. Whether asking a question at the grocery store or buying bus tickets, I had to punch phrases into my phone, even asking people to spell words for me, so I could decipher what they were saying. Our language struggles during our first week in Chile made us very motivated to start our Spanish program.

We spent a few days in Santiago recovering from jetlag, and then took an overnight bus south to the village of Pucón. Low, overcast clouds formed a gloomy, grey blanket over the quaint mountain town, nestled among the lakes and rivers of Patagonia's rugged northern region. During the summer and winter, tourists flocked to the area, enjoying its lakefront beaches, rafting tours, and nearby ski resorts. But the late autumn months left the town devoid of the tourist crowds. The famous Villarrica volcano remained hidden from our view, and the streets were quiet, with many of the shops and cafés closed for the off-season. However, our focus was on learning Spanish rather than seeing the scenery, so we eagerly started our immersion program with the hope we could overcome the language barrier. Unfortunately, a few sessions with Felipe convinced me our month-long course wasn't going to get us very far.

When my mentally-exhausting, three-hour dose of translating finally ended, I went to the girls' classroom where they were finishing up their lesson.

"*Mariposa, mariposa, mariposa! Es una mariposa!*" Ali yelled, jumping up and down with excitement and pointing to the butterfly their teacher had drawn on the white board.

"Ali! *Muy bien!*" the woman exclaimed. "*Eres una chica muy inteligente!*"

"*Gracias, Maestra* Karin!"

I retracted my previous statement. This month-long course probably wasn't going to get *Brian and me* very far. Our children, on the other hand, were already conjugating verbs.

As the girls and I stepped out of the language school into the chilly air, we discovered the clouds had finally parted. The sun had burned off the morning's fog, revealing a crisp, blue sky. The Villarrica volcano's perfectly symmetrical cone dominated the horizon, towering over the village with a dusting of snow on its peak.

In my first session with Felipe, I had told him about my concerns after the recent eruptions in the area. He'd given me a confused look and a shrug.

"The volcano is so far from us. More than fifteen kilometers," he said. "It is not to be feared. Volcanoes do not scare me. Those skinny clouds in your country, *those* scare me." He struggled to find the English word, moving one hand in fast circles. "You know, the wind comes and destroys the buildings?"

"Oh, you mean tornados?" I shrugged and added, "Those hardly ever happen."

He raised his eyebrows. "Every year we hear of these tornadoes *en los Estados Unidos.* They kill people! They destroy the towns! Our Villarrica erupts one time in forty years. And we know months before." He shook his head. "No, friend, *you* live in a dangerous place."

It turned out that when the Villarrica eruption began in the wee hours of the morning, Felipe and his family went outside to see mother nature's fireworks display. The entire town came out to share coffee and sweets with neighbors as they watched the historic event. A couple months later when the Calbuco volcano erupted and blasted a layer of ash over the community, the people of Pucón dusted off their porches and cars and went about their lives as usual.

While the girls and I walked back to our cottage that day, I couldn't take my eyes off the volcano hovering above the rooftops. Hours later, when evening fell, our family witnessed its nighttime glow for the first time. The simmering lava deep within the crater reflected against the cloud of steam floating above it, creating a fiery red disc in the pitch-black sky. The scene was ominous and foreboding and bizarre . . . and apparently, totally normal.

We settled into our routine quickly. The girls and I went to school for Spanish class first thing in the morning, and then Brian was tutored by Felipe shortly after my session finished. One rainy day, we returned just as Brian was heading out. The living room's wood paneling and two comfy sofas felt warm and inviting after our wet and chilly walk home.

"Hey, how'd it go today?" Brian asked the girls.

"*Gato* means cat! *Perro* means dog!" Ali chanted excitedly as she hopped into his arms.

He gave me a wry smile. "Something tells me these kids are going to be our translators pretty soon."

"Yep," I agreed. "My thoughts exactly."

"I just put more wood on the fire," he said as he set Ali down and loaded his Spanish book into his backpack. "Check it every hour so it doesn't go out on you, okay? I'm going to use the upstairs room at the school to do some client work after I meet with Felipe, so I probably won't be back until dinner."

I groaned. I hated dealing with the fire. In addition to the language barrier, the lack of modern heating systems in Chile had turned out to be another serious adjustment. Our cottage, like many homes throughout the Patagonia region, was heated solely with a wood-burning stove. For Brian, this was a fun element of life in Pucón because he had a macho affinity for building fires. He'd beam with pride as heat radiated from the black, pot-belly stove sitting in the middle of our living room.

"Feel that!" he'd say proudly, warming his hands. "Now *that* is one hot fire!"

He even seemed to find joy in his new ritual of getting up at 5:00 a.m. to restart the fire so the rest of us wouldn't wake up in an icebox. His enthusiasm bordered on pyromania. For me, on the other hand, tending to the fireplace meant burnt fingers, sooty clothes, and a good bit of cursing under my breath. I was not looking forward to stoking it all day in his absence.

After Brian left for his class, the girls and I sat down at the dining table to tackle their math and Spanish homework. They were finishing up a couple hours later when Liv looked around the room and blew into her cupped hands.

"Man, it's freezing in here," she said.

A wave of panic hit me, and I rushed over to open the stove door. *Dammit!* Sure enough, the fire was completely out. Not even a glowing ember remained. I sighed and pinched the bridge of my nose with the realization I'd have to start a fire to keep us from freezing all day.

"Well," I said, resolutely putting my hands on my hips. "How hard can it be, right?"

The girls stood around me as I crumpled up sheets of newspaper and pushed them into the fireplace. I piled some kindling on top, and then went out to our back porch and retrieved a couple logs from the wood box our landlord kept stocked for us.

"Do you guys know where Dad keeps the matches?" I asked the girls.

"He doesn't use matches," Liv said. "He uses that spark thing that's in the kitchen."

I was confused. "What? That clicker just makes a little spark to light the gas burners on the stove. It won't light a fire."

Emily interjected. "No, she means he lights a burner on the stove and then he lights a piece of paper on the burner and then he uses the paper to light the fire."

"Your father walks through the house with burning paper?" The three of them exchanged looks. "Yeah," they said in unison.

Against my better judgement, I decided to try Brian's tactic. *If he can do it, then I can do it.* I grabbed a piece of newspaper and twisted it into a little paper stick. Then I marched into the kitchen, grabbed the clicker, and lit the burner. I stood there for a moment pondering the logic of what I was about to do. The walk back to the fireplace was about fifteen feet. *Surely, I can cover that short distance without any trouble.*

I touched the paper stick to the burner and the tip burst into a little blaze. I quickly turned the knob to extinguish the stovetop, but I accidentally turned it the wrong way to the highest setting, erupting a wide circle of tall, blue flames. In the few seconds it took me to rotate the dial back to the off position, my paper stick had burned halfway down. I screamed and ran into the living room, but the breeze fanned the little fire in my hand even more. Suddenly, a burning piece of paper broke off and floated toward one of the couches.

"Oh my god!" I yelled as I attempted to simultaneously toss my blazing paper stick into the fireplace and wave the rogue flame away from the furniture. Unfortunately, I was unsuccessful on both counts. The burning paper came down squarely on the arm of the couch and my flaming stick landed right in the middle of the kindling box.

"AHHH!" I screamed. I stood there for a precious second, wavering between which of these two dangerous situations I should address first. *Fire on the couch? Or fire in the kindling? How did I get into this mess? And why in the world don't we have any matches?!*

"Mama!" Ali screamed. "Do something!"

Her voice propelled me into action. One hand brushed the flaming paper off the couch onto the hardwood floor where I stepped on it with my stockinged foot. Then I grabbed a glass of water from the table and dumped it into the kindling box. The flame extinguished with a quiet sizzle, and a little column of smoke floated into the air. The room fell quiet, and the four of us stood there looking at each other for a long moment. Liv scrunched up her nose and waved her hands at the smoke wafting through the room. I lifted my foot and inspected the black smudge on the bottom of it.

"Alright, girls, get your coats," I commanded. "We're going to the store to buy some matches."

Life in Chile continued to send me daily doses of blunders. I don't know if it was the language barrier and having to designate a significant portion of my brain power to my Spanish classes with Felipe. Or perhaps it was the sinus congestion I developed as a result of the smoky haze settling over the town each night, when all the residents started fires to heat their homes. Whatever it was, Chile returned me to the frequent moments of idiocy I'd experienced at the beginning of our journey. Seemingly simple tasks, like counting out change, ordering coffee, or even just walking down the street, could turn me into a bumbling fool. Because our family's blonde hair made us stick out like sore thumbs, I felt like people remembered me and my mess-ups too easily. "Here comes that crazy blonde lady who walked right into a parked car yesterday," I could imagine them saying.

Luckily, my daily fumbling was interspersed with the incredible beauty of Patagonia. I might have felt like an idiot some days, but at least I was an idiot living in a gorgeous place. From our cottage, we took short walks down to the shores of Lake Villarrica, a crystal-clear body of water mirroring the volcano that shared its name. Some days, we rented a car for a few hours and drove around the region, exploring its waterfalls and rushing mountain rivers. My cognitive difficulties still crept up during these little excursions, though. Despite finally getting to drive on right-hand roads for the first time in almost a year, I kept trying to drive in the left lane. Switching back to what should have felt normal created a total mental block for me. I turned into oncoming traffic so many times, I had to insist Brian do all the driving.

The icing on the cake came one day as I walked home from the store in the rain, awkwardly carrying bags of groceries in one hand and an umbrella in the other. As I crossed the main street of Pucón, a sudden wind popped my umbrella inside out. I tried to fix it, only to have another gust come along and pop it back into my face, which caused the metal frame to get caught in my hair. Bags hung off my arms while I attempted to wrestle the umbrella out of the massive tangle protruding from my skull. I managed to lurch my way across the intersection, and when I stepped onto the sidewalk a little old Chilean woman was staring at me. Her wide eyes and open mouth confirmed what I already knew to be true—I looked like an absolute nut job.

"*I Love Lucy!*" she said with a laugh, smiling at the younger woman walking with her. "*Ella es como la mujer de I Love Lucy!*"

The two of them laughed, and the old woman patted my arm sympathetically before they continued down the street, still chuckling over the spectacle of me. I felt an odd mixture of humiliation and pride. I mean, not everyone can pull off a great Lucille Ball impression without even trying.

The next morning brought us a beautiful sunny day, so our family decided to walk into town and check out Pucón's annual chocolate festival. As we passed the spot where I'd had my incident with the umbrella, I told Brian and the girls about it and had them laughing at my ridiculous behavior. Despite the chill in the air, the sun warmed our faces and gave me a light, amused attitude toward it all.

"You know, I might be getting dumber, but at least I'm finding it all mildly entertaining."

"Don't beat yourself up, Trace," Brian said, putting an arm around me. "You've been out of your career for over a year. Maybe you're just out of practice."

I stopped dead in my tracks and stared at him accusingly. "Out of practice for what? *Thinking?*"

Fear flashed across his face. "No! I don't mean . . . I don't think you're . . . I just—"

"Are you *agreeing* that I'm getting dumber because I'm not working at some *job?*" I pressed.

"No, no, no . . . I'm not . . . I don't . . . I don't know what I'm saying." He took a deep breath and smiled apologetically. "That came out totally wrong."

I rolled my eyes and relaxed out of my defensiveness. "No, it's fine," I said, as we started walking again. "Maybe I do need to get back to my career. My brain's been totally focused on elementary school math and travel itineraries for too long."

"Don't take anything from my stupid comment, Trace. If anything, your brain is working on overload lately." Seeing my doubtful expression, he continued. "I'm serious. Chile has been a huge learning curve for us, and you're the one dealing with most of it. You're always out in town running errands and using all the Spanish you've just barely learned. It's understandable you feel like your brain's a little fried sometimes."

"I hope you're right," I said. "I might have a hard time getting a job if I can't walk into a meeting without looking like a slapstick sitcom star."

We crossed the street to the town's large pavilion where the festival was in full swing. Crowds of people milled around the entryway and a man's voice boomed through large speakers.

"On the bright side," I added optimistically as we walked into the pavilion, "my Spanish is definitely getting better. I can actually understand what that guy's saying."

An enormous chocolate volcano occupied a wide platform in the middle of the hall, complete with a peak of white chocolate and powdered sugar. The facility was packed with people slowly making their way around to booths selling every chocolate confection imaginable. The girls hopped with excitement as we decided which direction we should go first.

"*Disculpe*," a voice said from behind us. I turned to see a man holding a clipboard and a microphone. "*Perdon, habla Español?*" he asked me.

"Uh . . . *sí*," I said warily, noticing the cameraman standing next to him.

"English?" he asked. I exchanged a look with Brian and nodded. The man continued. "We are with UCV Televisión and we are here for a story about La Festival de Chocolate. We would like to interview you about your experience today."

I laughed. "Oh no, you don't want to interview us."

"*Sí, sí,* we want to show the diversity of the people at this event."

I looked around the pavilion and quickly realized we were the only gringos in sight. Brian and I exchanged an amused smile at the bizarre idea of our Caucasian, blonde family being considered "diversity."

Brian nodded at the man and said, "Sure! My wife will do it. She speaks Spanish really well."

My mouth fell mouth open in shock.

"*Bueno!*" the man said and herded me over to a spot in front of the chocolate volcano.

"No, no, no this is bad idea," I protested as he talked to his camera man and shoved the microphone into my hand.

"You will be fine," he said distractedly. He pulled the girls over next to me and then stepped over the cord between the mic and the camera. "Just look here at me and answer my questions into the microphone. Okay? Okay. Here we go."

I shot Brian a scalding look as he stood next to the cameraman grinning.

"What do you think about the festival today?" the man asked.

"Uh . . . we like it," I replied.

"*Lo siento, en Espanol, por favor.*"

"Uh . . . nos . . . gusta . . . *gustan?*" My brain felt hollow, as though every Spanish word I'd ever learned had fallen out of my head and left a gaping hole.

"*Y sus hijas? Son sus hijas que disfrutan de la fiesta?*"

"Uh . . . *mis hijas . . . quiere . . .* I mean, *quieren . . .* uh . . . chocolate." This was going about as badly as it possibly could.

"*Cuénteme sobre el volcán de chocolate,*" he said, gesturing to the chocolate volcano behind me. I turned and looked at it for a moment.

"Uh . . . *es . . . grande. Y es . . .* uh . . . *bueno.*"

"*La familia va a estar comiendo mucho chocolate hoy?*" he asked.

Oh my god, what is this? The Spanish Inquisition?

"Uh . . . *sí*," I replied robotically. *"Estamos . . . comiendo . . . uh
. . . mucho chocolate."*

"Okay! *Perfecto!"* the man smiled and gave me an enthusiastic
nod he as grabbed the microphone from me. "Thank you very much!
You will be on the news this evening at seven o'clock!"

I sighed and palmed my forehead with embarrassment. Brian
came over as the two media guys walked off in search of another victim.

"That was . . . good," he said cautiously.

I punched him in the arm. "Why did you tell him I'd do that?
Way to throw me under the bus, Carisch."

He shrugged and gave me a pained smiled. "I thought your
Spanish would be better . . . but you were just nervous."

I looked at him and shook my head. "Not happy with you
right now."

He put an arm around me. "Come on, baby," he said, steering
me toward a booth. "You deserve some Chilean chocolate."

You're damn right I do.

When our language course ended in Pucón, it turned out we'd
learned a lot more Spanish than we realized. Everything we did felt
ten times easier than when we arrived in Santiago a month earlier.
We left town on a bus headed for Temuco, a bigger city where we
could rent a car for our week-long road trip up the Chilean coast. As
we bought our bus tickets, picked up the car, and found places to stay,
it became apparent how much we'd learned from Felipe. We may not
have been fluent, but we were definitely functional Spanish speakers.

Cruising north, we stopped in different coastal towns, each one
offering a unique view of the Pacific Ocean. We stood at the edge of
a lush forest filled with pine trees and emerald green grass, watching the water gently ebb and flow onto a smooth black sand beach.
Then, just a couple hours later, we were at the top of a rocky cliff
overlooking the loud, rumbling waves crashing against the boulders below us. One day as we walked the beach, a thick fog rolled
in, enveloping the five of us in a stark white, silent room. A little

while later, we warmed ourselves in the bright sunshine and watched expert surfers ride massive waves at the world-famous surfing spot *Punta de Lobos*. We stayed in big, bustling cities and small, quaint villages. Crammed ourselves into a tiny apartment one night, and then enjoyed sweeping ocean views from the porch of a rural cottage the next. This constant change in scenery and the kaleidoscope of experiences made our road trip through Chile seem much longer than it was. After just a few days, our life in Pucón felt very far away.

"Where are we on this map, Mama?" Ali asked one day, pointing to the Google maps screen I'd pulled up on my laptop.

I pointed to Valparaiso, the port city we'd driven into just a few hours earlier. "We're right here," I said. "And tomorrow, we'll drive this way." I traced my finger along a curved blue line on the map. "Then we'll be back in Santiago again, and we'll fly out to our next country."

Ali's eyes searched the screen. "Where's the United States?" she asked.

I clicked the button to zoom out the screen and North America came into view. "It's right here. Directly north of us."

"Wow," she said, raising her eyebrows and looking up at me. "We're not really that far from home."

Ali's statement struck me, creating an immediate tightness in my chest. Even hours later, as we walked Valparaiso's steep, winding streets filled with vibrant graffiti art, her words still echoed in my mind. *We're not really that far from home.* We'd been living the unusual existence of wandering nomads with little thought for the American life we'd left behind. But now, the return to normal was just a few thousand miles away. *What will our life look like when all this is over? Where will we live? Can I restart my career after so much time? Will the girls' transition back to school easily?* As we prepared to leave Chile, these and many other complicated questions tumbled around in my brain, fast-forwarding my thoughts to the big decisions we'd have to make at the end of this journey. It was hard to imagine what life would look like when it was over.

SEEING THE WATER

Incidences of helpful government corruption: 1
River-fording vehicles: 2
Possible exposures to tuberculosis: 1
Moments of life-changing clarity: 1

BOLIVIA

"Good evening, welcome to Bolivia," the woman said, reaching for our family's documentation without looking up from her desk. After flipping through our passports and forms, she added, "I will require proof of onward journey."

Brian and I exchanged looks.

I stepped closer to the counter. "It doesn't say anything about proof of onward of journey on the embassy web site," I said. "Our friends who live here told us we wouldn't need it."

The woman set the passports and papers down, and then folded her hands neatly on the desk. "I will need proof you will be leaving Bolivia within the thirty-day visa period before I can allow you to enter the country."

"Um . . . well, we don't have travel booked yet," Brian said. "We'll be here for a month and then we're going on to Peru, but we haven't bought any tickets."

"Our friends suggested we might want to take a bus to Peru instead of flying," I added. "We're talking with them this week and then planning our travel."

The woman looked at us blankly. "Bolivia requires each visitor have exit travel plans from the country."

Brian took a deep breath. "We understand that now, but we don't have anything booked yet, so what should we do?"

The woman looked back and forth between us, and then glanced at her watch. "Just one moment," she said, rolling her eyes before she picked up our passports and walked out of the booth.

When she was gone, Brian shook his head in disbelief. "Seriously? What the hell do we do now?"

I shrugged, and glanced at Em, Liv, and Ali standing behind us. They were so tired they were practically catatonic. Ali's droopy eyes suggested she might fall asleep standing up, so I put an arm around her to make sure she didn't tip over. I searched the room and spotted a row of folding chairs lining a wall. "I'm going to get the girls off their feet. I have a feeling we could be here a while."

Twenty minutes later, the girls were dozing in the chairs while Brian and I stood there waiting for the woman to return. Every other traveler had filed through the immigration lines. We were the only people left, except for an elderly janitor slowly pushing a broom.

A door opened and the immigration officer walked briskly back to her booth with our passports and several sheets of paper in her hands. "Okay. It is all prepared," she said as she sat down and placed the papers in front of us. "I have for you an itinerary for flights to Lima, Peru in thirty days."

"What?" Brian blurted as he scanned the document.

"These are plane tickets?" I asked.

"No, these are not plane tickets," she said perfunctorily. "This is an *itinerary* stating your family will go to Lima in thirty days." She gave us a tight smile.

"These aren't actual flights," I said with understanding. "It's just a document stating we're—"

"Leaving Bolivia in thirty days," she interrupted, her voice a bit louder.

"So . . . if anyone asks we just say . . . " Brian's voice trailed off as he looked over at me.

"That your family will be in *Lima, Peru* in *thirty days*," the woman repeated slowly, her voice heavy with impatience. She grabbed the itinerary, banged a stamp on the top of it and then set it aside. "I will need to make your photographs now."

Within ten minutes, we were walking out of immigration with our slightly shady Bolivian visas. We picked up our suitcases easily, since they were the last ones remaining in the baggage claim area.

"Why did she do that for us?" I asked Brian quietly as we wheeled our bags over to the customs X-ray machine. "Do you think she was expecting us to give her money for creating a fake itinerary?"

He began hoisting our suitcases onto the conveyor belt. "Well, if she did then she doesn't really understand how bribes work." He turned to the kids. "Girls, look alive. We need to get your bags through the X-ray machine."

Em, Liv, and Ali slid the backpacks off their shoulders, their tired eyes and slow movements making them look like little zombies. The airport employee working the X-ray put on his jacket while our luggage slid through the machine. As soon as the last of our bags came out, he punched a few buttons on a panel and it shut down with a quiet shudder.

Brian nodded his head back toward him as we walked out the terminal doors. "Honestly, this is probably one time where arriving this late worked in our favor," he said. "They all just want to get the hell out of here and go home."

"Misty Crowe! You haven't changed a bit!" I called out, walking toward my old college friend.

"Tracey Long, neither have you!" she said with a laugh as we hugged in the parking lot of the hotel. Her auburn hair and big brown eyes were the same as I remembered.

"What's it been? Seventeen years?" I asked.

"Ugh, we aren't that old, are we? Wow, so good to see you. How's the hotel? Did everything go smoothly with your flight and everything?"

"Eh. We ran into a little bump at immigration, but it all worked out. We finally got to our room at about two in the morning." I turned my attention to Misty's young son, who was balancing his way along a nearby parking block. "And you must be . . ."

He smiled up at me and extended his hand. "I'm Ciprian. Nice to meet you."

"Nice to meet you, too. One of my girls is over there on the playground if you want to introduce yourself." I pointed to Ali, who was climbing up the slide, and Ciprian ran off to join her.

Misty and I caught up on each other's lives while the kids played. She and I had been fellow Type A overachievers in college, and we met our senior year while serving as officers for a large student organization. After graduation, Misty took her passion and leadership skills into the Peace Corps. She'd been working to install toilets in a Bolivian village when she met her husband, Marco. He

managed a large farm outside of Santa Cruz de la Sierra, and Misty
had worked for various NGOs over the years. When she heard about
our family's travels, she reached out to me on Facebook and we
decided to make Bolivia part of our journey.

"I hate we'll be gone for so much of your time here," she said.
She and her family would be leaving for their annual trip back to
the United States about a week later. "But on the plus side, you have
a free place to stay while we're gone."

"Mama!" Ali called out as she ran over to us. "He says they have
a teeny tiny dog! And a tortoise too!"

I laughed and turned to Misty. "I have a feeling housesitting
for you guys might be the highlight of this trip for our girls."

"I hope so," she said, smiling down at Ali and Ciprian. "Well,
listen, we've got some errands to run, but we'll see you tonight at our
place. I'm excited to introduce you to our friends. I want you to have
some good connections here by the time we fly out." She paused and
gave me a knowing smile. "Something tells me you and my friend
Julie are going to get along very well."

"Hold on, ladies! It's about to get interesting!" Julie yelled. Her long
blonde hair cascaded down her shoulders from underneath a straw
cowboy hat, and her hands gripped the steering wheel with anticipation. I felt like I'd been thrown into a scene straight out of *Thelma
and Louise*. As Julie hit the gas pedal, I reached for the handle above
the truck's passenger window and glanced back at Misty, who'd
braced herself by clutching the front seat headrests.

"What did you get me into?" I said to her with a laugh.

"I don't know, but I'm in it with you!"

The truck's engine revved as we tipped down into the embank-
ment and the water rose up around us.

"Yee haw!" Julie howled as she drove us across the river. Only
the top of the truck's hood was visible above the muddy water. In
front of us, Marco's SUV had stopped on the opposite bank. I could
see the smiling faces of all the kids pressed up against the back
windows.

"Stay on the gas!" Brian yelled. He'd climbed out of Marco's car to take photos. "Keep going! Keep going!"

Within moments we were leaning back in our seats as the truck inclined up and out of the water, the back tires skidding in the mud before grabbing dry ground. I realized I'd been holding my breath when it suddenly came rushing out in a heavy sigh of relief.

I turned to Julie. "Lady, you have some serious off-roading skills."

"I know," she agreed. "Unfortunately, no one's figured out how to get rich as a professional off-roader."

Originally from Ohio, Julie and her husband, Alex, had come to Santa Cruz to volunteer at a children's home. For the past ten years, they'd worked for the organization while starting their own family in Bolivia. Two of their three children had been adopted from the children's home, where Julie and Alex now served as co-directors. They'd been friends with Misty and Marco for years, and their two daughters and son all attended school with Ciprian.

While Alex stayed at work to manage the daily activities, Julie served as our guide on a day trip to the Lomas de Arena park outside of Santa Cruz. After crossing the river, we bounced our way along rough dirt roads and across a series of smaller streams, eventually pulling up to the base of a colossal sand dune at least six stories tall. The kids immediately scrambled out of the SUV and went running up the hill.

"This is crazy," I said as I climbed out of the truck and looked up at the top of it, shielding my eyes from the sun. "How did this get here?"

"Yeah, isn't this a tropical climate?" Brian asked. "It looks like we're in the middle of the Sahara."

"It is a bit of mystery," Marco replied. "From what I understand, they do not know for sure how the dunes came to be here. But, trust me. They are fun. You will see." He winked and started the steep walk up.

After panting our way to the top, we took in the view spanning out around us. Lush wetlands ran along the dunes, creating a border of thick grassy fields against the light brown sand. I sat down and watched as the kids took flying leaps off the edge, screaming in delight when they landed and slid farther down the slope. It looked like fun, but I was hesitant. Eleven years of motherhood seemed to have sucked the playfulness out of me. I was always the one watching over things and keeping everyone safe, making sure no one got hurt, scared or abducted. Plus, this body of mine was pushing forty years of use. I might hurt my bad knee if I tried to act like a kid again.

Yet, seeing the sheer joy on our girls' faces, I felt a tug of childhood nostalgia. I remembered those days when I would run willy-nilly around playgrounds and climb trees with my friends. *When did I get so serious that I won't even jump off a sand dune?*

Movement out of the corner of my eye caught my attention, and I turned to see Brian launch himself off the hill. His deep voice boomed a loud "Woo hoo!" as he sailed through the air and landed at least fifteen feet below me, creating a monstrous cloud of sand.

"Nice one!" Marco called down to him.

Brian stood up and shook the sand out of his hair. Then he looked at me with that boyish grin of his. "Come on, Trace! Don't just sit there!"

He's right, you know. You dove with sharks, after all. Surely you can jump off a sand dune.

I stood up and leaned over to peer down the side of the hill, then backed up and took a running start, my bare feet hammering against the hard-packed sand on the top of the dune. When I reached the edge, I misjudged the distance and placed my last step into nothingness. Instead of bounding off the hill, I went tumbling head over heels and landed face first in the sand.

"Weak!" Julie yelled down. "You need a do-over, Trace!"

After a couple of tries, I found the rhythm of it, and every time I went free-falling down the dune, I'd couldn't help but giggle like a little kid. We spent the afternoon competing for the longest jumps and throwing somersaults into the sand. As the sun began to set, my whole body ached. Acting like a kid again turned out to be the toughest workout I'd had in months.

Life in Santa Cruz continued to be an ongoing adventure. Even mundane activities like transportation became heart-racing escapades. We walked through our neighborhood to the closest taxi stand, sometimes wading through ankle-deep puddles spanning the entire width of the street. After climbing into a cab, we were slung around the backseat while the driver cut across lanes and slammed on the brakes unexpectedly. The city's large, multi-lane roundabouts felt like carousels of confusion, with bizarre stoplights sometimes placed right in the middle of them. The quality of the roads kept things interesting as well. We'd be cruising down a smooth, paved street, and suddenly the driver would be erratically dodging potholes as wide as the car.

Julie, of course, handled driving around the city like a true local. When she took us out for excursions around town, I'd marvel at her ability to navigate a full-size van through the hectic streets of Santa Cruz while chatting away, not giving a second thought to the frenzied mess of traffic swarming around us.

She also served as my guide into the adventures of Bolivian cooking. With a large, modern supermarket just down the road from us, I'd mistakenly thought shopping for food would be one aspect of this country without too many surprises. Seeing familiar brand names, pyramids of shiny produce, and coolers of packaged meats, it felt like I was shopping in the United States again.

Uh . . . wrong. Things were not always as they seemed in my Bolivian grocery store.

The best example of this was the day I bought a plastic-wrapped whole chicken. Julie, Alex, and their kids were coming over for dinner, so I decided to make a traditional roast chicken with potatoes and carrots—a classic American meal to share with our new American friends. However, when I started prepping the bird, I got a bit of a surprise. I went straight to Facebook and messaged the only person I knew who could help me.

Tracey Long Carisch
2:42 p.m.
Problem. Bought a chicken for tonight. It has a head. Wtf?

Juliane Kozel
2:43 p.m.
Lol . . . Heads are the best part. People use them for broth and stuff.

Tracey Long Carisch
2:43 p.m.
Seriously? I have to cut the head off?

Juliane Kozel
2:43 p.m.
Chop chop

Tracey Long Carisch
2:43 p.m.
I've never done this before. Here goes nothing.

2:51 p.m.
OMG. This is not going well.

2:52 P.M.
I don't think I can do this.
It has all its organs, too.

Juliane Kozel
2:52 p.m.
Just reach your hand in and pull everything out. lol

Tracey Long Carisch
2:52 p.m.
In where? Like up its butt?

Juliane Kozel
2:52 p.m.
Yes, ma'am.

Tracey Long Carisch
2:52 p.m.
I can't believe I met you a week ago and we're having a
conversation like this.

Juliane Kozel
2:53 p.m.
You mean a conversation with the words "up its butt" in it? lol

Tracey Long Carisch
2:53 p.m.
Yes, that's exactly what I mean. How do they kill this thing if it still has a head on it?

Juliane Kozel
2:53 p.m.
You've heard the phrase choking the chicken, right? lol

Tracey Long Carisch
2:53 p.m.
Good lord. This thread just reached a new low.

3:01 p.m.
Holy shit! The feet are attached too!

3:03 p.m.
That's it! I'm done! Why package up a chicken in plastic and stick it in the refrigerated case if the damn thing hasn't been butchered?

Juliane Kozel
3:04 p.m.
lol . . . Welcome to Bolivia, friend. Sit tight. I'll come help you.

Tracey Long Carisch
3:04 p.m.
Stop your lol-ing and get over here!

My culinary experiences in Bolivia were a little traumatic at first, but I learned from a pro and soon Julie had me boiling chicken heads and feet to make a chicken broth for chicken soup. Cooking in the developing world turned me into a regular Wolfgang Puck.

Julie wanted us to see as much of Bolivia as possible, so she organized a trip to Santiago de Chiquitos, a rural region near the Amazon basin. Once again, Alex stayed back to manage the children's home for a few days while Julie served as our guide. We rented a Jeep for our family and followed her van five hours east, zipping by fields of sunflowers and buying snacks from roadside vendors. We passed teams of oxen pulling wooden carts and young boys leading donkeys packed with supplies. At times, we had to stop and wait for large herds of cattle to cross the highway.

When we reached the tiny, rustic town of Santiago, Julie pulled up to a quaint hostel with a red tile roof and a row of intricately-carved wooden pillars on its porch. The main building housed a restaurant, and behind it the guest rooms formed a horseshoe around a grassy courtyard, with cloth hammocks hanging along the covered walkways.

Our days in Santiago blended one into the next, with visits to the Kozel family's favorite spots. We relaxed in the bubbling hot springs of a jungle river and hiked through a high plateau meadow to reach an enormous natural stone arch. A steep walk took us up to a wind-blown overlook where the lush Amazon basin spanned below us like a green carpet a hundred miles wide. In the evenings, Julie's children toured our girls through town, stopping to browse through the little shops and play games in the central plaza.

One night after eating dinner in the hostel's restaurant, Brian, Julie, and I lined up in three hammocks along the walkway, each of us sipping beers we'd bought at the small shop across the street.

"It's so crazy you guys have gone all the way around the planet," Julie said, her face swinging rhythmically in and out view as she rocked in her hammock behind the pillar separating us.

"Yep. Technically, we've circumnavigated the globe," Brian said behind me. "Now we just have to keep going north."

"Are you going to try to get back for the start of the school year?" she asked.

A familiar tightness hit my chest at the thought of returning home before school started. I stayed silent, focusing my attention on a tiny spider crawling along the edge of my hammock.

After a long pause, Brian finally replied. "I don't know. That would probably make sense, but . . . " His voice trailed off.

"It's got to be weird for you guys to think about going back to a normal life after everything you've done," Julie said.

Maybe that's what's freaking me out. Maybe I don't want to be normal again.

"Do you know where you'll live?" she asked.

"No, we sold our house," Brian replied.

"But you're going back to Tennessee, right?"

"No, we're definitely going somewhere new. We want to raise the girls near mountains, so we're thinking probably Colorado."

"So, you don't know where you'll land yet," Julie said.

"Not exactly, no," he replied.

"And you don't know when you're getting there."

"Nope."

"Well, you don't know much, do you, Brian?" she said with a grin.

Brian laughed. "Apparently not. But, you know what, Julie? I think I kind of like it that way."

Me too, babe. Me too.

A few days after we returned from our Santiago trip, Julie connected us to some new volunteer work. While Alex watched all the kids at their house, Brian, Julie, and I went onto the streets of Santa Cruz with a young man named Lincoln, a leader in an organization called Youth with a Mission. We joined him on one of the nights he went out to help homeless drug addicts.

The drug of choice among Bolivia's young people was shoe glue. It was cheap to buy, technically legal to possess, and delivered an immediate, intense high. To be honest, I had some mixed feelings about this volunteer work. Throughout our travels, we'd met people living in dire conditions due to circumstances completely outside of their control. But drug addiction? We were going to spend our time and effort helping people who were making the choice to stand around on street corners sniffing glue? Something about it didn't sit well with me.

We met up with Lincoln in the children's home kitchen and spent a couple hours preparing food and organizing the donated clothing. At about 9:00 pm, we climbed out of Julie's van and walked along a busy main road armed with bags of sandwiches, stacks of paper cups, and thermoses of hot coffee.

We quickly encountered a large group of young men loitering in a grassy median, and when they saw Lincoln they shouted out greetings. Not knowing what to expect from the evening, Brian and I were surprised when an impromptu party broke out. Everyone was laughing and joking while we passed out our sandwiches and coffee. After a while, a group of young women showed up and the party got even wilder as the men teased them and snuck kisses onto their cheeks. I was pouring coffee, when I felt a wet slobbery smack on the side of my face and turned to see one of the young men staring at me with a drunken smile. I could feel a slimy patch of saliva on my cheek. *Gross.* As I wiped it away with my sleeve, I felt a hand on my arm and heard Julie's voice in my ear.

"Don't let them kiss you," she whispered. "A lot of these guys have tuberculosis."

I turned and gave her an open-mouthed, wide-eyed stare.

She grinned and patted me on the back. "Oh, don't be such a germaphobe. You'll be fine."

The silly stunts and laughter continued, but grim reminders of the sad reality were always there. Between their smiles and jokes, the young people pulled little tubes of shoe glue to their noses every few minutes. Some of them had put their glue into plastic soda bottles. They stood with one arm crossed over their chest and the other holding the bottle opening near their face where they could breathe in a steady stream of the noxious fumes. We learned most of the women with us worked in the sex trade, and they'd been at a nearby mobile clinic getting tested for HIV. One man began a show-and-tell session of his many scars—a stab wound here, a gunshot there, a machete slash, a cigarette burn. Lincoln was often in a serious conversation with someone, pressing a card into their hands with information about shelters where they could get help. The collective tragedy lay just below the jovial surface of the evening.

After an hour, we left the street party and made our way to other areas of the city. As Lincoln helped one young mother look through the bags of donated clothing, I watched her two small boys wander around on the curb collecting bits of trash. Some CDs. A soda can. A plastic bag. In another part of town, we found a group getting ready to go to sleep on the sidewalk. Among them was a young boy about Emily's age, sniffing glue from a plastic bottle. Despite the sharp chill in the winter air, the boy wore only a tattered t-shirt, so I set to work searching through our bags of clothing for a coat that would fit him. Julie walked up to help me.

"These young kids usually start sniffing glue when they're practically babies," she said as she rummaged through a bag. "Then they can't kick the habit."

I stopped and gave her an incredulous look. "Their *parents* give it to them?" I shook my head in disgust. "That's ridiculous."

Julie looked me in the eyes. "Sniffing glue gets rid of hunger pains, Trace. And parents hate watching their children cry because they can't get them food."

I closed my eyes with understanding. When I opened them, Julie was walking back over to the boy with a coat in her hand.

On our last stop of the night, a little girl about two years old toddled around us while Lincoln told her mother about a free child-care program. As they talked, the girl peeked out at me from between her mother's legs and smiled. Her dark curls poked out from underneath the pink hood she wore, creating a soft frame around her little face. I gave her a silly grin, and soon we'd started a game. Each time she peeked out, I flashed a goofy face, and then she'd laugh and hide again. After a couple minutes of this, she walked over and handed me the plastic Coke bottle she'd been holding, an expression of sweet expectation lighting up her face.

"Wow, gracias!" I exclaimed, gently holding the bottle like a prized possession.

She clapped her hands in delight and then ran back to her mother, letting out a bubbly, infectious giggle. And then it occurred to me why she was so excited to give me that plastic bottle. Because the grown-ups she knew liked to have them so they could sniff glue.

The little girl started up our game again, but this time when I gave her my silly smile, my eyes swept across the scene around us. Her mother and a couple other women took huffs from the little tubes of glue tucked in their fists as they talked with Lincoln. A few men pulled an old mattress out from a narrow alleyway and set it up on the sidewalk. A chilly wind kicked up, sending bits of trash whirling into the air. And there was this sweet child, still smiling at me. A little ray of light in the darkness of humanity.

In the days following our night on the streets of Santa Cruz, I kept thinking about the vast disparities between me and that little girl in the pink hood. Our two worlds couldn't have been more different, yet my brief glimpse into her life helped me see mine in a new way.

I grew up in the small community of Effingham, Illinois, a town surrounded by corn and soybeans in the heartland of America. We had a Walmart on the north side of town, a half-vacant shopping mall on the south side, and a massive grain elevator smack dab in the middle. It was a safe, quiet, and comfortable place where the Midwestern work ethic took hold at a young age. If you made responsible choices and worked hard, you'd have a good life. If you made bad choices, you'd face the consequences. That's the way life works. You make your bed, and then you lay in it.

This philosophy served me well growing up. I studied hard, stayed focused, and rushed around to extra-curricular activities. My parents were loving and involved in my life. They could afford to put good food on the table and nice clothes on my back, and they diligently saved up for my college tuition from the day I was born. I followed an easy path to a healthy, stable life.

Comparing my childhood to the little girl's, I remembered an insightful story I'd once heard. The voice of the late author David Foster Wallace narrated a video about two young fish swimming in the ocean. As the fish glided along together, they passed by an older fish. "Good morning, boys! How's the water?" the older fish called out to them. After he'd swum away, one young fish turned to the other and said, "What in the hell is water?"

That night on the streets of Santa Cruz, a little girl helped me see my water. My pure, clean, crystal-clear water. The stuff I'd been obliviously swimming around in for almost forty years. My water was a happy childhood in a stable family with three meals a day, a nice home, and a well-funded school. It was a father who took me golfing and bought me snow cones afterwards, and a mother whose career as a high school English teacher meant she understood the mind of a hormonal teenager. It was going off to college without worrying about student loan debt, and then meeting friends and professors who would change my view of the world. It was a life of middle class privilege, and all of it was such a given, so consistent and dependable, that I'd never stopped to really look at it before.

I'd never seen my own water.

Would I be the same person if I'd been swimming in that little girl's water instead? If I'd spent my life floating in a sea of uncertainty polluted with drug addiction, prostitution, and homelessness? If my mother had been a teenager addicted to shoe glue? If my father had been an alcoholic? If I'd been bullied or assaulted or abused? Would I be the person I am today if I'd grown up without the stable, happy childhood and a fully paid ticket to higher education?

Of course not. Everything in my life was the result of the water I'd been swimming in.

In that little girl's world, the easy road to a happy, healthy life didn't exist. Her options were limited to what she could see in that murky water. So, she's likely to follow the same sad journey as her mother, addicted to cheap drugs and living on the streets. Unless. . . .

Unless someone like Lincoln comes along. Someone with the compassion and determination to help clean her water. Someone who cares enough to change the tide and guide the flow of life down a very different path.

INTO THINNER AIR

Cases of mild to moderate altitude sickness: 5

Llama fetuses: Too many to count

Broken noses: 1

Silly photos: 341

BOLIVIA

"Lady, it's been so fun having you here," Julie said as she gave me a hug in front of the security line. She'd gotten up before dawn to drive us to the airport.

"We'll be back someday," I said. "Our corrupt Bolivian visas last five years. We should use them at least one more time, right?"

She laughed. "You better. And when we're back in the States we'll come visit you in your to-be-determined new hometown."

I smiled and picked up my backpack, feeling a tug of sadness. I was going miss my wild, funny, off-roading friend.

"Thanks so much for everything, Julie," Brian said, leaning down to give her a hug. "You went above and beyond for us."

The girls all took turns wrapping their arms around Julie's waist, and within minutes we were waving back at her as we followed the crowd through the security line.

A couple hours later our family squeezed into a tiny taxi cab in Sucre, Bolivia, elevation 9,200 feet. We'd decided to visit the famous salt flats in the southwestern part of the country. The journey to get there required a flight into Sucre, followed the next day with a five-hour drive up into the high mountain plateaus of the Andes. After getting checked in at our hostel, we headed out to explore for the afternoon.

Established by the Spanish conquistadors, Sucre couldn't have been more different from the grime and chaos of Santa Cruz. Gleaming white buildings lined the cobblestone streets of this quaint, colonial town. Courtyards with ornate fountains and immaculate landscaping sat in the middle of bustling shops and cafés. Women wearing the traditional local clothing of full, pleated skirts and bowler hats walked through the crowds, selling strawberries and homemade snacks.

We made our way to Mercado Central, an enormous building packed with booths selling fruit, vegetables, meat, flowers, and steaming hot plates of food. It was in this confusing and crowded maze of aisles that the high altitude started to catch up with us.

"I have a headache," Liv said quietly, scrunching up her nose as we passed a table loaded with stacks of fish.

"Me too, kiddo," Brian said, passing her a water bottle. "Keep drinking water. It will help your body adjust to the elevation."

I was hopeful we'd be able to sidestep altitude sickness, but by the end of the day all of us had headaches and Brian was stuck in bed nauseous and dizzy. This wasn't a good sign. The next day we were supposed to drive up another 3,000 feet to Uyuni, the small town situated on the eastern edge of the salt flats. Knowing that altitude sickness could get very serious very quickly, I began to wonder if we needed to cancel this little adventure.

Luckily, though, everyone felt much better the next morning, so we decided to go ahead with our plans. A battered minivan pulled up to our hostel first thing in the morning, and the quiet, serious driver helped us load up our bags. By 8:00 a.m. we'd settled in for our long drive across western Bolivia.

Less than fifteen minutes into the trip, the driver pulled up to a house on the outskirts of Sucre. He wordlessly got out of the vehicle and disappeared around the back of the building. Brian and I exchanged confused looks.

"Did he say anything about stopping?" Brian asked.

I shook my head. "Not to me."

About ten minutes later, he returned with an older gentleman, who climbed into the passenger seat. Without a word, the driver started the engine and turned back onto the road.

For a couple hours, we rode along a two-lane highway, which gently climbed its way up above the tree line to a desolate, rocky landscape. When we reached the town of Potosí, one of the world's highest communities sitting at over 13,000 feet, the driver suddenly turned off the main road. He zigzagged through town for a few minutes and finally parked on a small side street. He and the older man silently climbed out of the van and began walking away.

"*Disculpe,*" I yelled, knocking on the window. "*¿Donde estamos?*"

Seeming to suddenly remember he had five other passengers with him, our driver smiled. *"Almuerzo."*

"Apparently it's time to eat lunch," I said, pulling open the van door.

After our restaurant stop, we all climbed back into the van. The driver turned down various streets, going in the opposite direction of the main highway. Brian and I again exchanged confused looks as we went farther and farther into the town. I could feel a quiet panic rising in my chest.

Where in the hell is this guy taking us?

"Disculpe," I said loudly, leaning into the front seat. *"¿A dónde vamos?"*

He turned to give me a quick, slightly creepy smile and held up his index finger.

One? One what? One stop? One minute? One family delivered to a Bolivian crime syndicate and held for ransom?

Brian put a hand on my shoulder. "It'll be okay, Trace. Don't freak out."

I took a deep breath and sat back in my seat. After another minute or so, the driver stopped in the middle of an intersection, and the older gentleman quickly climbed out of the vehicle.

"See," Brian said. "Nothing to worry about."

I rolled my eyes. "So why couldn't he just tell me he was dropping that guy off? Would that have been so hard?"

Thinking we were finally getting back on the road, our driver confused us yet again when he took us to a nearby parking lot and got out of the vehicle. I just shook my head and laughed. About twenty minutes later he returned, followed by two local women wearing full traditional skirts and sun hats. Opening the van's sliding door, he motioned for Brian to go up to the front passenger seat. The two women climbed in, wedging me up against the van's window. I really didn't care we were picking up additional passengers, but this guy's complete and total lack of communication was seriously getting on my nerves.

For over an hour the van's tires squealed as we swerved around wide curves at unnecessarily high speeds. The two women kept their heads down and stayed absorbed in their knitting, while I stared out the window and willed myself not to throw up. At least the stomach-turning drive offered some beautiful scenery. An electric blue sky hovered above us, and below spanned a wide, flat valley, dotted with rocky outcroppings and bordered by the silhouettes of stark, rolling hills. When we came to a small village of mud brick buildings, the driver pulled the van to a stop on the side of the road and wordlessly got out.

Again.

From the backseat Liv let out a heavy sigh. "Good grief. Where is he going this time?"

"What is with this guy?" Emily added, pressing her forehead against the window to watch him walk away.

One of the women gave me a quiet smile and said, "*Coca.*"

Brian turned around. "What did she say?"

"*Él está comprando coca,*" she repeated.

"*Una* Coca-Cola?" I asked her.

She laughed quietly and shook her head, then elbowed her friend and whispered something under her breath. The two of them continued giggling as they went back to their knitting.

After almost half an hour, the driver returned to the van with a small, white paper bag in his hand. He climbed in and started the engine, but before he put the vehicle in gear, he opened the bag and started putting something in his mouth. From my seat directly behind him, I couldn't see what it was.

"What's he eating?" I asked Brian.

"Um . . . leaves." Brian's eyes followed the man's hand from the bag to his mouth and back to the bag again.

"Leaves?"

"Yeah, it's some kind of dried leaf. He's chewing them, I guess."

I watched the man reach into the bag for a fourth time. "That seems like an awful lot of leaves to put in his mouth."

The woman next to me looked up and gestured to the driver with one of her knitting needles. "*Es coca,*" she said.

"Oh, okay," I said, smiling and nodding at her like I knew what she was talking about. I leaned up toward Brian. "Remind me to Google '*coca*' the next time we have an internet connection."

We laughed at the surreality of this bizarre travel day and

watched the man stuff more leaves into his jowls. When nomadic life turned into a confusing enigma, as it often did, the best thing to do was just sit back, laugh, and wait for the next unexpected thing to happen. Travel was teaching me to let go of the control I thought I needed to have, and just put some faith in the unique experiences other people create in my life.

It was early evening by the time we rolled into the flat, grey town of Uyuni. Our five-hour drive extended to ten hours thanks to all the frequent stops and coca chewing. We dropped off the two women at the bus station, then continued on to our hotel. As the driver pulled our bags out of the back of the van, he smiled and shoved a business card into Brian's hand, nodding and making the universal sign for "call me."

"*Llámame cuando desea volver a Sucre, okay?*" It was the second time he'd spoken to us all day.

Brian smiled and nodded. "*Sí, sí,* okay."

As we walked into the hotel I looked at him. "We're seriously going to have him drive us back to Sucre?"

"Oh, hell no. I just didn't want to be rude."

I woke up standing at our hotel room door with the jittery, buzzing sensation that comes with waking up too fast.

What's happening? Am I sleepwalking?

Then came a knock and a little voice from the hallway. "Mama?" Liv's voice was shaky.

My subconscious mind must have heard the door of the room next to ours open and close. I'd apparently launched out of bed before I was fully awake.

"What's the matter, sweetie?" I said as I opened the door.

She stood in the freezing cold hallway looking miserable. "I feel like I'm going to throw up and my head hurts."

Why hello again, altitude sickness.

"I'm so sorry, honey." I wrapped an arm around her and walked her to the bathroom.

After spending the wee hours of the morning going back and

forth between the bed and the toilet with her, I was surprised when Liv woke up the next day magically cured. This was apparently the nature of altitude sickness. Miserable one minute, perfectly fine the next. Our 4x4 SUV arrived just after breakfast, and the driver introduced himself as Arturo. He was smiling, engaging, and pretty much the antithesis of our driver from the previous day. Arturo told us everything there was to know about his home.

The Bolivian Salt Flats had once been an enormous inland sea surrounded by mountains. The white sheet of sodium chloride goes down ten meters deep in some places, making salt mining a lucrative source of livelihood for local residents. Arturo took us miles out into the flats, our SUV speeding across the ground under a bright blue sky and a blazing sun. With the vast bleached landscape spanning out around us, he gave us advice for manipulating depth perception to create silly photos. Emily ready to crush the SUV under her foot. Me standing in Brian's shoe. A gigantic Brian leaning over to take a photo of the girls, who appear to be the size of mice. It's a surprisingly hilarious way to spend a morning.

Next, Arturo took us to Isla de Pescado, a fossilized coral reef rising up in the middle of the flats like an island.

"This is crazy," Liv said as she looked up at the fluffy, multi-armed cacti covering the hilly terrain. "I think Dr. Seuss must have visited here."

We hiked up a trail curving around boulders etched with tiny coral fossils, the relics of an ancient water world now basking in the Andean sun. When we reached the top of the hill, we were surrounded by miles of what looked like sheer white pavement, with only a few distant hills casting bumps on the horizon. Millions of years ago it had been a thriving coral reef in the sea, but time marched on over the millennia, slowly drying up an entire ocean and leaving a stark landscape behind. A human life was just the blink of an eye by comparison. This region hadn't changed in my thirty-nine years of life, and it would remain the same long after I was gone from this earth. These were the humbling, slightly depressing thoughts rolling through my head as I stood on a hill and looked out over miles and miles of white nothingness.

During the rainy season, the Bolivian Salt Flats are famous for the remarkable mirrored landscapes created by a thin layer of water blanketing the land. Brian had shown me some of these incredible images online, but with it being the dry season, we didn't expect to see this phenomenon ourselves. However, Arturo managed to make it happen for us. As the sun sank lower in the sky, he drove us out to an area of standing water. We stood in the shallows and marveled at the perfect reflections of clouds underneath our feet.

When the sun began setting, the sky transformed into a kaleidoscope of gold, magenta, and crimson. It felt like a dreamy hallucination, a painting created only in the imagination. A surge of awestruck wonder rushed through me as I watched the sun slowly disappear in a wavy blur and shoot vibrant colors across the atmosphere. My gaze locked onto the horizon, where the mirrored image of the sunset created a disorienting, magnificent collision of sky and earth. A familiar warmth wrapped around me, encapsulating my body until I couldn't feel my feet touching ground or the cool air on my skin. As I stared at the hypnotic scene before me, the sunset became an optical illusion, like a puzzle I felt compelled to solve. An image holding an answer I desperately wanted to find.

And then it came to me. A surreal dawning in the midst of a sunset. It was same feeling I'd had with the Buddhist nun that day in the temple. A recognition. A remembering. Stumbling upon something intimately familiar.

Hello. It's you again. I'm so glad you're here.

A swell of joy filled my eyes with tears and pushed the air from my lungs, leaving me breathless, as a discovery swirled through my brain and settled in my heart.

This is love.
The world is love in physical form.
This is why it's all here.
This is why we exist.
For love.

Suddenly, I felt the breeze on my cheeks again and pulled the salty, fresh smell of cool air down into my lungs. As goosebumps tickled my skin, I closed my eyes and smiled. Nature does this to us, if we let it. It reveals the energy flowing through all of us, weaving us into a divine connection we can't begin to understand. A constant, never-ending bond. The oneness hovering just below the surface of our individual realities. Always there. Always ready to be seen. Always waiting for us to recognize it again. And again. And again. This is the reason we have such beauty in the world. So we can see the beauty in ourselves.

"Bobo! NOOO!"

Ali's ear-splitting scream sliced through the check-in terminal at the Sucre airport. I looked down and saw her face contorted into a pained expression of grief.

"What happened?" I asked, scanning her for signs of injury.

"Bobo! Bobo!" she screamed and began scrambling around on the floor.

"She dropped Bobo and his nose fell off," Emily said.

I kneeled down to Ali, who held her teddy bear in one hand and the black round piece of plastic that had been his nose in the other. "Bobo!" she cried pathetically, sucking in shaky breaths through her tears. "He's broken!"

"Oh, baby, we can fix him." I gently pulled her chin up. "He'll be okay."

"No . . . look . . . he . . . he . . . HE HAS NO NOSE!"

"Ali, sweetie, we can glue his nose back on," I said, grabbing her by the shoulders. "He'll be fine."

She looked at me and took a deep breath. "Really?"

"Of course. We'll get him all fixed up, good as new."

Looking at her tattered, nose-less bear, it occurred to me that "good as new" would require a Velveteen-esque miracle, but at least we could get his nose back onto his little threadbare face. As we made our way to our boarding gate, I watched the girls walk ahead of me, all three holding the cherished stuffed bears they'd carried around the planet. Bobo, Pooh Bear, and Pooh Bear were the unsung heroes of this journey. Even though so much in our girls' lives had changed, those tattered companions had always been there, on every flight, in every hotel room, and in every temporary home.

When we landed in La Paz, Bolivia for our twenty-four-hour layover, my first order of business was to ask the front desk staff at our hotel for some glue. Just a few hours after his traumatic nasal injury, our little Bobo could smell imaginary things again.

We left the hotel with the intention of getting as much out of our brief stay in La Paz as possible. The city sits in the shadow of snow-capped Andean peaks, its streets and buildings ingeniously architected into the bowl-like valley it occupies. Cabled gondolas float on several lines above the city, transporting people up and down the steep hillsides. We wandered aimlessly down alleyways lined with colorful buildings and stumbled upon public squares where street performers drew crowds of spectators. We eventually made our way to the famous Witches' Market, a collection of shops and booths run by Bolivian witch doctors.

"That's a lot of llama fetuses," Brian said, grimly eying the line of shops in front of us.

Rows of tiny llama corpses hung from the store awnings on hooks.

I grimaced. "You can say that again."

"Why exactly did we bring our children here? This seems like a recipe for recurring nightmares."

"I blame TripAdvisor," I replied, staring at what looked like an authentic shrunken head.

The girls browsed the tables and examined little trinkets, doing their best to ignore the dead baby animals just inches from their heads. We learned about the fascinating, and rather grue-some, mystic traditions of the local area. Burying the fetus of a llama under a building was thought to bring wealth, health, and happiness to its occupants. Dried armadillos kept thieves away. Frog parts brought good luck, and powdered dog tongue would make your man faithful.

We wandered through the streets to Plaza Murillo, the city's main historical square, and came upon a small craft fair set up near the ornate, stone cathedral. As I scanned the artwork displayed on the tables, Emily walked up to me with an anxious look on her face.

"Mom, do you have any paper?"

"Um . . . no," I said distractedly as I examined a set of hand-painted ceramic plates, which I would never consider buying since there was no room in our luggage.

"Well, do you at least have a pen?"

I rummaged through my purse. "No honey, sorry."

She walked away, but returned a minute later. "Can we buy these?" she asked.

I looked at the fancy leather bound notebook and souvenir pen she was holding and gave her an exasperated sigh. "Emily, come on. We have plenty of notebooks and pens back at the hotel."

"Please, Mom," she pleaded. "This poem just came to me. It like totally popped into my head out of nowhere. I need to write it down. If I don't get these words out I'm going to lose them forever."

Poem drama? Seriously? Are we hitting the teenage years early?

I rolled my eyes, wanting to get back to my pointless browsing of useless trinkets I didn't need.

"Emily, you can write your poem down when we get back."

"But when will that be?"

"After dinner." I pretended to ignore her arm flailing and sighing, but a minute later she was back again.

"What if we went and found a store with really cheap school notebooks and stuff."

"Emily Sage Carisch, I said no!"

"Okay, okay, okay . . . geez."

GRIEF

Through Emily's eyes:

"Okay, girls. It's time to get ready for bed," Mom said.

I was copying the poem onto a new sheet of paper. I'd scribbled it out so quickly when we got back to our hotel room, I could barely read my own writing. It had been a relief to let the words come out. Now that I'd written it, I could stop repeating the verses I'd been saying to myself over and over.

I felt Mom's hand on my shoulder as I finished.

"Come on, kiddo. You need to get to bed or you'll be a zombie at the airport tomorrow morning."

I left the paper on the table and went into the bedroom to change. Then I brushed my teeth and climbed into bed next to Liv. That's when I heard Mom's voice.

"Oh my god!"

Her words were shaky. Shocked. Scared. Something wasn't right.

"Oh my god," she said again. She gasped. Or sobbed. I couldn't tell which. "Brian, am I reading this right?"

Liv and I stared at each other. My mind started racing. Someone had died. I knew it. I thought about my grandparents. I thought about my friends back home. Someone we cared about was dead.

I walked out to the living room, and Liv followed me. Mom was sitting at her computer, staring at the screen. Her hands covered her mouth. Daddy leaned over her shoulder reading words I couldn't see and shaking his head in disbelief. My head felt fuzzy. I had to know.

"Who is it?" I asked quietly.

Neither of them moved. They didn't take their eyes off the computer.

"Who is it?" I said louder.

Mom started sobbing, and Daddy pulled her up into his arms. He squeezed his eyes shut, and big tears rolled down his cheeks. I'd never seen him cry before. Then he finally spoke.

"It's Reuben."

When I remember that moment, my thoughts often go to Emily. To her experience of it all. At the time, I'd been in a vacuum. Caught in my own world, oblivious to the girls standing there watching our sorrow take hold of us.

I'd reread the email from Reuben's stepmother. And then read it again. And again.

This isn't right. I'm reading this wrong. There's a typo or something. A misplaced word that's changing the meaning of the message. This can't be right.

I heard words erupt from my mouth, like they were being spoken by someone else. Soon Brian was leaning over my shoulder reading the message, giving me a glimmer of hope he could snap me out of this confusion, tell me how I was misinterpreting all of this. I remember him pulling me up out of the chair, holding me firmly against his chest, his arms squeezing me tighter as each racking sob escaped from my lungs and burned its way up through my throat. I felt his shoulders shaking around me and knew he was crying, too.

Oh my god, this is real. Reuben is dead.

Diana's face flashed in front of me, and I squeezed my eyes shut as a wave of nausea churned my stomach. My beautiful friend. Their happy family. Their life in paradise. His work to end poverty and his incredible knowledge about the world. His funny stories and his country songs and his early morning swims. And his bike rides.

Killed that morning while riding his bike. His life ended doing something he loved so much. Hit by a van. A careless driver. A curvy road. And he's gone. Gone forever. Just like that.

An ache settled over me, a deep, dull pain that seeped into my bones. It was the first experience I'd ever had with real grief, and I knew it was a tiny fraction of what Reuben's family was going through. Diana. Leah. Ike. His parents. His siblings. A stabbing pain ripped through my gut as the enormity of their loss hit me.

Talking to the girls about Reuben's death was heartbreaking. He was the funny guy who'd crooned sad country songs through the house and cheered for them as they swung out over a rain forest pool. The one who'd read story books to Ali and set off fireworks on the deck. Who'd danced around with a Fijian music troupe.

"We're okay, Trace. We're going to be okay." I heard the shock in Diana's voice a little while later. We'd emailed and then connected on Skype. She and the kids were still at the hotel they'd woken up at that morning when Reuben left for the next leg of his ride. He'd planned to bike around the entire island while Diana and the kids met him at hotels each night. "The kids and I will get through this," she said. "I'm devastated, but . . . but, I'll get us through this . . . somehow."

"If you need someone else there, I'll be on the first plane, Diana." My voice cracked as I said her name.

"I know you would, but we're fine. His dad and stepmom will be here tomorrow. We'll be fine. We'll be okay."

I could hear her trying to convince herself. Trying to navigate this nightmare. A few minutes later, after we'd said good-bye and disconnected the call, I sat in front of my computer unable to move. I imagined Diana waking up the next morning. That brief instant when it would all feel like a bad dream, and then the intense, raging grief would crash in on her, tearing her apart as she tried to hold herself together for Leah and Ike. The shock wearing off and the reality sinking in.

I cried again. I cried for her. And for Reuben. And for everyone who'd known him. And for the world losing such a kind, generous man.

After we put the girls to bed, Brian and I sat around stunned and numb, trying to convince ourselves we needed to get some sleep. Even in this upside-down world where Reuben Summerlin was gone and nothing made sense anymore, our family still had an early flight to catch the next morning. The sun would come up and life would go on, even though thousands of miles away in the middle of the Pacific Ocean, my friend and her children would wake up without a husband and father.

I was walking to the bedroom with little confidence I'd be able to sleep, when I noticed a paper sitting on the dining table. Emily's neat handwriting filled the page, and I realized it was the poem she'd been wanting to write down that afternoon. The words she'd said she had to get out of her head before she lost them forever. I began to read.

A Little While
By Emily Carisch

Everyone is a candle in the darkness.
A candle brightening the nothingness into a world of wonder,
If only for a little while.
The candles go out, replaced by the new ones,
But as the light fades from the wick, the darkness brightens,
If only for a little while.
Something warmer and brighter and more welcoming,
Shedding its light and love and warmth into the world.
Even though the candle is gone, its light will remain.
Preserved in memory and love and hope,
If only for a little while.

A chill cut over my skin. It was like nothing Emily had ever written. Her poetry had always been sweet sonnets about nature or friends or things she liked to do. The kind of poems you'd expect to be written by a happy eleven-year-old girl. They were nothing like this.

The accident happened in the morning. Reuben had decided to get an early start on his ride since high temperatures were in the forecast. Diana said it was about 7:30 a.m. Fiji time when he died at the scene of the crash, hit head on by a van attempting to pass a slow-moving sugar cane truck on a curvy road. 7:30 Fiji time.

I thought back on our day and tried to remember when Emily had started talking about this poem. It was later in the afternoon, sometime between three and four o'clock, when we'd stopped at that craft fair and she'd begged me to buy her a notebook and pen. I calculated the time difference and sat stunned, staring at the words she'd written.

7:30 a.m. in Fiji was 3:30 p.m. in La Paz.

A flash of knowing struck me between the eyes, spilled down my spinal cord, and trickled through my nerve endings. I knew without a shred of doubt, this wasn't a coincidence. I wasn't reading into Emily's words and twisting her poem to fit my grief-stricken mood. Something mysterious and cosmic compelled my daughter to write this. I stared at the paper, her words written in her bubbly handwriting, and in that moment, I glimpsed the sacred knowledge we all share. It's deep within our souls, but we let ourselves forget. We let our egos convince us we're separate creatures occupying this planet, each of us confined to the limits of our bodies and the experiences of our individual lives. But the truth is, we're all connected. A collective mind binds us together through time and space, weaving us into that beautiful tapestry of life and death and love and fear, and it was this connection giving Emily's soul the knowledge that a family's world would soon tilt into tragedy.

The day the world lost an amazing man, I gained a belief I will hold for the rest of my life. We truly are One.

FINDING THE WAY HOME

Incan ruins: 5

Pails of water: 105

Pig pokes: 3

Southern belle gurus: 1

PERU

By the morning after Reuben's death, a memorial Facebook page had been set up for people to post their memories and condolences. We read story after story of Reuben's kindness, charm, and intelligence. As he worked to improve the lives of others, he'd touched the hearts of people around the world, and hundreds of them visited the memorial page to share their gratitude for having known him.

As our family got ready for our flight, the loss kept creeping up on me. Amid the busy travel day routine, I'd suddenly remember he was gone and my lungs would expel a heavy sigh. While repacking a suitcase . . . *Reuben is dead.* Loading into the taxi . . . *Reuben is dead.* Over and over and over again. Scenes of our fun times with him flashed through my mind, quickly followed by the unbelievable reality of my beautiful, fun-loving friend being a widowed mother of two. Our grief over Reuben's death left us in a numb haze for our trip into Cusco.

We'd arranged to rent a home in the Sacred Valley of Peru, a region carved into the foothills of the Andes by the Urubamba River. Our landlord, Isaias, picked us up at the airport and drove us an hour and a half on a curvy road descending into the valley. The terraced hillsides, architected hundreds of years ago by the Inca civilization, rose up on either side of us. My eyes followed the perfectly parallel lines of their retaining walls, each one separated by a narrow field of green crops. As we drove into Yanahuara, a tiny village on the road to Machu Picchu, Isaias pointed out the bus stop and a small store near our rental house. We pulled through a gate and into the yard of a beautiful home made of glass and stone overlooking the river valley. It had gorgeous hardwood floors, granite countertops, and stainless-steel appliances. It was by far the most luxurious home we'd rented on this trip.

However, we quickly realized the lack of heating in this lovely house was going to be a bit of an issue. Despite daytime highs in the 80s, overnight lows dropped into the low 30s, and we had only two small space heaters in the house. While I made dinner that first night in our state-of-the-art kitchen, the electricity suddenly went out, and we lost what little warmth the heaters had generated. Our family huddled under a pile of blankets and spent our first evening in Peru reading the stories on Reuben's memorial page until Brian's cell phone died. The dark, cold night seemed to mirror our sad mood.

When the sun rose over the valley the next morning, its rays streamed in through the floor-to-ceiling windows and warmed the rooms within minutes. With all of us still in a grief-stricken stupor, we decided to distract ourselves with a trip into Urubamba, the main town in the area. We caught the minibus down the road from our house and crammed in next to the locals, most of them staring at us curiously. Evidently, very few gringos caught the minibus in Yanahuara.

We found the town square and a little playground area, but the best entertainment proved to be Urubamba's market district. Vendors crammed into a collection of high-ceilinged warehouses, selling their goods out of burlap sacks and wooden crates. The women working the booths wore full skirts and broad-brimmed hats, with two long, black braids hanging down their backs. We watched them as they arranged flowers into bouquets, wove blankets on their looms, and spun llama wool into yarn. Every vendor was smiling and friendly, offering samples of the foods they sold.

My new favorite was *granadilla*, a hard-shelled fruit filled with sweet, crunchy, jelly-covered seeds. A little old man showed me how to crack a hole into the orange shell and then suck out the insides. It's sounds disgusting, but trust me, granadillas are like weird, slimy drops from heaven.

Ali was a big fan of them, too. As she sucked on one and slurped the seeds into her mouth she said, "Hey, Mama, I bet this is what it will be like if we ever eat a little animal's brain."

Yeesh. Maybe there's such thing as expanding your child's palate a little too much.

However, there was definitely one popular Peruvian food I knew the girls wouldn't come near with a ten-foot pole, and that was guinea pig. On that first day at the market, we passed several women sitting on the sidewalk with boxes of live guinea pigs in front of them.

"Oh, my goodness," Liv said as she leaned over to watch the little animals squirm around. "They're so cute!"

"I wish we could take one home," Ali crooned, reaching out to pet one on the nose.

Knowing these animals weren't being sold as pets, I used one of my most effective distraction techniques to get the girls away from them.

"Hey girls, let's go find out what the locals eat for dessert!"

We quickly found the market's cafeteria section, where vendors stood over their portable grills and whipped up steaming hot plates of Peruvian dishes. I was leading the kids toward the bakery section when we passed a line of barbeque booths. And that's when I saw them for the first time—skewered, grilled guinea pigs. Pigs-on-a-stick.

Oh, dear God, please don't let them see that.

I turned around, hoping the girls were looking in a different direction, but Emily was staring right at them. At first her face held a look of confusion, and then her eyes opened wide and her mouth fell open. She looked at me ready to say something, but I gave her a tight-mouthed stare and slowly shook my head. *No, we don't need to bring this up right now.* I could explain the Peruvians' culinary proclivity for guinea pig meat another time when the girls hadn't just been fawning over them.

Emily closed her mouth, opened it, and then closed it again. She looked sadly at the grilled guinea pigs as she walked by them. When we made it to a booth selling a wide array of chocolates and pastries, Ali and Liv eyed the selection eagerly.

"What are you gonna get, Em?" Ali asked.

Emily shot me a nauseated look. "I'm not hungry anymore."

◎ ◎ ◎

By the third day in our beautifully-architected rental house, the electricity came back on for good. But that afternoon, the plumbing system stopped working. A water main break near Yanahuara left the entire area with dry pipes. Luckily, we had a small creek running through our yard. Isaias brought us a couple buckets so we could haul in water for flushing the toilets and washing dishes.

"I am so very sorry for the problems," he said as he explained the situation. "I am told a large section of pipe is to be repaired. It is possible to take many days."

I sighed. "It's not your fault. We'll make do."

"Look, Mama!" Ali called as she sloshed a heavy bucket through the yard. "I'm like that girl in *Little House on the Prairie!*"

Yes, we were living like Laura Ingalls. In a designer house with granite countertops.

For the next week, the water would come back on for a few hours at a time, but then turn off again. It was annoying, but at least we were able to take showers every couple days. We hadn't been reduced to bathing in the creek . . . yet.

We ignored the little inconveniences of the house as much as possible and took the minibus around to the Incan archeological sites in the area. As we walked through the ruins at Ollantaytambo, Brian and I exchanged an ironic smile when we came across the Incan plumbing system. Water diverted from nearby streams still ran through the stone pipes and delivered a constant flow of clear water to the tubs and fountains in the ancient complex. Evidently, the Incans had one up on us when it came to plumbing.

Eventually the water service returned and we settled into our routine with homeschool work in the morning and trips to the market or an Incan ruin in the afternoon. At night, we huddled under blankets to stay warm and spent a lot of time reading through the posts on Reuben's memorial page. His colleagues who'd been with him in impoverished countries wrote about his resilience, intellect, and compassion as he implemented life-saving programs under the harshest of conditions.

Remembering Reuben's life made our household problems and transition into the Peruvian culture seem inconsequential. It wasn't until our second week in our little village that it occurred to me how different this country was compared to the others we'd experienced on this journey. I'd been walking through the fruit aisle at the market, heading toward my favorite granadilla vendor, when something bumped me gently between my shoulder blades. The market was extremely crowded that day and the aisles swarmed with people, so I didn't think much of it. Then I felt the nudge again, a little more sharply this time. I turned my head to glance behind me, but the aisle was so crowded I couldn't rotate enough to see anything. A moment later, a rough jab lurched me forward and caused me to stumble, almost knocking me into the little old woman ahead of me.

Alright, that's it!

I turned around to confront this rude person, but instead I came face-to-face with a dead pig. Balanced precariously on a man's shoulder, the animal stopped just short of hitting me in the face with its snout. I gave the man carrying it a slightly exasperated look, squeezed myself to the side, and waved my hand down the aisle, indicating he could go in front of me since he was in such a rush.

A few minutes later, after I'd reached my granadilla vendor, it finally occurred to me how weird it is to get poked in the back repeatedly by a dead pig. In fact, being any proximity to a dead pig is something that would have freaked me out not too long ago. Now, getting ramrodded by one was just par for the course. Another day at the market.

As the vendor weighed my granadillas, my eyes took in the scene around me. Men in traditional Peruvian vests and women with long black braids worked the booths, most of them speaking in their native tongue of Quechua. A llama ambled toward me, its back loaded with bundles of alfalfa as it trailed behind its owner on a rope. The next aisle over was the market's meat department, where I could hear the chickens squawking in their cages and see the bloody slabs of meat displayed on wooden chopping blocks. I was the only foreigner in the market and about a head taller than everyone else. As people walked by, they looked up at me, sometimes pointing at my blonde, frizzy hair. Everything about this situation would have felt bizarre and uncomfortable to the old me, and yet . . . it didn't.

A memory of Reuben brought a sad smile to my face. "You'll know you're a true world traveler when nothing's weird anymore," he'd said. "You start going through life expecting the unexpected." And he was right.

Seven hundred years ago, the Sacred Valley served as a spiritual and agricultural center for the Incan Empire. Farmers tilled the terraced land with ox carts and hauled their crops to market with llamas. In lieu of taxes, many citizens fulfilled their obligation to the government with *mit'a* labor, where a man from each family left his home to help build roads, work in the mines, or construct the empire's many temples. Incans worshipped the natural elements and the celestial bodies in the sky. Shamans presided over ceremonies designed to appease the gods and bring health and prosperity to the people. This civilization of proud and hard-working citizens rose to become one of the most expansive and powerful empires on the planet. Yet, when Pizarro and the Spanish conquistadors began their search for South American riches in the 1500s, the Incans were already dealing with the deadly effects of European diseases filtering down from North America. Faced with the military might of the Spaniards, the empire began to crumble.

However, the strong spirit of the Incans kept their beliefs and traditions alive, and the legacy of this ancient people remains strong throughout the Sacred Valley and much of Peru. For many locals, their way of life is very similar to that of their ancestors. They speak the indigenous language of Quechua and cultivate their farmland with the same methods they've used for centuries. Llamas still bring goods to market, and ox carts work in the terraced fields. The women wear traditional clothing, filling the streets with splashes of vibrant color. Living in our little Peruvian village often felt like stepping into a time machine and experiencing the past firsthand.

One Incan tradition attracting the attention of tourists and spiritual seekers is the use of *ayahuasca*. This hallucinogenic drink brewed from vines and leaves is consumed during healing ceremonies. Shamans serve as the intermediaries between the spirit and the human realms. Both the shaman and the participants drink this elixir of the gods to deepen their connection to the divine. Apparently, it can also cause quite a bit of vomiting and diarrhea, but these side effects are believed to be the cleansing of negative spirits from the body. People from around the world gather in the Urubamba river valley for ancient healing ceremonies, giving the region a very mystical and divine atmosphere. Hence, the name the *Sacred* Valley.

Even though Peru was a renowned stop for spiritual journeys, I'd been careful not to make the same mistake I'd made in Thailand. I'd arrived in that country expecting to launch myself into some kind of transcendent transformation, and ultimately, I'd been disappointed during our first visit there when it didn't live up to my expectations. I was careful not to ruin Peru by setting my sights too high. I didn't sign up for any shamanic retreats or spiritually-focused tours, and after Brian's happy pizza incident, I'd definitely ruled out the whole *ayahuasca* thing. I figured if this sacred region was meant to have a sacred effect on me, then it would unfold on its own. I didn't need to force it with a group meditation or a psychedelic episode.

Such was my attitude on the day we visited Machu Picchu, one of the most mystical places on the planet. I went with an open heart and an open mind, but left those preconceived notions of spiritual discovery behind.

Despite its divine reputation, visiting Machu Picchu turned out to be a highly-orchestrated logistical process. We had to purchase our tickets a week in advance, since only a limited number of visitors could enter the site each day. Then we booked an extremely expensive train ride to Aguas Calientes, the town sitting at the base of Machu Picchu mountain. Finally, we had to find a taxi driver willing to pick us up at an ungodly hour and get us to the train on time. Perhaps it was all this scheduling and coordination that put me in a rather pragmatic mindset as we made our way to this spiritual place.

When we arrived in Aguas Calientes, the intensity of its touristy-ness was a bit of a shock to the system. I'd imagined an authentic rural town with quaint markets and quiet streets, like the ones we'd come to know in Urubamba. Aguas Calientes was the opposite. Stepping off the train, we were accosted by a maze of vendor booths targeting tourists with every trinket and souvenir imaginable, from cheap key chains manufactured in China to intricate wooden sculptures priced in the thousands of dollars. Restaurants, hotels, bars, and coffee shops lined the streets, which were already packed with tourists by 8:00 a.m. After our days in a quiet Peruvian village, visiting Machu Picchu felt a trip to Disneyland.

This theme-park feel continued as we took a shuttle bus up a winding road of switchbacks and arrived at the Machu Picchu entrance. Long lines, organized with crowd control ropes, led us slowly up the steps to a team of ticket takers armed with clipboards and walkie-talkies. When it was our turn at the ticket booth, a staff member compared our tickets to our passports, making it seem like we were boarding an international flight rather than entering the ruins of an ancient city.

But then, everything changed as we walked up the stone path and Machu Picchu came into view. Set against a backdrop of green undulating hills, the terraced city is truly a wonder of the world. Its construction required the Inca to completely reshape a mountain, haul in millions of tons of boulders, and design complicated water diversion systems. As we walked along walls set with perfectly-aligned stones, our family embraced the architectural magnificence of the ancient city.

"My god," Brian said in amazement as he ran his hand across the smooth boulders, perfectly fitted together, like enormous 3D puzzle pieces. "Look at what humans can do when they put their minds to it . . . beautiful."

We navigated the paths in the central village of Machu Picchu, turning into the ruins of ancient homes and walking through the rectangular meadows, which served as playing fields for Incan sporting events. We eventually made our way onto a trail leading out of the city. Looking behind us, we could see the full panorama of the ruins, with lines of terraced fields descending down both sides of the mountain and the pinnacle peak of Huayna Picchu looming above it all. After about thirty minutes of walking, we arrived at the Sun Gate, the remains of a stone building where guards once checked Inca citizens in and out of the city. In this quiet place, far away from the crowds, I decided to meditate for a while. I wanted to see if the reputed spiritual power of Machu Picchu would have any effect on me.

As usual, meditating meant letting a myriad of thoughts stream through my brain first. I had to let the clutter clear out before a peaceful calm could occupy the space within my mind. I sat on a stone wall, looking out over the ruins and remembering what I'd learned about them.

An explorer named Hiram Bingham had rediscovered the area in 1911. He'd been leading an archeological expedition on a search for the lost city of Vilcabamba, when a local man told him about some extensive ruins high up on a nearby mountain. The village people called the place Machu Picchu, which meant "old mountain" in Quechua. When Bingham and his colleagues hiked up to it, they encountered some peasants who'd been living in a hut and farming the terraced fields around the ruins. A young boy led the explorers around his homeland, and showed them the Incan stonework hidden beneath hundreds of years of jungle growth. He'd probably been amused at their excited reactions to something he found so normal. Something that had been there his entire life.

I closed my eyes and slipped into that peaceful space where the world seemed to fall away and a numb, tingling sensation danced across my skin. I focused on my breath and my heartbeat and the warm breeze on my face. Colors began swirling behind my closed eyelids, and I listened intently to the sounds floating on the air. The rustling of leaves. Soft footsteps on the stones. The wind whistling in the trees. Soon, a few quiet words whispered through my mind.

It's been here all along . . .

I took a deep breath and heard it again.

It's been here all along . . .

And again.

It's been here all along . . .

Suddenly a tickle on my right hand snapped me back to reality. My eyes popped open, and I looked down to see a tiny insect walking across the center of my palm, meandering toward my thumb. I didn't wave it away. I just watched its little iridescent wings waddling along.

And I waited for something.

After a moment, that something came.

It was a story I'd once heard about a young woman seeking spiritual enlightenment. She was an American yoga instructor who'd been following the teachings of a Hindi guru. For years, she'd studied and meditated, feeling each day she was getting closer to her divine purpose, yet never quite reaching it. Finally, she decided to travel to India on a pilgrimage to see her guru in person. After a long journey, she arrived at his ashram, along with hundreds of other pilgrims. He was seated under a colorful canopy on a platform surrounded by offerings of fresh flowers. Following the lead of the other pilgrims, the woman reverently approached the guru, knelt in front of him, and brought her head down to the blossom-covered ground at his feet. She sat in this position waiting for the enlightenment she sought, hoping his presence would give her the insight she so desperately wanted to find.

And then, she began to feel it. It started as a mild numbness in the middle of her forehead on the spot known as the Third Eye, an energy center in the body believed to be the gateway to higher consciousness. *This is it*, the woman thought with excitement. *It's finally happening to me.* A rush of energy coursed through her, and in a flash, everything she'd ever questioned transformed into a wave of understanding. She felt overwhelming love, a blissful feeling of surrender to a sacred connection. Tears welled in her eyes as the warmth of her newfound enlightenment spread across her face and neck. *Thank you, thank you, thank you*, she repeated to herself.

After a few moments in this heavenly state, the numb feeling in her head morphed into a powerful, stinging sensation. She took a few breaths and tried to accept it, but the pain became worse and worse. Finally, she couldn't take it anymore. She sat up to rub the burning spot on her forehead and felt something drop into her hand. A bee was squirming on her palm. She stared at it for a moment and touched the welt swelling up between her eyes. Then, the woman laughed out loud as another wave of understanding flowed through every cell of her body. Kneeling in front of her guru hadn't brought this rush of enlightenment. The deep, universal understanding had been with her all along. She simply had to stop longing for something she already had inside her.

It's been here all along . . .

We have all of it with us all the time. The answers we seek, the peace we hope to find, the divine purpose we're meant to live. The patience and love and creativity and courage. We don't have to go searching for any of it. We simply need to pull back the vines on those parts of our souls covered up by dense jungle foliage, so we can rediscover the beauty we've hidden away from the world.

"There's something I want to do, but I think it might freak you out a little," I said.

Brian raised one eyebrow provocatively. "I'm intrigued."

I rolled my eyes. "Get your mind out of the gutter. It's not that."

He feigned disappointment, then smiled.

"I want to go somewhere on my own," I said. "I want to take the bus out to Lake Titicaca and stay there for a couple days."

"Okay," he replied. "Is this supposed to freak me out?"

"I don't know, I just figured you wouldn't love the idea of me traveling alone."

Brian laughed and shook his head. "Trace, one thing I know with absolute certainty is that you can handle yourself anywhere. I'm not worried."

"Okay, then. I'm going to book it for later this week. You and the girls will be on your own."

"That's fine with me. Luckily, we won't starve since we have access to take-out food now," he said with a smirk.

A few days earlier, we'd left our remote little village in the Sacred Valley and moved into an apartment in the heart of Cusco. Our lovely glass house got too cold for us, so we found a two-bedroom apartment in the city with easy access to the historic sites and a better heating system.

Cusco was saturated with evidence of Inca architecture and traditions. Spanish colonial churches and government buildings had been built on the stones of ancient foundations, their perfectly-joined masonry creating the walls of the alleyways around the main square. Narrow streets paved with cobblestones slanted precipitously up from the city center and led to picturesque courtyards with fountains and little craft markets. A maze of staircases snaked its way through neighborhoods built into the hillside, with little dirt trails veering off from the steps and leading to rows of houses.

On the morning of my trip to Lake Titicaca, I crept out of our silent apartment before dawn and got a taxi to the bus station. Eight hours later, I arrived in Puno, a large town squeezed in between the shores of Lake Titicaca and the hills surrounding it. I took a cab to the hotel I'd booked for my stay, but when I arrived they gave me some bad news. They'd given my room away.

"¿Por qué? Tengo una reservación," I said. I'd even confirmed my reservation with a credit card.

The man shrugged, pointed to his watch, and said, "Es tarde."

"What? It's four o' clock! That's not late," I said in English. My Spanish skills often went out the window when I was irritated.

The man stepped away from the counter and came back with a woman who spoke English. "I am so very sorry for this problem," she said calmly. "We can arrange for you to stay at another hotel in town. It is a bit more expensive, but they will give you a discount for your trouble. You will like it. It is very nice."

The taxi drove me to the outskirts of Puno and turned onto a causeway leading out to a small island. We curved up a hill and through the trees to arrive at the lustrous front entrance of the Libertador Hotel. With the sun beginning to set, the building's white exterior and tall windows reflected a soft shade of pink. I paid the driver and walked up the steps into a sleek, modern lobby with white walls reaching up to wood plank ceilings. Tall windows running along the east side of the hotel offered an unobstructed view of Lake Titicaca as the sunset cast millions of sparkles over the water. My little solo retreat was turning out to be a lot more luxurious than I'd anticipated.

The next morning, after stuffing myself at the gourmet breakfast, I walked down to the island's dock with some of the other guests and boarded a boat that would take us out onto the lake. I stood on the boat's upper deck feeling the cold morning air nip at my cheeks as we glided through a narrow corridor in the tall reeds. These were called totora reeds, our guide told us, and they were used extensively by the Uros people we'd be visiting that morning. The Uros not only build their homes, furniture, and boats with the reeds, but they also use them to construct the islands they live on. Hundreds of years ago, their ancestors figured out an ingenious way to avoid the expanding Incan Empire and later the Spanish conquistadors. By tying the reeds together, detaching them from their roots, and then laying meters of cut reeds over the top, the Uros architected the little islets they called home.

By the time we arrived in the Uros community, the sun's rays had warmed up the day. Our boat pulled up to one of the islands, and when we stepped onto it our feet disappeared into the spongy layers of crisscrossed reeds. Our guide translated as an Uros family gave a short talk about their island home and the traditions of their people. While it seemed a little contrived and overly touristy, the locals seemed authentic in their love for their lifestyle and heritage. As we boarded our boat again, I began thinking about this community's ability to maintain their way of life as the modern world changed around them.

We skimmed over crystal clear blue water on the way to our next stop—Taquile Island. Our guide's voice came over the boat's speaker system to tell us we were nearing the border between Peru and Bolivia, which cut through the middle of the lake. "If you look straight ahead you will see the Bolivian Andes mountains on the other side of Lake Titicaca," his voice announced.

I stared across the water and felt the grief slide down my shoulders. Every time I thought of Bolivia, my mind went straight to the horrible day we learned of Reuben's death.

"You're lookin' awful sad on an awful pretty day," a deep voice said. I looked over and saw an older gentleman standing nearby, his large forearms leaning back against the railing of the boat's upper deck. He extended one hand toward me. "I'm Dave."

I shook his hand and smiled, happy to have a distraction from my sad thoughts. "I'm Tracey. Where are you from, Dave? Your accent sounds familiar."

"North Georgia, born and raised."

I nodded. "I lived in Chattanooga for about nine years."

"Well, heck, we're neighbors then! Small world!"

"We don't live there anymore, but we liked it. It's a beautiful area."

"You here with your family?" he asked.

"No, actually, for once they aren't with me. My husband and kids are back in Cusco. I came out here for a solo trip."

"Little break for Mom?" he asked with a wink.

"Something like that."

"Well, that's pretty adventurous of ya. I can't imagine my wife ever travelin' in a foreign country on her own. You guys live in Cusco?"

"No, we're just staying there for now. We're kind of . . . on this . . . around-the-world trip thing. We live in different countries for a while."

"No kiddin'? How long you been traveling for?"

"Um, I guess we're coming up on a year and a half now."

"Hot damn!" Dave leaned over the railing and shouted below. "Debbie! Hey, Deb, get on up here, honey! I got a lady here you need to meet!" He turned back to me. "So how many kids you got? How old are they?"

"We have three girls. They're eleven, nine, and six."

"And you've been travelin' around the world with them for a year and a half? I'll be damned, that's amazin'. How many countries you been to?"

"I think we're at about twenty-two or twenty-three, maybe. But some of them we only visited for a few days."

He slapped his leg and shook his head. "Holy shit, that's the craziest thing I ever heard. I love it!"

An attractive older woman I presumed to be Debbie emerged from the boat's circular staircase and walked up to stand next to Dave. He put a beefy arm around her and said, "Honey, you gotta hear this. This lady and her husband have been travelin' with their three kids for almost *two* years and they've been to *dozens* of countries."

And so began my stint as the pseudo-celebrity guest speaker of our little tour group. As we disembarked from the boat and walked up a hill to the village, Dave, Debbie, and others peppered me with questions about our trip. Where we'd been, which places we liked the best, how our daughters had handled it, how we found housing and health insurance and volunteer work. This nomadic life of ours had come to feel normal. It was strange talking about it with people who found our travels so intriguing.

In the village, we walked among a people who lived as their ancestors had lived, most of them never leaving their island home. The men all wore long cloth hats, the color and position indicating their age and romantic status. We learned that three months before a young couple was married, the woman would cut off her long black hair and weave it into a wide belt, which she gave to her husband as a wedding present. These traditions had gone on for centuries. The only change in recent years had been the daily appearance of a few dozen tourists, who'd come onto the island to eat lunch, take photos, and buy some handcrafted souvenirs. The recent tourism had been a boon for the Taquileans' local economy, but it had little impact on their way of life.

When we returned to the hotel that afternoon, I'd planned to find the hiking trail circling the island, but a fog rolled in and the sky began streaming down a steady drizzle. I decided to trade in my hike for a glass of wine by the lobby's fireplace. I was tucked into an armchair reading when I heard a familiar southern accent.

"Well, hello there!" Dave called out as he and Debbie walked through the lobby. "Long time no see. Whatcha drinkin'?"

"Oh . . . uh, Sauvignon Blanc," I said.

"That's Deb's drink, too. I'll be right back." As he strode off toward the bar, Debbie sat down gracefully on the chair across from me.

"He's buyin' ya a drink, whether ya want one or not," she said with a grin.

"That's nice of him," I replied, closing my book.

"He can't stop talkin' about your family's trip. He's a little envious, I think." She watched him walk up to the bar and start chatting with the bartender. "Dave's always been the adventurous one. He would've loved to take our boys on a journey like yours, but I suppose I'm the cautious balance to his wild heart. I tell him he married me just to keep himself alive." She let out a breezy laugh and placed an elbow on the arm of the chair, letting her chin rest elegantly on the tips of her fingers. Everything about her oozed gentility. She tilted her head to one side and asked, "How long is this journey of yours gonna last, darlin'?"

I took a deep breath. "I don't know. My husband and I have been talking about that lately. At one point, we thought we'd be in the US for the start of the school year, but that's just a couple weeks away and we don't have tickets back yet. So . . . " I shrugged. "We don't know what we're doing."

"Do you want to go back? Don't you miss your life at home?"

My eyes went past Debbie to the large window behind her. The darkness outside created a mirror, leaving only my reflection looking back at me from the glass.

"Yes and no, I guess," I said quietly. "I mean, we miss our families. The girls haven't seen their grandparents since we left, so that can be hard at times. And I miss having a home. You know, a place that's really ours. But . . . " I paused for a moment, then shook my head. "No, I don't miss the life we had before."

Debbie gave me a quizzical look and waited for me to go on.

"We were just . . . so damn *busy*. Always going, going, going, running from one thing to the next." The words tumbled from my lips in a flurry of reawakened frustration. "I was working these crazy long hours and waking up in the night remembering some email I needed to send or a report I needed to update, and then I couldn't go back to sleep until I'd gotten up and done it. And we had our girls in all these activities, so when I wasn't working it felt like I spent most of my time in the car, driving all over town to get them to soccer or dance or art class or whatever else I'd signed them up for. And I was trying to make the house perfect all the time, for some crazy reason. Like I thought *Southern Living* was going to walk in for a photo shoot at any moment."

Debbie laughed and gave me a sympathetic look.

I shook my head and continued. "I just never felt totally relaxed. Ever. I was constantly thinking about the next thing I had to do. The next meeting. The next errand. The next house chore. One day, my husband and I realized our life had become this big, messy, stressful . . . blur."

Debbie smiled. "Well, everyone sort of feels like that, sugar," she said. "Life gets crazy. That's just part of being a young family."

"Is it, though? I mean, does it really have to be?" I looked at my reflection again as the memories of our busy American life rolled through my head. "I didn't really know my kids when we were that family. Hell, I didn't even know myself. We were so caught up in chasing something, but we never stopped to ask what exactly we were chasing . . . or *why* we were chasing it."

"Well, it sounds to me like you did stop to ask yourself that," Debbie said. "Otherwise you wouldn't be on this trip, would you?"

I nodded. "Yes, that's true. That's the reason we did this." I took a deep breath and braced myself to speak the words I'd been holding back for months. "And that's why I'm scared to go home. I'm afraid as soon as we settle into a normal life again, we'll lose everything we've gained from this experience. We'll get sucked right back into the rat race. All that keeping up with the Joneses. Stretching too far for the next rung of the ladder. Before we know it, we'll be back right where we started. Stressed and overscheduled and just . . . *chasing.*"

Saying the words, I felt that tightness in my chest again. The one that would grip me every time I thought about going home. Finally, I knew what it was. It was fear. Fear of losing the balance we'd finally found. Fear of letting go of the relationships we'd built with one another. Fear of forgetting the woman I'd become.

I looked at Debbie, this woman I barely knew, and let the words spill out like a confession. "What if I go back and forget everything I've learned about myself on this journey?"

Debbie leaned forward and looked me in the eye. "Honey, I realize I just met you, but I'm very good at knowin' people. And I'm telling you, you are not the kind of person who's goin' to forget who you are."

My eyes instantly filled with tears and I let out a half-laugh half-sob. "Sorry . . . I just . . ." I wiped at my eyes and nodded, feeling the truth of her words. "Yes, thank you . . . you're right. I won't forget."

Debbie leaned forward and patted my knee. "Don't you be scared to go home, honey. It's just the next part of your family's adventure."

I wanted to reach out and hug her. Wrap my love around this woman who'd given me exactly what I'd needed at the exact moment I needed it.

"Alrighty, here we go!" Dave's voice boomed from above us. His fingers were wrapped around three glasses, two with white wine and one with an amber liquid. Debbie and I reached up and took a wine glass from him.

"What're we talkin' about, ladies?" he asked as he eased himself into the chair next to Debbie's.

She gave me a wink and raised her glass in a toast. "Darlin', we're talking about new adventures."

The next morning, I woke up before dawn and went out to watch the sunrise. I sat on a bench overlooking the lake and shivered in the cold, still air, watching the fog from my breath float out into the darkness. The horizon slowly brightened, painting the soft puffy clouds with pastels, and soon the sun's golden rays shot across the lake. The air instantaneously warmed, and I peeled off my jacket before walking down a hill to the hiking trail circling the island. The path curved along the shoreline and wrapped around enormous boulders, some of them so tall and narrow they resembled soldiers standing at attention. I climbed onto a large, flat rock and looked out over the reeds of the shallows to the glistening waters beyond.

You are not the kind of person who's going to forget who you are.

As Debbie's words floated through my mind, I closed my eyes and smiled into the warmth of the sun. I thought about going home, and this time the tightness in my chest never came. That fear was gone, because I knew she was right. Our family's adventure had forever changed me.

Or maybe it had simply helped me remember who I really was. The separate inner voice I'd once had in my head was different now. Observer Tracey had lost her judgmental edge and let go of her scathing criticisms. She seemed to have blended into the core of my being, helping me find my center, look for life's lesson, and use those lessons to feed my soul.

This was the honesty Reuben had talked about. It was what he'd meant that day when he'd said happiness came down to being honest with yourself and the world. No more mask. No more self-judgment. No more resisting those aspects of life deemed to be frustrating or unfair. Just the easy authenticity that comes with complete and total acceptance of everything and everyone, including me. I'd learned how to connect with my higher self, maybe not all the time, but enough to remember what it felt like. Enough to know the difference. And Debbie was right. I would never, ever forget.

WHY HELLO, DYSENTERY

Friends and family: 9

Inspirational tour guides: 1

Fecal colors: 11

Hospital visits: One too many

NICARAGUA

After I returned from my weekend at Lake Titicaca, Brian and I sat down for a big discussion about our family's future. We'd already made plans to meet friends in Nicaragua, but we were uncertain what would come after that. Would we go to more countries in Latin America? Maybe even make a quick visit to the US and then head out to Europe again to continue the journey? We kept stalling on deciding what we should do next, and admittedly, I was the primary cause for the procrastination. That tense fear in my chest had led me to avoid any discussion of going home. Until now.

"I'm ready for it be over," I said to him my first night back. The girls were in bed, and Brian and I were sitting on the couch sharing a bottle of wine. "I've had a fear of ending this because I felt like we'd get sucked back into that rat race we were in." I reached up to his hand on the back of the couch and laced my fingers through his. "But I think we're stronger than that."

He smiled and looked at me for a long moment before gently pulling me into his chest. "I'm ready, too. I'm ready to see what this new version of us can do back in the real world." He kissed the top of my head as I leaned against him, feeling a relaxed confidence flow through me.

It's time to go home.

The next day, we booked our plane tickets to the United States. Our family would spend a month at a house in Granada, Nicaragua, with different groups of friends and family coming down to stay with us. After the month ended, we'd fly back and start rebuilding our American life.

It turned out I didn't have to do much planning for this last leg of our journey. Our friends had offered to take the lead on booking a rental house for all of us, and after eighteen months as the designated travel agent, I happily handed over the role. We combined our funds and wound up renting a gorgeous place with a garden, a pool, and even a housekeeper. The day we arrived, our first set of visitors greeted us at the door.

"Maddie!" Emily squealed at the top of her lungs as she threw her arms around her best friend. The two of them immediately dissolved into giggles in their giddiness over seeing each other again. Within seconds, Maddie and her little brother, Benji, had disappeared into the house with our girls.

Jay and Emily Perry, longtime friends from Chattanooga, helped haul our bags into the home's open courtyard, where flowering tropical plants surrounded the pool and crept up the garden's stone wall. Plush patio furniture, woven hammocks, and a massive dining table sat beneath the red tile roof surrounding the courtyard. Ornate wooden doors opened to high-ceilinged bedroom suites, each with its own air-conditioning unit and private bathroom.

"Nice work finding this place, Em," Brian said as the adults settled into patio chairs and the kids splashed in the pool. "This house is amazing."

"Yeah, it's working out really well so far," Em said. "We got here the day before yesterday and the location is fantastic. Everything in Granada is in walking distance."

"It's perfect," I said. "And I can't thank you enough for doing the work to find it."

"I figured you'd done your share of travel planning for a while."

I laughed. "Yeah, you can say that again."

"How many places have you guys stayed in on this trip of yours?" Jay asked.

"Including this one, we're at seventy-nine," I said.

He shook his head. "Damn, that's a lot of work."

"Yep," I nodded. "I can assure you, looking for housing is definitely one thing I *won't* miss about traveling."

"Yeah, but think of all the other stuff you have to do," Jay said. He stuck out one hand and began ticking things off on his fingers. "Get a car, find a house, get your storage unit, move in, start the kids in school . . . Have you guys even decided where you want to live when you get back?"

"Jay, please stop," I said in warning tone. "I'd rather take the head-in-the-sand approach for the time being. Just let me enjoy my beer, okay?"

He flashed me an ornery smile. "Don't you have to change your health insurance, too? And you sold all your furniture, right? So, you basically have to buy everything new. And how does all this travel affect your income taxes?"

"Oh my god!" I yelled, grabbing a throw pillow and tossing it at his head. "You're evil!"

He threw me a wink and took a swig from his beer. "You guys might be all worldly and evolved after this trip of yours, but I'm still the same old Jay."

I rolled my eyes and laughed. "Yeah, I noticed."

It was good to be with old friends again.

I decided to avoid the overpriced modern supermarket in town and instead took my friend Em to Granada's main *mercado*. When we stepped into the pungent labyrinth of booths, my eyes methodically scanned the cluttered aisles looking for vendors selling the things I needed. I examined yucca root, picked out whole trout, and got into a friendly debate with one vendor over which mangos were ripe. When I stopped to buy a bag of chicken claws in the meat aisle, I noticed Em staring at me with an amused look on her face.

"What?" I asked.

She shook her head and smiled. "You're just . . . different. I mean, you're buying chicken feet, Trace."

"They're for making broth," I said defensively.

"No, I get it. It's just kind of amazing how comfortable you are with all of this." Em opened her arms and gestured to the chaos around us. "This place is definitely not a typical trip to the grocery store, you know?"

I looked around for a moment and saw the market through her eyes. The dark, cramped, low-ceilinged booths with filthy, sticky floors. The flies buzzing around us and landing on the food. Plucked chickens hanging on hooks and pyramids of glassy-eyed fish. I tried to remember at what point this had become normal to me.

"Yeah, I guess it's a little overwhelming at first," I said.

She laughed and put an arm around me. "Luckily, I have you to do our shopping for us."

Em and I settled into easy roles for the two weeks they were with us. I handled most of the shopping and cooking, and she took the lead on researching excursions for our families. She found a tour business just a couple doors down from our house, and when she told the manager we'd be there for a month with a rotation of different guests coming through, he gave us some big discounts on scenic trips around the area. Every few days we were off somewhere exploring. Hiking around Masaya Volcano. Zip lining through the rain forest. Boating around the little islands in Lake Nicaragua.

As new groups of friends and relatives arrived and departed from the house, our family repeated the tours, seeing the same thing but with different people on a different day. Usually, no matter where we were going or who we were with, we were being led by our favorite guide, Mario.

When we first met him, I had no idea what an inspiring man Mario would turn out to be. As he led us up steep, sandy volcano hikes and down into rocky caves filled with bats, he didn't seem any different from the other guides bringing tourists to the parks around Granada. But as we got to know him, we learned Mario had a unique and inspiring story.

"To learn English is very important in Nicaragua," Mario told me one day during a drive out to Laguna de Apoyo, a crater lake formed from an extinct volcano. "From the time I am a boy, I want to learn because with English I can work with tourists. Tourist work pays much more money, but it is very hard. No English in our schools. I must teach myself."

"You taught yourself English? That sounds impossible," I said, thinking back to our classes with Felipe.

"Well, a good thing happened to help me learn it," Mario said. "I got very, very sick." He laughed at my confused expression before explaining. "You see, three years ago, I have pain in my leg and it is very . . . how do you say it . . . big."

"Swollen?"

"Yes, very swollen. So, I go to a doctor and he tells me it is a tumor. A cancer tumor. He must cut it. But here in Nicaragua, we do not have much hospitals. I wait months for the operation. And the tumor grows more big and more big. To walk is very difficult. My family has a farm. The work is not possible for me. Then, one day, I decide a very important thing. I decide God gives me this tumor. I must create good from it. So, I learn English. A friend give me English books and CDs and every day I sit and I study and study and study. Soon, my English is good." He smiled proudly.

"But what about your leg? How long did you have to wait for your surgery?" I asked.

"Eight months," Mario said. "The tumor is very big, but I have no fear. I am excited and I am very grateful because now I can have a good job with the tourists." He unconsciously rubbed his leg, and I noticed for the first time how thin his thigh was under his jeans. "After the operation, it is very hard because the doctors take much of my muscle. But, this is no problem. I am so happy with my English. And because I am happy, my body heal very fast and I start this job."

I shook my head in amazement. "That's incredible, Mario," I said. "I have two normal, healthy legs and these hikes you've taken us on are still challenging for me."

"Yes, it is very hard in beginning," Mario said with a shrug. "Some days, I have much pain. But now this leg is strong. Even stronger than before. *I* am stronger. I can tell you, my life is better because of my cancer. Without it, I do not have my English. My tumor is a blessing for me." Mario paused and smiled. "God will always give us what we need. We must have faith and see the goodness in everything . . . even in things we believe to be bad."

We got to know Mario a little better with each tour we took. When he learned we were interested in volunteering, he invited us to help at the youth English class he taught through his church.

"It will be good for my students to hear your American accents," he said. "You will like them. They are very fun, but . . . I think your daughters stay at your house with your friends. It is not dangerous for gringos in my village, but maybe not very safe."

Not entirely sure what to make of his paradoxical comment, Brian and I decided it couldn't be that bad or else he wouldn't have invited us. One evening Mario and his friend, Miguel, picked the two of us up for the drive out to their village church. I sat in the cab of the truck with Miguel, while Mario and Brian rode in the open bed. Soon we'd left the paved streets of the town and were winding along dark, dirt roads lined with small shacks and chicken-wire fences.

As we approached a stop sign, Miguel pointed ahead and said to me in Spanish, "Very dangerous here. I do not stop." He slowed down as we came to the intersection and, seeing no other cars, hit the gas pedal to speed through it. Then he glanced over at my nervous expression and smiled reassuringly. "Do not worry. Church is safe."

It was a reminder that, despite our house's location in the tourist-filled safety of Granada, the country of Nicaragua was still plagued by the high crime rates accompanying war and widespread poverty.

After a half hour of driving, Miguel pulled the truck up to a large concrete pavilion with a rusty metal roof. A wooden stage at one end held a podium and several small amplifiers. Stacks of plastic chairs lined the walls. A large, ornate cross had been mounted behind the stage.

Mario began the class by introducing us as the "special gringo guests," and then we spent two hours speaking English with a dozen Nicaraguan teenagers. We discussed favorite foods, family members, job aspirations, and other topics covered in the evening's vocabulary lesson. Brian and I tried to enunciate and speak slowly, but Mario still had to help the students understand our accents.

As I watched him with his class, I thought back on my conversation with Mario about his cancer. *We must have faith and see the goodness in everything . . . even in things we believe to be bad.* Although I'd come to believe in this perspective, I hadn't mastered it like he had. I could certainly see the value of life's hurdles in hindsight, but to find something good in a frightening situation like cancer? That kind of wisdom requires a unique faith.

Listening to the laughter of Mario and his students, I felt a familiar serenity wrap around me, sliding a delicious numbness down my shoulders and across my skin. This kind, simple man exuded optimism and hope in every word he said. Being around him felt like reaching enlightenment by osmosis. Our perspectives form our thoughts, our thoughts shape our actions, and our actions create our reality. Only when we accept this truth can we embrace every hurdle we encounter in life with gratitude. I let my brain swim in this blissful mindset as I laughed at the students' jokes and answered their questions about life in the United States.

Soon Mario brought the class to a close and gave out the weekly homework assignment. We helped him stack the chairs while saying good-bye to the students, and walked out of the pavilion under a canopy of stars. I looked up into the sky and took in a deep breath of warm, humid air, the organic scents of farmland lacing through my nostrils.

Then suddenly, out of nowhere, a dark thought flashed through my brain, shooting a cold jolt down my limbs. It reverberated in my ears like a record scratch sound effect and stopped me in my tracks.

"You coming, Trace?" Brian was already in the back of the truck with Mario.

"Yeah . . . I'm coming." My voice sounded heavy and hollow.

I walked across the dirt parking lot to the truck, feeling a weight of sadness pressing against my shoulders. When I climbed into the front seat, Brian leaned over the door and gave me a concerned look. "You okay, babe?"

I nodded and closed the door. But I wasn't okay. All my sanctimonious, one-with-the-universe musings dissolved, replaced with the angry contradiction now barreling through my brain. And it changed everything.

What about Reuben? How could anything good ever come from the world losing a man like Reuben Summerlin?

After our night at Mario's English class, I teetered on the edge of anxiety. As we began our last week in Nicaragua, the serene confidence I'd found on this journey began to crumble, with little threads of uncertainty snaking their way through my synapses. All that accepting the world as it is and having faith in the unfolding of life as a beautiful tapestry . . . . It was all a lie when I held it up to the tragedy of losing Reuben Summerlin to a careless driver.

Two months after the accident, I'd finally admitted how his death contradicted everything I'd come to believe. I'd been subconsciously pushing the conflict away, hoping it would leave me alone and let me go on living in the blissful little philosophical bubble I'd created for myself.

But now the bubble had popped.

On top of this transcendent turmoil, I was dealing with the logistics of our return to the United States. When Brian and I weren't entertaining the family and friends visiting us in Granada, we were researching cars and housing markets. Just like Jay said, I had to figure out what to do with our storage unit, how to change our health insurance, and how to account for foreign-earned income in consecutive, partial tax years. The endless list of items on the to-do list made me want to climb into bed, pull up the covers, and sleep through it all. I'd left the United States an uptight, overscheduled yuppie, and now I seemed to be returning as a disillusioned, apathetic hippie.

"Going back is turning out to be more work than it was to leave," I said to Brian one night as we lay in bed. A cool breeze blasted out of the AC unit above us and drowned out the noise on the lively street outside our window.

"Yep. But we'll get through it. It'll all work out."

"Maybe we should go back to that option of visiting all the grandparents for a few weeks and then heading out to Europe again," I said. "You know, just make another loop around the planet for old times' sake?"

He laughed into the darkness. "Just be wandering nomads for the rest of lives, huh?" He turned onto his side and squeezed my hand. "Don't stress out, Trace. It'll all come together. We just have to take it one step at a time."

I knew he was right. But I felt overwhelmed and disillusioned, and I was mourning Reuben's death all over again.

This is the crux of spiritual growth. It's a very two-steps-forward-one-step-back process. At least, that's the way it seemed to work for me. I would experience several weeks of euphoric highs and easy clarity, only to follow them with a confounding low period. And this time, it was serious. I could feel myself sliding down into a pit of spiritual despair. I tried to claw my way out of it, putting on a happy face and laughing with our friends and family, but that panicked me even more. I was turning back into the woman I'd once been, the one who looked so confident and put-together on the outside, but struggled through confusion and insecurities on the inside.

My eighteen months of spiritual growth seemed to be unraveling before my eyes. The age-old question we humans have wrestled with for millennia had finally blocked my enlightened path, and I couldn't find my way around it.

Why do horrible things happen to good people?

No matter how much I meditated or practiced yoga or searched for the value in life's hurdles, this was the cruel reality I knew I could never accept. It was the spiritual lesson I simply couldn't learn.

But then one day, a good thing happened to help me learn it. I got very, very sick.

It started off as a headache. Within a couple hours, the rest of my body hurt and I had a high fever. At first, I thought it was the flu, but then I remembered I was in Central America and it could be something much worse. Dengue fever or the chikungunya virus or even malaria. I lay in bed miserable, both physically and mentally, as I worried over the prospect of being seriously ill in a developing country. When my stomach began cramping and I was forced to take up residence in the bathroom, I actually breathed a sigh of relief.

This is probably just food poisoning. Something I ate. It'll be over in a few hours. No big deal.

But after two days of constant misery, it was a big deal. I was a sweaty, putrid, writhing mess. I couldn't leave the toilet for more than a few minutes, so I wound up lying on the floor next to it in a pathetic heap. When we'd first arrived at this house, I remembered thinking the bathroom was a little weird—a yellow tiled room with a toilet at one end and a slanted floor leading to a shower head and drain at the other. No curtain or barrier to keep the water in the shower. Just one continuous plane of tile. As I lay there in misery, I finally appreciated the ingenuity of this unusual design. This was a bathroom perfectly constructed for food poisoning victims. I could splay myself across the floor half-naked, with my ass near the drain and the moveable shower hose within arms' reach. Easy cleanup.

I spent most of my time staring at the bathroom's tiled walls and replaying movies in my head. Brat Pack eighties flicks, Oscar winners, classics from the forties. It was an effective strategy for keeping my mind off the cold sweats and abdominal cramps, much better than just lying there anxiously awaiting the next wave of torture. Scenes from *Dazed and Confused* were rolling across my mind's eye when a quiet knock echoed around the bathroom.

"Babe?" Brian's voice said. "Are you okay?"

That's so weird. My husband kind of sounds like Matthew McConaughey.

Brian knocked again. "Trace? Can I come in?"

"No!" I yelled. *Don't let him see you like this! The man watched you push three babies out of your vagina, for God's sake! He's seen enough grossness out of you for one lifetime.* "No, don't come in! Please. I'm fine, Brian." I tried to sound less miserable than I was. "I just want to be alone, okay?"

"Do you need anything? Can I get you some more water?"

"I have water."

"But are you drinking it? I brought it to you hours ago."

"Yes. I'm trying."

"You can't get dehydrated, Trace. You have to keep drinking."

"I will. I am."

"Is there anything I can do for you?"

"No, Brian. Please just leave me alone."

"Alright. But don't lock this door, okay? I need to be able get to you if you need me."

"Okay."

Soon after he left, the next wave started. I knew the routine at this point. First, the beads of sweat popped out on my forehead, and then my heart began to pound in my ears. I started crawling toward the toilet just as the cramps hit. Knowing I only had a few seconds before the volcanic eruption began, I moved as fast my weak body would go. On this round, I managed to make it onto the toilet in time. Progress.

When it was over, I crawled back down onto the cool tile and relished the brief euphoric relief coming right after one of these horrible episodes. I lay there staring at a decorative tile stuck halfway up the wall. Amid the bathroom's plain mustard yellow squares, a few ornately-painted ones had been placed in random spots. This one showed a woman with a basket on her head, standing next to two large arched doorways. For some reason, it brought to mind a British film I'd seen years ago called *Sliding Doors*, so I closed my eyes and tried to recall the opening scenes.

Gwyneth Paltrow's character goes to work, gets fired, and misses a subway train as she's trying to get home. Then, the scene does a fast rewind and replays, but this time she manages to make it onto the train. From that point on, the movie's story line splits, and two versions of the character's life unfold. In one, she misses that train and her life seems to fall apart. In the other, she makes the train and everything keeps getting better. The audience is left to believe that this seemingly insignificant event of missing a commuter train ruined the woman's entire life . . . until the end of the film. And then we see what she would have lost if she hadn't gone through all the pain.

The scenes of Gwyneth and her costars dissolved as dizzying swirls of color began spinning around me. Loud ringing filled my ears and a disorienting vertigo overcame me, tilting the room at odd angles. The sensation kept getting worse and worse, and I felt myself panicking and gasping for breath, trying the grip the slick tiles below me. I couldn't move. I couldn't scream. I could only squeeze my eyes shut and pray for it to end, but the spinning surged, increasing in speed and intensity, like getting sucked into a whirlpool.

Then, a memory from childhood floated to the surface. Being on my elementary school's merry-go-round and relishing the bizarre pull of gravity as I circled around and around. The smiling faces of my friends set against a blurry background while we chanted "Faster! Faster! Faster!" I began to feel a rhythmic pattern in the spinning, with waves of energy coursing through my body at the top of each rotation. I surrendered to it, remembering that weird pleasure in being dizzy and out of control.

And then, it all abruptly stopped. Everything went still and silent. Black and peaceful. What happened next was the most surreal, mysterious experience of my life. Maybe it was dehydration.

Maybe it was a toxin-induced hallucination. Maybe I passed out on that slanted tile floor and fell into a lucid dream. Whatever it was, it felt like a conversation with the divine.

We don't get to see the other story line.

The calm, quiet words seeped into my brain, radiating a warm, numbness at the top of my skull.

We don't have a crystal ball telling us what might have been if things had gone a different way. We may not understand the importance of the events we draw into our lives, but they are there for a reason. It's up to us to use them all for growth.

But why do horrible, tragic things happen? How can anything good come from the evil in the world?

There is no evil. There is only the opportunity we create. Both as individuals and as societies, we draw into our experience what we need to grow. We cannot grow unless we are challenged. Pain, grief, and anger bring us the opportunity for joy, love, and expansion.

No. No, I can't accept that. I refuse to believe Reuben Summerlin's death could create joy and love.

Then you miss the divine purpose of his human experience. Just like his presence, his absence will impact the world in tremendous ways. Reuben's life on Earth was a gift and, whether or not you choose to accept it, his physical death was a gift as well.

But why do some people have to make this sacrifice? Why do some people live long, happy lives and others have to suffer or die young?

Because a single human experience is not all there is. We are part of the collective consciousness and each of our souls understands the role it intended to play when it came into this physical world. Our higher selves know what we are here to learn and what we are meant to teach others. There is no death. There is no real suffering. There is only the end of one perspective into the human experience. Life is energy, and energy cannot be created or destroyed. It only changes form, opening us to the infinite range of universal possibility. All that can exist. Every potential manifestation. In bringing this forth, the human experience expands existence to the next level.

The only question to ask as the events of our lives unfold is this: How is this serving me?

Look for the opportunity you have brought into your experience. Do not simply revel in what you like and condemn what you hate. Seek to understand how all of it can serve you. See the value it brings. Give it the power to take you to a higher level and guide you on the evolutionary path you're meant to follow. Welcome it all with open arms.

The good.

The bad.

The everything.

It is from this state of unconditional allowing that you will create the physical reality your higher self has chosen.

I don't know how long I lay drifting in and out of this surreal place. At some point, the conversation dissolved from words and into waves of understanding. There were no more explanations, just a surrender into acceptance. A primal inner knowing beyond rational thought.

This is faith. I believe in this with everything I am.

And then . . . silence . . . darkness . . . peace.

When I finally opened my eyes, the bright bathroom light beamed down on me like the sun, blinding me for a moment. I blinked and took a deep breath. My skin felt cool and dry. The cramps were gone. My muscles were relaxed.

Slowly and carefully, I stood up and braced my hands against the wall. Once I'd gained confidence in my balance, I slowly peeled off the sweat-soaked T-shirt I'd been wearing for days. With steady hands, I connected the showerhead back to its wall mount and turned on the stream. A jet of cold water blasted my skin, but I didn't flinch. I stood there letting the cascade run down my neck and shoulders, feeling the gradual change as the water warmed to a steamy heat.

When I came out of the bathroom, clean and calm for the first time in what felt like an eternity, it was nighttime. I slipped into bed next to Brian, and he woke with a start.

"Hey," he muttered groggily as he sat up. "Hey, baby, are you okay? Do you need anything?"

"No. I'm fine."

"Is it over?" he asked.

I lay down on my side, sinking into the soft bed and feeling his strong hand move up and down my arm. "I'm not sure it's completely over, but the worst of it is."

"God, I'm so sorry, honey." He curled his body around mine. "I'm so sorry you're going through this."

"It's okay." I could feel the weight of sleep sliding over me like a heavy blanket. "I think I needed this to happen."

"What?"

But I didn't answer. I was too tired to explain the great mysteries of life.

The next day, I visited the hospital in Granada where I was diagnosed with dysentery. As the doctor checked my hydration levels, we engaged in a thorough discussion on the nature and frequency of my bowel movements. Were they yellow? Green? Red? Runny? Foamy? Did they have mucous in them? Did they burn? Was there cramping? Vomiting?

Um, yes. All of the above.

My doctor sent me home with a handful of prescription slips and directions to the nearest pharmacy. Over the next few days, my intestines slowly recovered, but soon other family members fell victim to the microscopic warriors of Nicaragua. Liv went through a shorter version of the digestive onslaught I'd experienced, and I sat in the bathroom with her one night, empathizing through her cramps, cold sweats, and moments of delirium. Emily and Brian had several days of diarrhea, and one evening during dinner Ali projectile vomited all over the table.

So, yeah. Good times.

This is all serving me. This is all serving me. I repeated it to myself like a mantra. I decided my soul had heard me pondering the idea of continuing this trip, and it decided to offer a very loud and clear opinion on the matter. *Oh, so you think it's a good idea to keep traveling, do you? Well, here you go, honey. Maybe some demonic intestinal bacteria will change your tune.* It worked. The more time our family spent in the bathroom, the more excited I was to return to the United States.

On the day before our departure, everyone was feeling good again so we took a trip over to the coast and visited Playa Coco. Brian and I soaked up the sun and sipped on coconuts, while the girls dug in the sand looking for shells.

A few craft booths sat in the shade of some palm trees, so I told the girls they could each buy a little trinket as a souvenir of our time in Nicaragua.

"Not too expensive, though," I said to them. "Your budget is like two or three bucks."

Ali leaned over a table and gently ran her fingers over a necklace made from tiny shells. After admiring it and eying the price tag, my six-year-old looked up at me and asked, "Hey Mama, what's the US exchange rate for Nicaragua?"

PREPARE FOR LANDING

Countries visited: 24

Miles traveled: 65,272

Volunteer projects: 56

New adventures: To be determined

USA

"Ladies and gentlemen, the aircraft will soon begin its descent. At this time, we ask that you stow any carry-on items you may have removed from the overhead compartments. Flight attendants will be coming through the cabin to collect any trash or unwanted items."

Emily and Ali started handing me cups and wrappers without prompting. It was the twenty-seventh time they'd heard this announcement over the course of our journey, so they knew the drill.

Brian leaned up from the aisle seat behind me and gave my arm a squeeze. "Alright, Trace," he said. "You ready for this?"

I smiled at the memory of him saying almost the exact same thing to me when we pulled up to JFK International at the start of this adventure. At the time, I hadn't been sure. Our kids were in various states of psychological turbulence, and we had no idea what to expect from this nomadic life. Back then, I wasn't sure any of us were ready for what lay ahead.

It was a little astounding to think back on everything we'd experienced together. All those exotic places we'd visited and the unique people who'd come in and out of our lives. Some of the most poignant moments floated to the surface of my mind. Watching a security guard chase peacocks in Prague changed my relationship with my daughters. Buying plane tickets for Ebola-ridden Africa dissolved the part of me controlled by other people's opinions. Giving reluctant pediatric medical advice to my neighbor in Thailand helped me let go of judgment and accept people for who they are. Sitting with the Cambodian nun taught me to follow my joy instead of my guilt. Seeing a little girl's life in Bolivia gave me a new understanding of my own. And losing a dear friend challenged everything I'd come to believe.

"Ma'am, her seat needs to be in the upright position." Startled from my thoughts, I looked up to see the flight attendant gesturing to Ali's chair.

I reached over and pushed the recline button, just as Emily turned from the window and said, "Ali, look at those islands down there." She put her arm around her little sister and helped her lean across so she could see out.

I watched the two of them huddle together, then turned to look over the seat at Liv, who was engrossed in the inflight magazine. I tried to imagine what the next few weeks would bring for our girls. Reuniting with grandparents they hadn't seen in so long. Moving to a new town. Unpacking their things in a new home. Settling into new schools.

Our family's return to normalcy would bring our most dramatic transformation yet. As we found a home in the mountains of Colorado, we would realize just how much we'd changed. Our house would be smaller, our possessions fewer, and that hectic schedule packed with activities and obligations would no longer be an option for us. We would stop collecting stuff, and start collecting our stories.

This journey had taught us that happiness would never be found in what we owned or what we accomplished. It couldn't come from the house we lived in or the car we drove or the career success we might someday acquire. The only thing that can bring us true happiness is the current moment we're living in. Life isn't about running around, trying to do all the things that might make us happy at some point in the future. Life is about being happy *right now*. Every minute we spend stressed or worried or frustrated is a lost moment of happiness we can never get back. The key to a happy life is to simply fill up our days with as many happy experiences as possible. Stack up those moments of laughter, joy, bliss, and love until life is overflowing with them. And when we string all those moments together, we'll have lived that happy life we were looking for.

Over those eighteen months of travel, I rediscovered something I'd lost when I was a stressed out working mother. It was a truth my higher self had always known, but the frazzled mom had forgotten over the years. Our journey helped me remember again.

My life isn't happening to me. I'm happening to Life. I'm a powerful force. Part of the expanding universal field creating the planets and the stars, the forests and the flowers, the newborn babies and the ant baskets. No matter what happens around me, I choose my outcome. I can look for the lesson to be found in every experience, and then use those lessons to grow. To learn. To create something beautiful. To be the woman I'm meant to be. Each and every day, I'm writing my story. We're all the authors of every chapter and every page in our books. Only when we take responsibility for our lives will we write the stories we want to read. We'll become our own heroes, embracing every plot twist with an open mind and an open heart. Living for those precious right-now moments.

In our new American life, our family would choose happiness in as many of our right-now moments as possible. It would be a conscious decision we'd make every day, and we'd keep pushing ourselves to be *more*. More joyful, more inspired, more accepting, more connected, more fulfilled. Wanting something more isn't condemning what we have. It's simply the whisper of our higher selves, daring us to grow. Pushing us to rediscover the wisdom already inside us.

But sitting on that airplane, I wasn't sure of any of this yet. I hoped I could bring it all with me when we settled back into American life, but as the wheels touched down on the runway, our future was just a nebulous, hazy cloud of family visits and to-do lists.

"Ladies and gentlemen, welcome to Miami International Airport where the local time is 2:35 p.m."

Ali screwed up her face and looked around in confusion. "What!" she cried. "I thought we were going back to the United States!"

I heard Brian's laugh from behind me.

"We are, Ali," I assured her. "Miami is a city in Florida. We have a layover here and then another flight. Don't worry. We're definitely back in the United States."

"Oh, okay. I thought we got on the wrong airplane or something."

When the seatbelt light dinged off, everyone stood up to gather their carry-ons, but Emily sat motionless, staring out the window. "This is crazy," she said in disbelief. "Everything looks so different. This airport is humungous. And so *clean*."

As we made our way up the jetway and through the terminal,

I noticed Liv staring at the other travelers walking by us. She shook her head and said, "It's so weird they're all speaking perfect English. I can totally understand everything they're saying. It's like I'm eavesdropping or something."

At Immigration, we submitted our documentation through a facial recognition scanner, a stark contrast to the less modernized border checkpoints we'd experienced. We thought we were done with the process, but then an immigration officer stopped us and looked through our passports.

"So, why aren't these kids in school?" he asked reproachfully as he studied Liv's face and compared it to her photo.

Brian and I exchanged a look. "Um . . . they're being homeschooled right now," I said.

"So? Homeschool kids don't have school on Mondays?"

"Well, this is a travel day for us, so . . . no. Not on this Monday."

"Alright, whatever," he muttered, shoving our passports toward me.

As the five of us walked through the bright, shiny hallway into Customs, Brian threw me a smirk. "You think that guy is a truant officer in his spare time?"

I laughed. "Maybe he's just really concerned about our country's standardized test scores."

"Oh, no!" Emily cried, slapping a hand to her forehead. "I totally forgot about those stupid tests! Yuck. Can we avoid them if we just keep homeschooling?"

"Um, no," Liv said firmly. "No offense, Mama, but I'm seriously ready for normal school."

Brian slipped his arm around my shoulders. "Hear that, Trace? I think these kids are firing you from your teaching gig."

"Yeah, well, I'm not sure I was ever really cut out for that job."

He laughed and squeezed my shoulders.

As I looked up into those twinkling blue eyes of his, the enormity of what we'd done together hit me. We'd let go of the rat race and jumped onto a roller coaster journey. Now we were coming back to the start of the track, the train clicking our family to a stop. A giddy, relieved, let's-do-it-again joy coursed through me, filling my eyes with emotion and sending a tear down my cheek.

"Don't cry, Trace." He reached over to wipe the tear away. "Everything's going to be great."

"I know." I said with a smile. "I'm not crying because I'm scared. I'm just so damn proud of us for doing this crazy thing."

He stopped walking and pulled me into a hug.

"Me too," he whispered in my ear.

We stood there in the middle of the corridor, my head nestled into the curve of his chest as travelers rushed passed us.

When he pulled back and looked down at me, his eyes were glistening. "Thank God for our midlife crisis, right?" he said with a grin.

I laughed and planted a kiss on his lips. "You can say that again."

A vision of myself in that wine bar bathroom flashed through my mind. A raccoon-eyed, sweaty, hyperventilating mess with a stain down the front of her shirt, trying to talk herself out of a panic attack.

We must have faith and see the goodness in everything . . . even in things we believe to be bad.

Brian leaned down until his forehead pressed against mine. "Are you ready for the real world, babe?" he whispered.

I closed my eyes and smiled, the lessons of this adventure reminding me how far I'd come. I took a deep breath and looked up at him. "After almost forty years, I can say yes. Yes, I'm finally ready for the real world."

Brian took my hand and gave it a squeeze. And then we followed our girls into a new version of normal.

The privilege of a lifetime is being who you are.
—Joseph Campbell

ACKNOWLEDGEMENTS

First and foremost, I must thank this amazing family of mine. Brian, Emily, Liv, and Ali, you will always be my inspiration for living an authentic, no-regrets life. Without Brian's encouragement and ongoing support, I wouldn't have had the guts to start, much less finish, this memoir. I also need to express my deep gratitude to Keri Todd, Jolina Karen, Kathryn Grohusky, Mari McDonald, Linda Štucbartová, and Keri Randolph, my friends and beta readers who gave me valuable feedback and guidance as I wrote this book. Another big thank you goes out to my brother, who served as my editor, cheerleader, and philosophical guru while I grappled with the insecurities of the creative process.

With regards to our trip, I want to thank my parents and in-laws for managing their concerns as we trekked their granddaughters around the planet, as well as for sharing their insight while I worked on this book. Thank you to the Rotary Clubs in the countries we visited. They welcomed me with open arms as a visiting Rotarian and connected our family to many of the volunteer projects we worked on during our travels. Our family would also like to specifically thank the following organizations who gave us the opportunity to volunteer and join their communities for a little while as we contributed to various volunteer projects. Our family has seen firsthand the wonderful things these organizations do for the world.

Pink Crocodile in Prague, Czech Republic
The Red Cross in Labin, Croatia
Cherokee Gives Back in Addis Ababa, Ethiopia
Sale Enat in Addis Ababa, Ethiopia
Berhan Yehun in Addis Ababa, Ethiopia
Koh Samui Dog Rescue Center in Koh Samui, Thailand
Caring for Cambodia in Siem Reap, Cambodia
Journeys Within Our Community in Siem Reap, Cambodia
Te Kākano in Wanaka, New Zealand
Living Heart Peru in Pasic, Peru
The Meeting Place in Cusco, Peru

And finally, thank you to all of you, the readers, for coming on this journey with us. I hope this book brings opportunity to connect with many of you so we can share our no-regrets, right-now moments with one another.

PHOTOGRAPHY OF EXCESS BAGGAGE

Images from the Carisch family's journey have been organized into digital galleries for each chapter of the book. You can explore this photographic storytelling at:

www.traceycarisch.com/photos

REFERENCED BOOKS AND AUTHORS

The Power of Now by Eckhart Tolle

The Four Agreements by Don Miguel Ruiz

The Fifth Agreement by Don Jose Ruiz, Don Miguel Ruiz, and Janet Mills

Taking the Leap by Pema Chödrön

ABOUT THE AUTHOR

TRACEY CARISCH is a speaker and consultant, who enjoys long walks in the woods and the occasional Netflix binge-watching session. She lives in the mountains of Colorado with her family, their two dogs, and a cat who also thinks he's a dog.

Author photo © Brian Carisch

SELECTED TITLES FROM SHE WRITES PRESS

She Writes Press is an independent publishing company founded to serve women writers everywhere. Visit us at www.shewritespress.com.

Peanut Butter and Naan: Stories of an American Mother in The Far East by Jennifer Magnuson. $16.95, 978-1-63152-911-5. The hilarious tale of what happened when Jennifer Magnuson moved her family of seven from Nashville to India in an effort to shake things up—and got more than she bargained for.

This is Mexico: Tales of Culture and Other Complications by Carol M. Merchasin. $16.95, 978-1-63152-962-7. Merchasin chronicles her attempts to understand Mexico, her adopted country, through improbable situations and small moments that keep the reader moving between laughter and tears.

Gap Year Girl by Marianne Bohr. $16.95, 978-1-63152-820-0. Thirty-plus years after first backpacking through Europe, Marianne Bohr and her husband leave their lives behind and take off on a yearlong quest for adventure.

Postcards from the Sky: Adventures of an Aviatrix by Erin Seidemann. $16.95, 978-1-63152-826-2. Erin Seidemann's tales of her her struggles, adventures, and relationships as a woman making her way in a world very much dominated by men: aviation.

Renewable: One Woman's Search for Simplicity, Faithfulness, and Hope by Eileen Flanagan. $16.95, 978-1-63152-968-9. At age forty-nine, Eileen Flanagan had an aching feeling that she wasn't living up to her youthful ideals or potential, so she started trying to change the world—and in doing so, she found the courage to change her life.

Pieces of Me: Rescuing My Kidnapped Daughters by Lizbeth Meredith. 978-1-63152-834-7. When her daughters are kidnapped and taken to Greece by their non-custodial father, single mom Lizbeth Meredith vows to bring them home—and give them a better childhood than her own.